PLACE IDENTITY, PARTICIPATION AND PLANNING

EDITED BY CLIFF HAGUE AND PAUL JENKINS

Routledge
Taylor & Francis Group

LONDON AND NEW YORK

First published 2005 by Routledge
2 Park Square, Milton Park, Abingdon, Oxfordshire OX14 4RN

Simultaneously published in the USA and Canada
by Routledge
270 Madison Ave, New York, NY 10016

Routledge is an imprint of the Taylor & Francis Group

© 2005 Editorial and selection, Cliff Hague and Paul Jenkins; individual chapters, the contributors.

Typeset in Akzidenz Grotesk by GreenGate Publishing Services, Tonbridge. Kent
Printed and bound in Great Britain by The Cromwell Press, Trowbridge, Wiltshire

British Library Cataloguing in Publication Data
A catalogue record for this book is available from the British Library

Library of Congress Cataloging in Publication Data
Place identity, planning and participation / edited by Cliff Hague and Paul Jenkins.
1st ed.
        p. cm. – (RTPI library series)
    Simultaneously published in the USA and Canada by Routledge.
    1. Regional planning–Europe. 2. City planning–Europe. 3. Local government–Europe.
    I. Hague, Cliff. II. Jenkins, Paul, 1953– III. Series.
    HT395.E8P56 2004
    307.1'2'094–dc22   2004007064

ISBN 0-415-26241-0 (Hbk)
ISBN 0-415-26242-9 (Pbk)

The new planning is less codified and technical, more innovative and entrepreneurial. It is more participatory and concerned with projects rather than whole urban systems. Planning expertise is increasingly sought not only by the state, but also by the corporate sector and civil society ... What is controversial is not urban planning per se, but its *goal*: whether it should be directed chiefly at efficiency, reinforcing the current distribution of wealth and power, or whether it should play a distributive role to help create minimum standards of urban liveability. (United Nations Centre for Human Settlements, 2001)

CONTENTS

PART 1
OBJECTIVES, THEORY AND CONCEPTS

PART 2
RESEARCH INTO PRACTICE

LIST OF FIGURES

LIST OF TABLES

LIST OF BOXES

NOTES ON CONTRIBUTORS

Cliff Hague is Professor of Planning and Spatial Development within the School of the Built Environment, Heriot-Watt University. A past president of the Royal Town Planning Institute, he is currently president of the Commonwealth Association of Planners.

Marilyn Higgins is Senior Lecturer within the School of the Built Environment, where she teaches and undertakes research on design quality and sustainable environment, planning education and its interface with practice, and management in planning.

Paul Jenkins is a Reader within the School of the Built Environment, where – as Director of the Centre for Environment and Human Settlements – he teaches and undertakes a range of research and professional planning, housing and environmental issues, with a particular focus on the rapidly urbanizing world and governance issues related to human settlements.

Karryn Kirk is a Research Associate at the School of the Built Environment. She is active in planning research in urban regeneration and European spatial planning and governance.

Harry Smith is a Research Associate at the School of the Built Environment and linked to the Centre for Environment and Human Settlements. He is active in planning and housing research in the UK and the developing world, with a particular interest in community involvement in development.

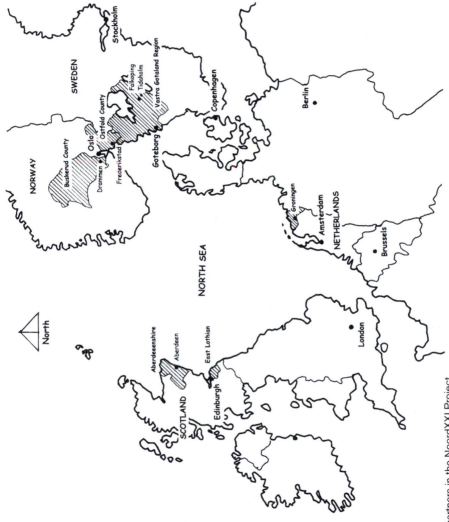

Figure 0.1 The partners in the NoordXXI Project

This book grew out of the authors' involvement in a contract research project under-taken during 1999–2001 as part of Interreg, a European Union programme that fosters trans-national co-operation amongst local authorities in particular, and seeks to translate ideas from the European Spatial Development Perspective into practice. The Interreg IIC project entitled 'Quality by Identity: Beyond Traditional Spatial and Economic Development' and led by the Dutch NoordXXI Foundation involved part-ners from the Netherlands, Norway, Sweden and Scotland (Figure 0.1). All of these partner regions faced challenges stemming from urban spread and economic change that impacted on the identities of towns and rural areas. The inspiration behind the NoordXXI project was the idea that the authentic identity of rural areas around growing cities constitutes a radical solution to spatial development prob-lems. The central concerns were with spatial planning, local identity and economic development. The aims were to 'influence the spatial development of each region based on a stronger local identity' and thereby to contribute towards more sustain-able development.

To assist them, the partners invited a number of academics to attend their meetings and to undertake research under contract for the project. Thus this research was driven initially by the priorities and timescale of our clients, within a framework that they had devised and agreed amongst themselves. Although most of the research was undertaken by the authors of the chapters in this book, Professor Paulus Huigen from the University of Groningen, who had been involved in research on rural identities (Haartsen, Groote and Huigen, 2000), made important contribu-tions in the early stages and undertook some of the contract research, with his assistant Bart J.M. van der Aa. Furthermore, Professor Arne Bugge Amundsen, from the University of Oslo, was able to bring into the project a strong theoretical insight about the nature of place identities. Professor Morten Edvardsen, from the Norwegian Agricultural University, and Erna Wenche Østrem (a planning practi-tioner) also undertook contracted work on the Scandinavian partner regions. Staff and students from the Norwegian Agricultural University worked on design projects with their opposite numbers from Heriot-Watt University's School of Planning and Housing in Edinburgh. Thus the Interreg project stimulated a wide range of acade-mic/practitioner international collaboration.

It is not uncommon for internationally comparative research to be heavily reliant on case studies, and for such case studies to be chosen in a pragmatic rather than scientific manner. Attempts to collect systematically comparable data from the partners were made within the Interreg project, but not prior to its initiation. Difficulties posed by differences in definitions, data availability, legislation, institutions and planning cultures are endemic in trans-national research, and our study was no exception. Barriers of language, a common problem in European work, were overcome by the high quality English amongst the Dutch and Scandinavian participants. However, time was limited and the questions the researchers had to answer were those posed by the practitioners, not by research or academic peer groups.

As part of the final stages of our contracted research we proposed that this could be of benefit to a wider audience of academics and practitioners, and that we would like to draw broader conclusions from the research that surpassed the specific contracted research objectives. This was agreed by the NoordXXI management team, who provided initial support for us to get a book proposal to the publisher. This book is the result therefore of a re-visiting of the contract research through a broader lens and with wider objectives. In so doing we are in effect using this opportunity to refine hypotheses which draw on substantially wider literature and analysis. As such the veracity or not of these hypotheses will require wider 'testing' than we are able to do through our own research activities in planning – this is further elaborated in the concluding chapter.

Publication of our findings through this book allows for peer evaluation of how thorough and convincing the methods and answers were. Our feeling is that what might have been sacrificed in terms of methodology was more than compensated for by the gains that came from working with practitioners and in a consciously international context. Like most contract research, this book is a product of team work, rather than of a single author. Though in the end it was the Edinburgh-based part of the team who wrote the book, it would not have happened without the collaboration of our colleagues in the University of Groningen, the University of Oslo and the Norwegian Agricultural University. We hope that this book reflects these benefits, in particular by focusing on issues of direct relevance to practising planners in a number of countries, while also bringing social scientific concepts into real life/work applications. If this is the case, the Interreg project will have made a wider and positive contribution to the development of spatial planning.

Cliff Hague and Paul Jenkins
Edinburgh, July 2003

FOREWORD

The idea to use regional identity in encouraging regional development came from the North of the Netherlands, a region that many Dutch people view negatively as the real outback of the country. For several years the three northern provinces – Groningen, Drenthe and Friesland – that comprise the North had tried to improve its image. Amongst their initiatives were:

- an advertising campaign with the slogan 'The North is on top of the Netherlands' (the play of words links its location on a map with the idea that this is the best part of the country);
- *Noorderbreedte*, a journal focusing on the spatial qualities and development in the North of the Netherlands, which reached a wide circulation;
- a number of research projects that the University of Groningen was involved in;
- a regular open conference focusing on regional and spatial development called the Keuning Conference (named after the founder and first professor of the Faculty of Spatial Sciences at the University of Groningen – H. J. Keuning), organized in order to create a network including politicians, planners and the public.

Technically the conferences were organized by the NoordXXI Foundation, which was created for this specific purpose. The foundation has a board of five members and the following organizations are represented:

- Eo Wijers Foundation – a national foundation for the promotion of spatial design;
- *Noorderbreedte* – the journal published in Groningen on landscape, cultural history, nature and the environment in the provinces of Friesland, Groningen and Drenthe;
- The Faculty of Spatial Sciences of the University of Groningen.

The partners in the NoordXXI Foundation had developed ideas around the term 'identity strategy' for some years. This strategy is to generate:

> spatial concepts whose roots lie in the potential and qualities (such as the valuable natural setting and cultural landscapes) of the North (of the Netherlands) themselves and not based on developments in urban areas as the Randstadt. The activities have in common that they seek spatial

concepts that are not only anchored in the identity of the region, but also strengthen and develop this identity. This new strategy means, amongst other things, identifying and experimenting with techniques to increase awareness and involvement of everyone in the region – from politicians to children, from planners to scientists – and stimulating dialogue within the region (Holt and Collins, 2001: 11).

A local project was first established in the North of Netherlands. The elements of the project were organized as four sub-projects known as 'pillars'.

1.   The first 'pillar' was entitled *Imagination* and it comprised a competition for landscape architects, spatial planners and related professions to identify a long-term strategy for the North of the Netherlands that did not replicate the policies applied in the Randstad.
2.   The second 'pillar' was called *Policy* and it looked at how a vision for the future development of the rural landscape could be worked out that reflected the identity of the area and its inhabitants.
3.   The third 'pillar' was called *Know How*. It focused on how to communicate these new ideas about the landscape and planning to a wider audience.
4.   The fourth 'pillar' was *The Future*, which looked at ways to involve people, and in particular young people, in spatial planning.

The partners behind the NoordXXI Foundation wanted to take this concept into a wider regional setting like the North Sea Region and looked for international funding. The opportunity came when the Interreg IIC programme was launched in 1997. At the first partner-seeking conference, organized in June 1997 in Gothenburg, participants from East Lothian Council in Scotland and the Østfold Research Foundation (STO) from Norway attended a presentation given by the NoordXXI Foundation. Later in 1997 the same persons were invited to a workshop in Groningen in order to discuss a common project and how to prepare an application for the Interreg IIC North Sea programme.

Parallel to developing the content of a project, both East Lothian and STO started to look for other possible partners. In Norway the counties of Buskerud and Østfold found the ideas of the NoordXXI project outline interesting and became partners. Both counties had experienced a huge decrease in employment in their manufacturing industries. In Østfold long-established industries like the shipyards in Fredrikstad and Moss, and the tyre factory in Askim, had closed down. The local councils were working hard to fit new activity into old estates. In Buskerud many of the paper mills along the Drammen river did not produce any paper any more. However, unemployment had not risen very much as most people who had lost a job lived within 30–90 minutes travel time from Oslo and could commute to new employment quite easily. Population statistics also showed another stream of people from the Oslo area, moving to the south of Buskerud/Drammen and to northern parts of Østfold in order to find affordable housing.

In Sweden the new region of Västra Götaland, a merger of three traditional counties, decided to join in. They needed to establish a new identity for the region and looked for ways to do this. In Scotland Aberdeenshire joined – having a similar settlement structure and facing rural decline but also growth of commuting into Aberdeen – with a view to learning from partner regions across the North Sea. In addition to the six official partners, other local authorities have been involved as case study areas or collaborators, notably some lower tier local authorities within the Scandinavian partners, and also the City of Aberdeen.

The partners submitted a first project application in March 1998, and received a preliminary approval by the end of May. A revised application was resubmitted in October and the project was finally approved in December 1998.

A characteristic of the partner regions is that most of their inhabitants live 30-90 minutes travel from a major employment centre like Oslo, Gothenburg, Edinburgh, Aberdeen or Groningen. There are more options for work and access to private and public services than in the more peripheral parts of regions character-ized by very low population density and economies based on primary industries and steady out-migration.

Thus the project built on the idea that for many people living in NoordXXI regions there will be a trade-off between the benefits of living in a familiar and safe rural or small town environment and the cost of commuting to the city to find employ-ment. The planning approach in the NoordXXI regions was seen as being different from both the pure allocation and congestion planning problems of the cities and the focus on accessibility and service supply applied to the more distant areas. A challenge in the spatial planning of NoordXXI regions was the threat of the transfor-mation of the small towns and the surrounding rural landscape into extensions of the large urban areas with the consequent loss of their identity. The European Spatial Development Perspective (CEC, 1999) proposed new urban–rural relationships across Europe. The NoordXXI Interreg project sought to explore the possibility of such relationships in four countries around the North Sea.

The aims of the project were to:

*   introduce new concepts for spatial planning;
*   learn from one another by comparing different models of urban and rural development;
*   identify new interdisciplinary approaches with special emphasis on how to involve the public, and especially young people, in the planning process;
*   strengthen the identity of each participating region.

In order to fulfil these aims the partner regions needed well-qualified assistance. One option was to hire one or more consulting companies. The other was to invite academic institutions to take part in the different activities involving both teachers and students. We chose the latter strategy, hoping that the experience from the NoordXXI project could also be used as background for teaching. We also wanted academic documentation of the findings in the project to be aimed at a wider audience than the few people normally reading reports from consultants. This book is thus the final part of a series of 68 different publications that came out of the project.

Normally it is difficult to undertake experiments in planning, but the NoordXXI project gave this rare opportunity. By bringing students and professors together from two universities (Heriot-Watt University and the Norwegian Agricultural University, NLH) to investigate the potential of two similar towns – Askim in Østfold and Ellon in Aberdeenshire – we established a trans-national network also involving local planning officers and politicians. We gave the students an opportunity to listen to young people, create unbiased scenarios on how the towns should develop and present their ideas to the local politicians.

Staff from Heriot-Watt and NLH, together with others from the University of Groningen, additionally undertook a systematic comparison of the regions in the project. We also used academics to clarify new concepts (like identity) and describe planning methods in order to establish a common understanding and terminology among the people taking part in the project. Academic staff were further invited to the four main plenary sessions in the project, to give introductions under the different themes, run workshops and summarize the discussions.

A special focus in the project was on youth participation in planning. Several practical experiments and activities were undertaken in all countries. A lot of young people from the different regions were involved in different projects, such as youth exchanges, workshops, conferences, planning projects and follow-up meetings. The youth involvement activities consisted to a great extent of good examples of mutual learning between the regions. The idea and format of youth councils were adopted in a couple of regions as a result of the experience transmitted from other partners in the project. This focus on youth participation was subsequently expanded to include a study of various experiments in wider participation in planning in the partners, and led to the linking of the concepts of place identity and participation as the theme of this book.

Overall, the work undertaken in the project has led to changes in planning approaches among several of the partners, especially concerning the image, environment and appearance of towns. In the local master planning we can see a greater emphasis on social and environmental as well as economic factors. Another clear conclusion among the partners, based on the experience from the NoordXXI project, is that public participation should be introduced at an early pre-plan stage in addition to consultation on prepared planning proposals.

In summary, NoordXXI was an innovative project that fostered co-operation between planners in four countries around the North Sea: Norway, Sweden, the Netherlands and Scotland. It also brought together practising planners and academics, whilst additionally involving politicians and young people. It was made possible by the support of the project partners – the councils of Aberdeenshire, Buskerud, East Lothian, Østfold, and Västra Götaland, and the lead partner, the NoordXXI Foundation, in which the Province of Groningen played the key role. We also acknowledge the support provided through the Interreg programme from the European Regional Development Fund. This book is therefore the outcome of new forms of collaboration that are developing in Europe around the theory and practice of spatial planning.

Øivind Holt
Halden, Norway, March 2003

ACKNOWLEDGEMENTS

The research this book draws on would not have been possible without the interest and determination of the local authorities that were involved as partners in the NoordXXI project: Province of Groningen and Province of Overijssel in the Netherlands; Buskerud Fylkeskommune and Østfold Fylkeskommune in Norway; Västra Götaland in Sweden; and Aberdeen City Council, Aberdeenshire Council and East Lothian Council in Scotland. This collaboration was skilfully steered by Øivind Holt and Pete Collins, who also provided the encouragement for us to produce this book.

Invaluable academic contributions to the gestation and development of the NoordXXI project were made by Arne Bugge Amundsen at the University of Oslo; Paulus P.P. Huigen at the Faculty of Spatial Sciences, University of Groningen; and Morten Edvardsen at the Norges LandbruksHøgskole.

We also particularly thank our colleague Harry Smith, who tirelessly and efficiently helped prepare the final typescript. The time he put into this was generously covered by Edinburgh College of Art initially, and later by the School of the Built Environment, Heriot-Watt University. We are also grateful to Helen Ibbotson at Routledge for her support and patience through the period it took to complete the manuscript.

We should give special thanks too to Askim Kommune, as without their help we would not have undertaken the design-focused part of the project. Similarly the communes of Tidaholm and Falköping were active participants in the project and in the research.

ABBREVIATIONS

BSE	Bovine Spongiform Encephalopathy
CABE	Commission for Architecture and the Built Environment
CEC	Commission of the European Communities
DATAR	Délégation à l'aménagement du territoire et à l'action régionale
DETR	Department of Environment, Transport and the Regions
ESDP	European Spatial Development Perspective
ESPON	European Spatial Planning Observatory Network
EU	European Union
GDP	Gross Domestic Product
IT	Information Technology
LA21	Local Agenda 21
MP	Member of Parliament
NGO	Non Governmental Organization
NLH	Norges LandbruksHøgskole (The Norwegian Agricultural University)
NPPG	National Planning Policy Guideline
NSR	North Sea Region
NWMA	North West Metropolitan Area
ODPM	Office of the Deputy Prime Minister
POP	Provinciaal Omgevinsplan
RTPI	Royal Town Planning Institute
STO	Østfold Research Foundation
UDAL	Urban Design Alliance
UK	United Kingdom
UNCED	United Nations Conference on Environment and Development
USA	United States of America

PART ONE

OBJECTIVES, THEORY AND CONCEPTS

CHAPTER 1

PLANNING AND PLACE IDENTITY
CLIFF HAGUE

INTRODUCTION AND OUTLINE

> Cities and regions are facing great challenges as a consequence of globalisa-
> tion. In many ways cities are the driving force of the global economy. The
> challenge for the future is to determine how this force can pull with it an entire
> region without compromising our identity. In other words we must remain locally
> anchored in a changing global world (Hans Schmidt, Minister for the
> Environment, Denmark, in *Ministry of the Environment, Spatial Planning
> Department*, 2002: 2).

Place identity is attracting increasing interest both from practising professional
planners and politicians as well as in social science research. In this book we aim
to ask some basic questions. Why has concern for identity moved centre-stage in
planning? Who put it there and what/whose identity is being expressed? What
spatial planning policies, institutions and practices are prescribed to deliver that
identity, and why? What role does public participation play? In raising such
queries we hope to bridge the theory/practice divide, and to demonstrate what
can be achieved by engagement and critical interaction between the academic
community, the community of planning practitioners and the elected politicians
whom they serve. We are encouraged to venture into this blurred interface
because that was how the NoordXXI Interreg project worked and, as described in
the foreword and the preface, that project underpins the empirical part of our
book.

The book thus seeks to connect theory and practice. The first three chapters
are largely concerned with theory and concepts. This opening chapter will explore
the concept of place identity by drawing on a literature from cultural studies and
geography. The chapter then addresses the question of what are the implications of
changing perceptions of place identity for planners. Chapter 2 looks at the economic and geographical forces that are changing place identities, and develops an
analytical framework to differentiate between space, place and territory to assist in
the application of theory to practice. Chapter 3 then looks at theories which explain
the political context of these changes, and develops propositions about the participation of individuals, actors in civil society and lobbying groups in forms of
collaborative planning.

The second part of the book applies and develops these ideas in relation to planning practice. It is European practice that is analysed, both at a trans-national scale through the spatial planning concepts and policy instruments being developed at the level of the EU, and also the national systems and local practices in four countries: Scotland, the Netherlands, Norway and Sweden. Thus Chapters 4 to 9 broadly work through a hierarchy of spatial scales. Chapter 4 is concerned with the place identities being created at a trans-national scale, but also introduces the planning systems in each of the four countries. Chapter 5 looks at regions, Chapter 6 is about identity in strategic planning, and Chapter 7 analyses participation and Local Agenda 21 as channels for developing local narratives of place identity. Chapter 8 looks at the planning of urban expansion around and beyond the edge of the city in the context of narratives of compact and sustainable cities. Chapter 9 looks at urban design as a means of creating and sustaining place identity. The final chapter then returns to the main themes running through the book. It attempts to contribute to a necessary critical debate about spatial planning practice and about the involvement of planners in the fashioning of new place identities. In doing this it advances some propositions about theory and the relation between academic research and practice-based contract research.

WHAT IS PLACE IDENTITY?

As Urry (1995: 1) observed,

> The understanding of place is a complex theoretical and empirical task requiring a range of novel techniques and methods of investigation … most social theories deal unsatisfactorily with the nature of place because they have not known what to do about time, space and nature.

'Place' is more than a location. Relph (1992: 37) said that 'place' meant 'those fragments of human environments where meanings, activities and a specific landscape are all implicated and enfolded by each other.' Similarly, Rose (1995: 88) observed that 'places are infused with meaning and feeling'. In this way we distinguish place from the more abstract and functional notion of 'space' and from 'territory', which is a politicized demarcation and control of space. These distinctions are developed further in the next chapter. For now we will focus on how ideas of place are formed and communicated.

As the quotations from Relph and from Rose in the previous paragraph suggest, 'place' implies some mix of memory, sensual experience (in particular visual, but possibly also aural and/or tactile) and interpretation. We might say that a place is a geographical space that is defined by meanings, sentiments and stories rather than by a set of co-ordinates. Thus 55 degrees 57 minutes north and 3 degrees 13 minutes west is not a place, but when we call that same space 'Edinburgh' it becomes a place. Though latitude and longitude identify a location, they do not give identity to a place. It is interpretation and narrative that give identity and it is identity that transforms space into place.

It is not surprising therefore that words like 'character' and 'identity' are used by planners, especially in respect of conservation and the impact of new developments on existing townscapes or countryside. However, the underlying meanings are rarely decoded, and the presumption is typically that place is defined above all through visual qualities. The concept of place identity that most frequently underpins planning and design is the *genius loci* view of place (Norberg-Schulz, 1980). This notion implies that there are essential natural characteristics that identify a place, and that, in effect, these are latent and will structure, but also be released by, a sensitive design solution. Of course there are objective physical realities in a place – e.g. slope, orientation, vistas, etc. – and we would also agree that there are personal and highly individual reactions to any place, and that these are triggered not only by physical features but also by less tangible meanings and memories. However, we would also contend that the capacity to see, unravel and impart values and meanings to such aspects is not a purely intuitive, spontaneous and subjective skill, but rather a socially learned and mediated process. In other words the experience – or the design – of place is relational rather than primarily subjective. This means that our capacity to identify a place *as* a place is shaped by what others tell us about the place, and filtered by our own socialization, as shaped by class, age, gender, ethnicity, nationality, professional education, etc. As Rose (1995: 89) commented, 'although senses of place may be very personal, they are not entirely the result of one individual's feelings and meanings'. It is this process of receiving, selectively reconstructing, and then re-communicating a narrative that constitutes identity and transforms a space into a place.

The word 'identity' is based on the Latin pronoun *idem*, which means 'the same'. Thus identity is what is central, real and typical to something or someone (Amundsen, 2001: 5). This usage of the word comes from psychology and psychiatry; for example, an individual unsure of him- or herself might be said to have an 'identity crisis'. However, even this notion of identity, as core and integrated values and characteristics through which a person defines him- or herself, implies the interaction between an individual and others. The process of developing even an individual identity, while seeming to be quintessentially subjective, is one that is fundamentally social; that is to say it develops through interaction between the individual and others in the society, both directly and indirectly.

The idea that the meanings and identity imputed to places are relational rather than only subjective means that from an infinity of possible identities for any place, we can discern some shared, even dominant ones. Indeed, as Rose noted, feelings about place are embedded in sets of power relations. This does not mean that those with most power necessarily determine the dominant feelings about a place – such a reading would be a crude version of Marx's famous dictum that the ruling ideas are the ideas of the ruling class. In societies of difference and division places have a particular symbolic significance, and their fabric, meanings and identities are contested. For example, in countries of Central and Eastern Europe street names or even the names of cities were changed by the Communists when they came to power, and then further changes were made after 1989. In Moravia, Zlin, the planned company 'town in gardens' of the Bata shoe company became Gottwaldov, in honour of the Czech Communist leader to whom a statue was erected in the main square. However, Moravians still called it Zlin and the original name was restored (and the statue removed) after the Velvet Revolution. This is just one example of how place identity is contested and linked to power.

Both Rose (1995) and Amundsen (2001) pointed out that a group identifying with a place, and so establishing what they have in common, is simultaneously establishing a relation of difference with other places and other social groups. In place identity there is a relation based on similarity, *and* a relation based on difference. These are social relations – places, as places, should not be seen in psychological terms. Put crudely, identity is about 'us' and 'them', or more neutrally about 'us' and 'the others'. 'We' share common experiences, cultures, tastes and histories that set us apart from the rest. Identity then is more than a psychological status (important as that is). Also it is more than a passive output from social structures. It is something that is shaped between individuals, groups and others in the wider society, as a basis to claim authenticity, originality and singularity, even ownership. It is thus a dynamic, potentially powerful force that influences policy and practice. Again the example of Zlin/Gottwaldov illustrates the point. For the Communists, the name Zlin was part of the bourgeois identity of the town owned by the Bata company. It was the 'other' which would be transformed into Gottwaldov, with the name change, Gottwald's statue, and the practices of 'actually existing socialism' all contributing to the new identity and the associated narratives of the Party. After 1989 a similar process restored Zlin in negation of the 'other' that had been imposed for 40 years through 'Gottwaldov'. Thus when we look at place identity, and especially when we explore place identity as an input to policy and action, we need to be aware of 'the other', or counterpoint, to that identity. As societies have become more diverse and fragmented (e.g. in relation to gender, ethnicity or lifestyle) the claims to authenticity and singularity at the core of place identity need to be assessed critically.

Amundsen (2001) recognized a tension, even a contradiction, in the concept of identity. Identity implies a form of essentialistic thinking. That is to say that identity is depicted as something that cannot be changed; it is an expression of what you *are*. In such essentialism there always lurks the possibility for conflict with those others whose identity is radically different from ours. Groth (2002) suggests that there are two strands to discourses on identity. One of these he calls 'ethnos'; it is about inherited cultures and emotions that bind individuals into a community. This is the essentialistic version of identity. The other strand is 'demos', whereby through rational arguments citizens and society enter into agreement about common rights and responsibilities. Identity involves consciousness, knowing and acting on that knowledge, and as it is about the relation between individuals, groups and others, the nature of identity must be social and contractual. This is to say identity is contingent on ideas and interpretations, actions and reactions; it is something that is formed through discourses and can change and be cross-cutting, so that those who share one identity may not share others. Groth (2002: 17) says that in the demos strand 'identity is likely to be polycentric rather than monocentric, formed as it is by citizens organizing their own life in their own interests, however within a common legal framework of society'. In other words, the interpretative notion of identity is that 'essentials', 'authenticity' and 'distinctiveness' only become such through interpretation, communication and action within a context, and not in isolation.

The point then is that the basis of claims to authenticity in place identity need critical scrutiny. Authenticity claimed by and through a single place identity based only on ethnos can be exclusionary and repressive. Through demos we would expect there to be multiple identities that may be shared or contested, and such identities would primarily be generated by the everyday life of the people themselves within a framework of tolerance and the rule of law. Again Gottwaldov can serve as an example, though in a slightly paradoxical manner. The paradox is that forging of state socialism in Czechoslovakia had to invent its own authenticity – based on class and class struggle, and to negate more traditional claims to authenticity rooted in the past. This meant rolling out the inherited cultures of the Communist Party as the new ethnos for Zlin, an all enveloping culture which everyone would be expected to follow. In contrast the restoration of Zlin after 1989 was inextricably linked to the reclaim of demos.

Our argument can be summarized as follows. Places *are* places (and not just spaces) because they have identity. Place identities are formed through milieux of feelings, meanings, experiences, memories and actions that, while ultimately personal, are substantially filtered through social structures and fostered through socialization. Thus place identities are relational – i.e. they are formed in relation to other people, other places and other identities for that place. Therefore, place identities are encapsulated within power relations and are likely to be contested. It follows that it is important to ask 'Whose place identity is it?' and 'How has it been constructed and agreed?' Claims to authenticity and essentialism are often at the heart of place identities. While such claims often assert legitimacy by reference to history, that is to say that a place is seen as 'always having been ...', as we argued in respect of Gottwaldov, there can be other grounds. The point is that authenticity is imbued with what may amount to a sense of moral superiority and is seen as non-negotiable and exclusive. Therefore we need to ask whether place identities have been imposed or negotiated, while also being sceptical about the monopolistic claims often associated with notions of authenticity.

Where does planning practice fit into this line of reasoning? We see planning as being about place-making; that is to say that a key purpose of planning is to create, reproduce or mould the identities of places through manipulation of the activities, feelings, meanings and fabric that combine into place identity. Planning is a set of institutions, ideas and practices that sits within a social context and is embedded in power relations. Thus, while place-making is more central to the profession of planners than to most other social groups, the planners do not have a monopoly on the power to determine a place identity. In particular, planners (as agents in planning systems, economic development agencies, etc.) are likely to be used as a conduit through which politicians and economic interests promote *their* versions of place identity. At the same time planners have to be able to engage with local residents and other members of civil society, for whom places may have very different meanings and identities. In planning practice this process is encapsulated by the term 'public participation'. Therefore place identity, participation and planning are intimately intertwined, and this book is concerned with understanding their interrelations. We attempt this through developing propositions from an academic literature in this first part and then using these to structure an analysis of planning practice.

Our main concern is with how narratives of place identity are constructed and contested in the context of spatial planning – i.e. through practice and participation in the social sphere – rather than exploring the cognition of an individual. Inevitably this means that, as researchers, we are ourselves engaging in interpretation of the communications and actions that take place in and around the spatial planning process. Such interpretations might be deemed to be ephemeral and subjective. However, Amundsen argued that public expressions of identity amount to 'cultural realities' and that symbols and language (and we would add actions and interventions for design, investment or disinvestment in a place) are as real as people's personal feelings or inner thoughts.

Inhabitants' feelings about an area are difficult, but not impossible, to research. Raagmaa (2002) used questionnaires to measure regional identity in a small town and two rural communities in Estonia. In addition, the 'Lifestyles in Rural Wales' project (Cloke, Goodwin and Milbourne, 1998) interviewed almost 1,000 households and used open-ended questions to probe perceptions of cultural issues linked to rural Wales as a place. In the NoordXXI project we also used open-ended questions to explore perceptions of place identity amongst the project's partners, and Amundsen (2001) undertook some empirical work focusing on perceptions of place identity in the Norwegian town of Askim and in Tidaholm in Sweden. Haartsen, Groote and Huigen (2000: 13) noted that the main means of analysing representations of rural identity are through questionnaires and/or through 'cultural or popular indicators' such as paintings, advertisements, television and other media. They cite the work of Frouws (1998), who used a wide range of reports and public debates as source material to develop a typology of discourses over the future of rural areas. To focus only on explicit declarations of place identity or to rely only on empirical methods such as questionnaires would be to miss some of the most crucial aspects. These concern how identities are constructed, contested and changed. The next section of the chapter probes the theory that can offer answers to these questions.

DISCOURSES, IMAGINED COMMUNITIES AND EVERYDAY LIFE

The work of Anderson (1983) is a way to approach issues of place identity, as both Rose (1995) and Amundsen (2001) noted. In his seminal study, Anderson analysed nationalism and the formation of national identities in the nineteenth century. He coined the term 'imagined communities', since the process of building a nation required that people identify themselves with a symbolic community that was wider than their actual local or regional one. Thus, as Amundsen explained, inhabitants of say Østfold County in Norway could imagine that they shared a symbolic community with people in other, distant parts of what was to become the state of Norway – e.g. Finnmark or Bergen – though they were unlikely to have visited those places and had differences in language, clothing, customs and other aspects of daily life. Thus the symbolic community extended well beyond the traditional place-bound network of neighbours, colleagues, relations and friends.

Anderson's argument was that national identity was the output of a process of deliberate cultural construction. As Amundsen (2001: 8) observed, 'The people of Norway or Sweden "are" not Norwegians or Swedes in any objective way. They can, however, "see" themselves as Swedes or Norwegians.' Norway became an independent state in 1905, the culmination of a process of constructing national identity. Through such efforts identity became related to a bounded geographical space, and national identity and its territorial form, the nation-state, was arguably the dominant mode of place identity within Europe through the twentieth century. Such attempts to build identity with the nation-state in situations of ethnic, cultural and religious division were often bitterly contested by the 'other' whose own identity and claims to authenticity were being repressed through making them a 'state-less nation' (e.g. in Ireland, Catalonia, the Balkans, etc.). Indeed, analyses of nationalism as cultural construction have tended to understate the spatial issues involved. Yiftachel and Hague (2002: 168) argued that the focus on the nation-state obscures other

> dynamic 'spatialities' [that] often run across, 'below' or 'above' the putative, flat and stable 'national homeland' … The links between space, development, and collective identities and group relations are thus *reciprocal*. That is, while political processes create spatial outcomes, these outcomes in turn, create new political dynamics.

The example that Groth (2002) cites to illustrate the 'demos' strand of identity illustrates this very point. Historically, European market towns and trading cities were parties to statutes not only at national level, but also with their own citizens and with each other across national boundaries, e.g. through the Hanseatic League.

If imagined communities, and the 'communal myths' at their foundations, can be constructed at a national level, there is no reason to suppose that a similar process, and a similar analysis, cannot be advanced at other scales – trans-national, regional, urban and local. Indeed, Amundsen (2001) argued that the identity processes at national, regional and local levels (and we would add trans-national and urban too) are both 'complementary and contradictory'. The national discourse had to explain inter-regional differences, while simultaneously downgrading them and containing the risks of protest. Arguably the emergence of the Committee of the Regions within the EU is an indication that the nation-building project did not entirely extinguish counter-narratives based on regional identities. Certainly in the case of one of our NoordXXI countries, Scotland, the 1980s and 1990s were marked by increasing political disaffection from the institutions of the centralized UK state, culminating in the creation of a devolved parliament in Edinburgh in 1999. This is one example of a nation-state having to renegotiate the terms of its dominance, refashioning rather than abandoning its own place identity.

We thus interpret planning for place identity as a process of developing a discourse, even writing a narrative. It is a selective way of imagining, acting and communicating about a place. Seen in this way, planning is a set of inter-linked discourses of words and graphics, procedures, decision structures, legal requirements and limits. Within these structures narratives about places can be written. Such narratives are likely to take the form of stories, interpretations, explanations and prescriptions. Of course, planning is neither a static nor a homogenous discourse, nor is it undifferentiated or unambiguous. Different national legal systems and intellectual or disciplinary traditions distinguish planning between different countries and through time. The dominant planning discourse at any one time or place is a negotiated outcome arrived at through a set of power relations that will generally seek to reproduce those same relations.

The basic argument in this book is that planning discourses in Europe, historically the products of national governments and social democratic ideologies, are being challenged to accommodate new narratives of place identity. This is because the nation-states are being weakened from above (by globalization and the emergence of the EU as a trans-national political entity) and from below (by resurgent regions, settlements and civil society). Furthermore, fiscal and political crises have blighted social democracy, forcing a transmutation into pragmatic, centrist 'Third Way' politics in which identity and electoral popularity occupy the core ground conceded by class-based politics. Thus planning is intimately involved in the cultural process of creating and disseminating meaning and modes of perception that help form collective identities (and individual ones too, presumably) that underpin action, while simultaneously marginalizing other possible place-related discourses and actions. Can planning practices change – or be changed – to facilitate the construction, communication and implementation of narratives of place identity that are relevant and feasible today? Whose interests define those place narratives?

This is not a process monopolized by planners, nor are planners assured a driving role. As Duncan and Barnes (1992: 7) noted, 'Places are intertextual sites, because various texts and discursive practices based on previous texts are deeply inscribed in their landscapes and institutions'. We need to be alert to the tensions between the new narratives of place identity and other narratives concerning that place. Past and present realities cannot be easily erased in favour of some ersatz new identity, even if those with power wish to do so. Identity is closely tied to memory, and though it would be wrong to posit some common 'folk-memory' in societies that are increasingly diverse, mobile and exposed to a plethora of outside influences, memory and tradition remain important reference points in any construction of place identity.

Similarly, the construction of place identity should not be reified, or depicted in monolithic and functional terms even if an elite such as leading politicians, bureaucrats and business figures is united in an identity-building project, as is often the case. The vibrancy of everyday life necessarily sets the structures within which place communities are imagined, experienced and changed. De Certeau (1984) drew a distinction between the 'concept city' of 'utopian and urbanistic discourse' that underpinned the origins of rational urban planning, and the more messy and experiential discourses of place. De Certeau wrote that 'the ruses and combinations of powers that have no readable identity proliferate; without points where one can take hold of them, without rational transparency, they are impossible to administer' (1984: 95). In other words, the essence of planning is the presumption that deliberate 'top-down' action can translate a desired place identity into an actual place identity, but the reality is that a myriad of actions of others, the normal practice of everyday life in the city, will subvert such intentions. The gap between planners' narratives of sustainable development and the lifestyle and living choices of ordinary people are a contemporary expression of this tension. There needs to be dialogue between the elite and the public. As Groth (2002:19) puts it,

> The construction of urban identities should be formed in a broad partnership-dialogue on visions for the 'first order' development of the city while at the same time leaving room for a multitude of 'second order' dialogues with the citizens and cultural and social movements.

In summary, Haartsen, Groote and Huigen (2000: 2–3) claimed that in academic debate broad agreement seems to have been reached on the following points about place identity in relation to regions:

1. Regional identities are *by definition* a social construct: they are ascribed by people to an area, and are not 'natural' or 'objective' characteristics of that area.
2. Constructions of identity are based on specific perceived characteristics or qualities of the area; and
3. As the future is not yet known, these perceptions always lean on the past.
4. Regional identities are *by definition* contested. Different people and/or institutions, who have different interests in the area, may proclaim different regional identities.
5. Regional identities are *by definition* contextualized. It is important to deconstruct the context of ascribed identities (who is proclaiming this identity and why?). This requires unravelling the power balance between claimants in the political arena.
6. Regional identities are *by definition* processes. Identity is a dynamic concept which changes with its changing context. The power balance between claimants may change; their goals may change; new claimants may arrive in the arena; new functions may arise; etc.

In short, there will be multiple, contested identities for any one area. The key questions are how does spatial planning construct, integrate and exclude identities, and what are the relationships between identities, participation, policies and actions?

COMPONENTS OF REGIONAL AND LOCAL IDENTITY

How are we to take these challenging concepts from social science and begin to apply them to explorations of the way that planning and design articulates, and impacts on, local and regional identity? What characteristics is a geographical area deemed to contain? Amundsen (2001: 10–11) identified four elements typically present in a place identity, which frequently are combined in some fashion. These were:

- spatial qualities that distinguish the place from others – e.g. location, but also infrastructure, communication and architecture;
- characteristics or qualities of the inhabitants that distinguish them from inhabitants of other places – e.g. values, customs, physical appearance;
- social conditions and social relations between the inhabitants;
- culture and/or history, seen as a unifying element that again connects the inhabitants to tradition and again distinguishes them from 'the other'.

Amundsen further suggested that analyses of local and regional identity could proceed by asking the basic questions: what, who, how and why?

'*What*' is the specific content of the identity? The four bullet points above give some indication. However, we have already used the term 'narrative' in relation to place identities, and it is an important concept in relation to 'what?' Place identity is unlikely to comprise a disconnected and fragmented set of images and statements. Rather place identity is likely to take the form of a narrative, 'a coherent story with high and potent argumentative and symbolic value' (Amundsen, 2001: 13–14). The narratives will typically link and explain the components of a place identity, and implicitly or explicitly prescribe some action, while tacitly or explicitly rejecting other actions. Because our concern is with place identity and planning, it is important to analyse what aspects of the place, what components of the area, feature in (or are conspicuously ignored, or ruled illegitimate by) the planning discourse about identity.

For example, the NoordXXI project revolved around a narrative that depicted the partner regions as rural areas around expanding cities, places where people live 'in a safe and well-known environment' but have to commute to work from areas where jobs in traditional primary and manufacturing sectors are declining. Further absorption into commuting would undermine this traditional identity and deny the potential of that identity to generate an economic, environmental and lifestyle alternative to the remorseless spread of the city. The priorities of spatial planning and economic development should be changed to work towards this end: 'quality by identity'. Thus the project sought to work within the planning discourse in each partner region, but to challenge and change policies, procedures and practices so as to create and implement place narratives based on 'identity'.

Amundsen (2001) suggested that the identity narrative is a narrative of roots, belonging and structures, and these features can be seen in this vignette of the focus of the NoordXXI project. For example, the notion that people 'have to' commute because of a decline in local employment excludes the alternative reality of people from urban areas staying in their existing job in the city but choosing to move to housing beyond the urban fringe and to commute. Similarly, Amundsen hypothesized that place narratives express a conflict of interest between 'our' community and others. In NoordXXI the local large city, and its dominance, was 'the other', a familiar tension in any city regional planning situation.

Amundsen (2001) also highlighted the likelihood that there would be conflicting narratives of identity, linked to plurality and diversity in social structures within a region. Little attention had been paid to that possibility in the initial design of the NoordXXI project, though once research began it became clear that there were indeed different identities. However, we would take this argument a stage further. Given the economic restructuring of space that is ongoing, analysis needs to be alert to the particular conceptions of place that are at the root of global use of space. How do the filters that privilege competitiveness, mobility, market choice and consumerism translate into stories about, and spatial plans for, places? Chapter 2 seeks to build a base of definitions and concepts that can be used to explore such questions in later chapters.

The 'who?' question raises issues of power. Narrators can be individuals, such as local historians, architectural conservationists or other individual experts on identity, though Amundsen (2001: 15) suggested that to be successful they would probably have to have been seen to be 'one of us' within the place community. Local or regional groups can also be narrators of place identity, examples being employer or trade union organizations, amenity bodies and environmental activists, etc. Thirdly, there are public institutions, which include the media and political parties as well as planners and other officials. More than the rest, these operate on what we call 'territory' (a concept explained in Chapter 2), and have the power to publicize and act on their narratives, though such narratives are likely to be more eclectic and consensus oriented than those of individuals or groups. Chapter 3 explores the nature of participation and involvement in the making of place narratives and these themes are then assessed in NoordXXI practice examples in later chapters.

How and where are place narratives articulated? Planners typically use quite a restricted set of 'texts' to communicate. The written plan and accompanying map is probably the main one, though it may be supplemented by exhibitions, newsletters, or reports to politicians. Typically they are operating what Amundsen (2001:17) called a 'consensus genre'. In contrast 'outsiders', those with less access to power, may resort to a 'conflict genre' to challenge a dominant narrative, e.g. a provocative letter to the press or a demonstration. There may be negotiation or the exercise of power, cooperation or ongoing challenge and dissent. However, if we accept that 'all texts are narratives' and, following de Certeau (1984: 95), that 'the ruses and combinations of powers that have no readable identity proliferate', then we should also expect that part of the identity of a place will be constructed by everyday practice. Such practice will use space and place in a way that is not accessible in a formalized and explicit text, but nevertheless constitutes a real discourse about place. For example, if people commute from an area, the public transport timetables and the traffic queues in the rush hour are themselves potent expressions of place identity. It is also important to recognize the 'invisible' hand of those outside the locality – such as central government or the global purveyors of commodities and brands – in defining such place identities.

Box 1.1 gives an example of the 'what', 'who' and 'how' of place narratives, emphasizing the significance of everyday practices and the exclusion of such narratives from orthodox planning practice. Though Belfast is exceptional in terms of the intensity and form of conflict over place identity, it highlights the centrality of place narratives to civil society and their reproduction through practices that organize space and demarcate territory.

Finally, we should note the model of regional identity formation proposed by Paasi (1986) and summarized by Raagmaa (2002), though this primarily relates to the formation of regional units, rather than the more open-ended concerns of Amundsen and of the NoordXXI project. This involves four 'shapes' that occur simultaneously. These are defined as the constitution of the territorial shape, the symbolic shape, the institutional shape, and the emerging socio-spatial consciousness of the inhabitants and the establishment of the region/locality in the regional system. The territorial shape is about achieving boundaries and some kind of status as a territorial

Box 1.1 Place identity and planning in Belfast

Neill (1999) reviewed place identity in Belfast, a city where memory is extensively embedded in a physical environment that carries deeply meaningful symbols to contesting social groups on either side of the sectarian divide. It is a city where par excellence there has been spatial construction of national identity (Ireland or the UK). For example, as Neill noted, Stormont, the parliament building designed in the 1920s for the statelet of Ulster that emerged after the partition of Ireland, is 'read' very differently by unionists and nationalists in the city.

In Belfast, enclosed communities either side of the sectarian divide demarcate their territories by a host of visual symbols. Murals, painted kerbstones and community facilities define the identity of these places. Moving through or along the edge of these spaces – especially in parades or marches – reaffirms or challenges the narratives of place identity.

In this situation of intense and contested place identity, planning as a statutory practice has operated in a narrowly technical and professional manner. Neill quoted an official government report that stated: 'typically, the issue of a divided society has not been explicitly mentioned or addressed within planning documents in Northern Ireland'.

Source: HMSO, 1997: 43

unit. The symbolic shape will entail icons such as a name, a language or dialect, as well as landmarks and infrastructure, or traditions, lifestyles and cultural outputs. The institutional shape includes the formation of values and organizations to maintain the image of the region and mobilize its symbols. Such institutionalization helps to form a popular regional socio-spatial consciousness that is reproduced through everyday practice and lived space.

In summary, in discussing the '*why?*' of local identity, Amundsen (2001: 18) wrote 'All narratives, all public messages are related to intentions – open and hidden, internal and external, conscious and unconscious, functional and structural'. In such a multivariate situation the combinations are potentially bewildering. However, we can probe the relations between identity narratives and the values and interests they advance.

PRACTICAL QUESTIONS

This chapter has argued that there is a new concern for place identity within planning, as evidenced by the NoordXXI Interreg project from which the book has been developed. However, planners do not have a monopoly on the place identity process; indeed, many existing institutional structures and ways of practising severely limit their capacity to produce anything other than technical and legalistic narratives. However, changes in places and in governance are themselves likely to restructure such practice and are already creating new and important narratives of place identity that challenge or sidestep the planning discourse. Thus we feel that a clearer understanding of the role of planning practice in creating, maintaining or changing place narratives is important, a theme we develop at the end of the book.

We have identified ways to begin to interrogate place narratives: Amundsen's 'what, who, how, why?' However, we have also sought to stress the need to be alert to less explicit, but potentially important, place narratives formed out of everyday life and out of the power of global consumer culture. From this platform we pose a number of practical questions that were encompassed in the NoordXXI project on 'Quality by identity'. The rest of the book will address these questions:

* Does the spatial setting, the environmental experience of the place where people live, affect the language and consequently the construction of narratives? How do different groups of people, or people from different places, construct narratives about places?
* What narratives of place identity are currently embedded in the development of spatial planning as a European project? In particular, where does the European Spatial Development Perspective fit in?

- To what extent does national legislation and policy on planning and related legislation on land and development create or restrict opportunities for the development of local or regional narratives of identity?
- How does planning for place identity, as described through NoordXXI, relate to the broader spatial visions of the future Europe, and what is their emerging role in relation to global competitiveness and changing governance patterns?
- How are regions changing? Can we build a typology of regions, and spatial planning interventions, in terms of their dynamics towards or away from distinctive place identity?
- Participation: how do the culture and practice of public involvement in spatial planning relate to narratives of identity?
- Identity, sustainability and settlement patterns: what are the implications for spatial planning in relation to infrastructure, economic development, housing and landscapes? Who gains and who loses?
- Local place identity and urban design: how can planners identify local narratives of place identity and use them in urban design?

CHAPTER 2

SPACE, PLACE AND TERRITORY:
AN ANALYTICAL FRAMEWORK
PAUL JENKINS

This section examines the concepts of space, place and territory and their relevance to spatial planning, as an analytical contribution to the changing role of planning. It has been felt important to define these terms as they are used in various ways in planning literature, often without clear definition, and yet – it is argued here – they have significantly different conceptual bases. The terms are defined below, and the inter-relationship between them is also illustrated in Table 2.1. It is this relationship that is examined in the subsequent sections, as the chapter argues that the changes in the concepts and their relationships need to be taken on board in our changing view of the role of spatial planning in society.

SPACE, PLACE AND TERRITORY AS ANALYTICALLY DISTINCT CONCEPTS

The term 'space' is used here to denote physical location, which underpins the other two concepts of 'place' and 'territory' in that these relate to physical attributes. There are two main conceptual approaches to space. One sees this as abstract and real, existing whether it is 'filled' or not – framing and containing all physical elements. This concept of 'absolute space' is opposed by the approach which postulates that space exists only through definition of the things it contains – i.e. that space is relational (Madanipour, 2001). Although this distinction may seem abstract and far removed from the practicalities of planning, it is important to establish here that it is the *relational* quality of space which concerns us, whether space exists outside of this in its own right or not.

Geographical identification of *space* as such is undertaken in relational ways, using latitude, longitude and altitude, the first being arbitrarily defined in a specific historical (and political–economic) context through Greenwich, the second in relation to the earth's spherical attributes (i.e. the equator as widest circumference most distant from the poles) and the third in relation to sea level, also relationally defined. Techniques of spatial positioning have moved on a lot from the compass and star chart, yet geographical positioning systems also measure space relationally. However, strongly associated with spatially existing elements are economic values placed on physical resources – whether for consumption (e.g. coal) or other use (e.g. river transport). The existence of certain physical attributes thus affects the micro-economics of places, as well as the distance between these spatial locations having macro-economic implications, overlaid with territorial definitions – i.e. economic geography.

Place on the other hand is seen as being the predominantly socio-cultural perception and definition of space, and is an important element of social identity – whether individual or collective – and can be understood as social geography. As the previous chapter has stressed, in an increasingly complex society, overlapping definitions of *place identity* exist – again both individual and collective. The manifestation of these forms of social identity is what has been termed 'mind-maps' whereby we register physical space mentally. Thus if asked to describe, for instance, the area which they live within, members of the same household will define this area differently, based on their perception and activities within it, and will use different physical attributes to describe this. More than this, an individual household member is quite likely to use different mind-map references when describing the same area to different people, and would probably describe the same place in different ways with the passage of time.

Place is also a relational concept as it is defined as the relationships between elements perceived in multiple ways through socio-cultural filters. Multiplied manifold times, this would seem to create perceptual chaos, but strong socio-cultural groupings create their own 'traditions' of mind-maps, or 'collective myths' ('permanences' in Harvey's 1996 analysis), which are then used as a means of collective communication and identity. However, as noted above, increasingly complex societies include increasingly wide diversification of socio-cultural groups, and thus multiple mind-maps and expressions of place identity exist for any specific space. These place-based forms of social identity are often deliberately created or moulded by institutions – football teams being an example which operates at the local, city, national and increasingly international levels.

Although place in this analytical framework is predominantly defined in socio-cultural terms, there are also important micro-economic aspects to this as socio-cultural values underpin much of the local economy. A simple example is the proverbial estate agent's definition of the three important aspects to selling a house: location, location and location. The importance of location in this case is defined by socio-cultural values, whether access to 'good' schools, other amenities or general aesthetic and social character, but has economic expression. While this has been a well-established feature of the micro-economy, the importance of place is increasingly stressed at a meso- and macro-level also.

We define *territory* here as essentially the governance context of space – as limited generally by formal (or legally constituted) boundaries that are spatially determined, and of course mapped and even physically created (e.g. fenced). The dominant manifestation of this is still perhaps nation-state boundaries, with their strong macro-economic significance as nation-states manipulate economic inter-change through laws and taxation. The creation of nation-states has always entailed the creation of *territorial identities*, a process that is in flux, in terms of both nation-state changes and the relationship with sub-national and supra-national entities (Le Gales, 1998). In general, nation-state boundaries are becoming of less importance in macro-economic terms as changing technology permits faster and greater flows of resources (or more accurately less physical grounding of the control of resources) and distance has less (or different) economic importance. The opposite situation exists concerning the flow of labour, with boundaries becoming more strictly defined and policed, with a subsequent increased tendency to challenge this through forms of migration.

An aspect of the changing macro-economic importance of nation-state bound-aries is the development of wider macro-regional boundaries, mainly driven by economic considerations, but with strong political significance. The EU is a clear recent example of this, but macro-regional groupings, with greater or lesser political implications, are being created worldwide. These all entail the creation of new terri-torial identities in some form or other – a simple example in Europe being the EU form of passport and its associated cross boundary rights. This changing economic context – often referred to as 'globalization' – is examined below, as this is one of the major factors affecting the relationships between the concepts used here.

Other than the nation-state, territory is defined at sub-national levels through a wide range of local authority boundaries: provincial, municipal, etc., as illustrated for some of the countries in Europe in Chapter 4. However, the simplistic definition of 'localities' based on these has been increasingly challenged. Attempts to define locality which reflect the micro- and meso-level economy are being developed,[1] and these also express an intention to reflect some of the socio-cultural elements of place, although this is a much more ambitious target (for example Coombes and Wymer, 2001). There is wide recognition, however, that in developing new territorial identities, whether at a macro-regional level, city/city region or locality level (i.e. meso- and micro-regions), the sense of identity plays an important role. Hence a sig-nificant literature and practice of 'place-marketing', and 'place-making' in planning has developed (e.g. Kearns and Philo, 1993; Gold and Ward, 1995; Fitzsimmons, 1995; Griffiths, 1998). It is argued that the dominance of the nation-state as the economic unit of global importance is becoming diminished and the city/city region at the meso-level has become more important. Thus Andersen (2002: 36–7) points to the fall of the Iron Curtain as changing European territory, and says:

> The importance of the states has diminished in tandem with a growing number
> of organizations becoming more important for European integration. In particular
> the EU, with its single market, has become the dominant non-nation-state actor,

and increasingly performs the overall national planning and co-ordinating functions regarding economic and commercial relationships. At the same time, local and regional authorities have acquired increasing responsibility for commercial and employment development and, thus, also for the welfare of the population.

While this is undoubtedly so to some extent, nation-states retain sovereignty and are in no danger of imminent disappearance (Herrschel and Newman, 2002). However, there is also no doubt that the forms of institutional and territorial relationship between cities, regions and national territories in Europe are changing, as they have over time (Le Gales, 2002).

Table 2.1 attempts to capture and relate key elements of the above definitions. This chapter argues that there is a changing emphasis between the various categories outlined in the table, i.e. in the relationships between forms of knowledge and perception which this analysis relies on: socio-cultural values, economic trends and governance processes. *These all have implications for place identity and territorial identity.* In other words, there is a trend for changes in power structure between territorial definitions, with a relative decline in importance of the nation-state as an economic unit, in relation to larger macro-economic and smaller meso- and micro-economic units. In parallel there is a trend to manipulate socio-culturally defined identities to underpin these territorial changes, within the context of the governance regimes that operate. These governance regimes are themselves changing, albeit much more slowly, as traditional forms of authority and sources of legitimacy are queried – mainly by new elites exerting their 'voice', but also by marginalized groups 'exiting' the formal political and economic system.

Table 2.1 The relationship between space, place and territory in different spheres of knowledge and perception

	Space	Place	Territory
Physical	geographical identification	'mind-maps' and cultural signifiers	mapping
Economic	natural resources and distance factors	micro-economic factors	macro-economic factors – e.g. taxation, tariffs, economic concentration
Legal/ political		allegiances, acceptance of the legitimacy of the governance regime	boundaries and definition of authorities and powers
Socio-cultural		social identity	'formal', or administrative, identity

GLOBALIZATION, COMPETITIVENESS AND PLACE IDENTITY

While identity is a psychological and cultural concept, as described in Chapter 1, and place a geographical one, as described above, we would assert that contemporary concerns for place identity are probably most significantly rooted in economic change and globalization as a manifestation of this. Space is a key element in capital accumulation, labour control, and the reproduction of power and knowledge.

For example, in the nineteenth and twentieth centuries, urban economic growth was a major characteristic forging place identities within Europe. While a range of forces at different spatial scales impacted on any one place, the identity of the town was defined primarily by its economic base, and bolstered by the imagery of the associated infrastructure. Thus Sheffield in England was famous as a steel town where cutlery was made, and there were ports like Gothenburg in Sweden, fishing towns like Fraserburgh in Aberdeenshire, and seaside resorts whose identity was signified by 'miles of golden sand'.

Globalization, and the increasing mobility of capital that underpins this concept, has led to a more comprehensive context for competitiveness, and has changed the economic/place identity relation in barely a generation. Thus Castells (1989: 348) has spoken of 'the historical emergence of the space of flows, superseding the meaning of the space of places'. Similarly, Harvey (1989:14) talked of 'a world that capital treats as more and more place-less', while for Robins (1991: 13) there has been 'the disarticulation of place-based societies'. In parallel, despite growing global restrictions, intensified movements of population (and hence labour) have made places more diverse, but it is the movement of capital that has most drastically changed place identities.

From the 1970s a new international division of labour developed in which labour-intensive industrial production shifted to concentrate in locations where labour was cheap and well controlled. At the most basic level, the huge loss of manufacturing jobs – for instance 2.8 million in Great Britain between 1971 and 1989, over a third of the total (Barke and Harrop, 1994: 93) – devastated traditional identities. In the new age of consumerism, mobile capital and the service and high-technology economies, traditional identities and their associated institutions became potential barriers to reinvestment, the attraction of capital and the reconstruction of the economic and infrastructure base of settlements. If, as Rutherford (1990: 19) has suggested, 'identity marks the conjuncture of our past with the social, cultural and economic relations we live within', then such drastic change in so short a time was bound to create tensions about the identity of places.

While the urban and industrial centres underwent drastic economic change in the 1970s and 1980s, rural Europe remained largely sheltered from the impacts of global competition. The phrase 'you cannot buck the market' was applied to steel workers and factory hands, but not to farmers. The EU in particular, while espousing the merits of free competition, heavily subsidized agriculture, and hence sustained the identity of rural areas, through the Common Agricultural Policy, and tariff barriers against producers from outside the EU (see Cloke, 1992). However, changes in agricultural practices, in response to competition and changing subsidy regimes, did impact on the structures of agricultural production and on rural land-scapes and ecosystems associated with traditional practices.

More specifically, at the end of the twentieth century, anxieties about possible reform of the Common Agricultural Policy and public loss of confidence in food safety under industrialized agricultural production systems have prompted an eco-nomic crisis in the countryside. The changes imply a restructuring of place identity through processes of rural diversification. Meanwhile rural identities are also pres-sured by urban mobility, through commuting, new house building, inter-regional transport infrastructure and tourism. The empirical research this book is based on highlighted these effects and their immediate causes, as well as the reaction of the current planning systems to these, and hence we try to delve into the causes and their effects on the planning system.

Although likely to change in future, the competition and the associated decon-struction and reconstruction of place identities in the past 50 years have been greatest in urban areas. Concerning reconstruction of these identities in the face of macro-economic change, the USA, with its traditionally decentralized governance system, strong mayors and active business groupings, led the way with a number of major and economically successful attempts to redefine the identity of de-industrial-ized urban centres. Baltimore in Maryland, on the east coast of the USA, is perhaps the paradigmatic example. It is a city of 750,000 inhabitants in a wider metropolitan area of two million. Industrial decline and loss of people and jobs to the suburbs began in the 1950s. A partnership of local business, developers and the city coun-cil turned the Inner Harbour area into a range of retail and leisure uses. Throughout the whole renewal process attention was paid to achieving quality in the architecture and much effort went into a campaign to improve the city's image. 'Although this is an area difficult to define, image-related elements have a big impact on the business climate and the willingness of entrepreneurs to participate in the future of a city' (de Jong, 1991: 194). The near hegemonic status of Baltimore as a 'best practice' that has been aped in many places across the globe, does indeed demonstrate the importance of 'image-related elements', since the regeneration of the Inner Harbour is somewhat cosmetic. It does not go more than three blocks into the city, nor, more fundamentally, does it provide the city with a new economic purpose. The marketing image (and its benefits to Baltimore) is more potent than the actuality.

Such success stories prompted practical imitation, much debate and acade-mic theorizing. Holcomb (1994) argued that place competition required the transformation of traditional industrial cities into 'post-industrial' service centres, through both a re-imaging of place *and* a remaking of the built environment. Crilley (1993: 233) noted that architecture had become 'an integral part of the incorpora-tion of cultural investment and policy into urban growth strategies, as cities struggle to attract inwards investment'. Thus the definition of space through architecture, urban design and development at the local level can be a key driver in the recon-struction of place identity at the level of the city or agglomeration.

In Europe, Paris and Barcelona set the pace in the use of spectacular architec-ture to embed their identity as places. There was no shortage of admirers or followers among national governments, and the EU itself complemented and spurred market place competitiveness through its own initiatives. For example, Glasgow was a city whose identity had been defined by the work of the shipyards and by a romanticized militant working-class culture based on the politics of 'Red Clydeside' in the years fol-lowing the First World War. By the 1980s the shipyards were closed and thousands of other jobs in manufacturing had also been lost. One response was the city's rep-resentation as the European City of Culture for 1990. This newly created identity was not without contest. McLay (1988) contrasted the city of culture with the 'Real Glasgow', the 'Workers' City', arguing that 'it has nothing whatever to do with the working- or workless-class poor of Glasgow, but everything to do with big business and money: to pull in investment' (McLay, 1988: 1).

Notwithstanding such critiques, there has been a growing recognition that there are important spatial and place dimensions to globalized competition. While economists still hold that competition is between firms, not places, a body of writing has developed contending that place-related factors influence the competitiveness of firms. Porter (1990: 158) argued that 'Internationally successful industries and industrial clusters frequently concentrate in a city or region, and the bases for advan-tage are often intensely local.' Porter's view was that competitiveness of nation-states, and of related sub-national places, is influenced by policy interven-tions. In the 1990s less weight was accorded to traditional economic reasons for explaining the dynamics of new industrial agglomerations, and more emphasis was given to social and institutional factors. Amin and Thrift (1995: 100) highlighted the importance of 'relationships of trust; a strong sense of common industrial purpose; social consensus; local institutional support for business; and agencies and tradi-tions encouraging innovation, skill formation and the circulation of ideas'.

A shared vision for the development of the locality has thus come to be seen as an essential part of a successful partnership. The core argument made is that globalization has increased the importance of actions at the level of the city or agglomeration to influence competitive advantage, so that local government together with local civil society has the capacity (but also faces the imperative) to foster and sustain innovation and business competitiveness. Thus Kresl (1995: 51)

included institutional flexibility, public–private sector co-operation and urban strategy as factors determining urban competitiveness, alongside more traditional
concerns with infrastructure, amenities and location, etc. Amin and Thrift (1995)
brought many of these ideas together in the concept of *institutional thickness*,
which they saw as a key factor in shaping capacity for local action. This implies a
host of bodies – e.g. firms, financial institutions, chambers of commerce, training
agencies, trade associations, local authorities, development agencies, unions, government agencies – building coalitions in which the individual interests merge into a
collective representation, and a common enterprise.

Similarly, a body of theory focusing on the power and importance of local coalitions has developed within political science. Known as regime theory, it recognizes the
complexity of governance as the state's local role has come to be shared with a range
of private sector bodies. Power then resides in networks that have the capacity to get
things done. A leading proponent suggested that 'In a complex, fragmented urban
world, the paradigmatic form of power is that which enables certain interests to blend
their capacities to achieve common purposes' (Stoker, 1995: 55). While this literature
has concentrated on the urban scale, we suggest that in the context of early twenty-
first-century Europe, similar dynamics are evident at least at regional and arguably at
trans-national scales (see also Herrschel and Newman, 2002; Le Gales, 2002).

Writing from Estonia, Raagmaa (2002: 55) has suggested that public authorities have to struggle to create a favourable business climate while also improving
the living conditions of the citizens. In these circumstances, 'knowingly designing
regional identity … with its 'institutional thickness' based on common social space
and local culture' is a way of steering institutional change and 'painful reforms without a danger of social collapse'. This is a subject we develop in the next chapter, and
also in the empirical research related later in the book.

In summary, our argument is that from the 1970s onwards structural economic
change re-worked space and, in the process, undermined many 'traditional' aspects
of place identity, certainly at the city and regional level. However, in parallel, the new
globalized elements of the economy, together with competition through nation-state
and supra-national bodies like the EU, put a new premium on spatial collaboration of
a diversity of players in partnerships. Some form of shared place identity has been
seen as important in rallying and sustaining such networks. That identity, if geared –
as it usually is – to attracting and/or retaining investment, must necessarily be congruent in at least some significant respects with business interests and the promotion
of competitiveness. This usually means that there will be a tension between the new
identity and traditional identities and/or identities adhered to by social groups
excluded from the coalition. Thus Castells (1989: 350) urged: 'At the cultural level,
local societies must preserve their identities and build upon their historical roots,
regardless of their economic and functional dependence upon the space of flows.'

The basic thesis of this chapter is thus that macro-economic changes are leading to macro-, meso- and even micro-level changes in territorial identity at the same time that socio-cultural rates of change are increasing and thus multiplying place identities. For example, global changes have led to the closure of traditional port-related industries, and as we have already indicated, the Inner Harbour regeneration in Baltimore has changed the identity of the area immediately adjoining the harbour, but has also given Baltimore itself a new global identity. However, socio-cultural changes, such as the increasing importance of young professionals in urban housing markets, or the growth of marginalized migrant communities (sometimes characterized as 'the Third World in the First World') have superseded the relative homogeneity of many places in the mid twentieth century.

Furthermore, place and territorial identity is increasingly important and contested in underpinning governance: as class has waned as the basis of political identity, spatial and ethnic identities have become more significant. For example, intra-party divisions over the powers of the EU vis-à-vis the British nation-state – and its 'unique identity' – were a significant factor in the political collapse of the Conservative Party from the mid 1990s. Hence there are opportunities, even imperatives, to construct new forms of political legitimacy and territorial identity with new, or adjusted, socio-cultural values. Place identity (encapsulated in new jargon such as 'knowledge city' or 'sustainable region') is a key component in this process, and participatory forms of spatial planning are potentially significant discourses for construing such narratives of place identities. Referring back to Table 2.1, these changes can be summarized in the analytical framework as in Table 2.2.

However, we will also argue that whether these changes in territorial and place identity lead to broad public benefit or not – and how this is defined – is an under-developed issue in contemporary planning theory and practice. In relation to the changing context of governance, our research identifies that changing territorial relations provide opportunities and demands for wider negotiation forums on spatial planning issues, but many of these operate informally, and there is a danger that these are manipulated for the benefit of specific groups as opposed (or in addition) to that of the broader public. Arguably the role of state redistribution through the welfare state based on nation-states – i.e. the political economic context that planning 'grew up' within – is changing and the new territorial and place identities emerging create both opportunities and threats to such concepts of broad public benefit. As such, public benefit needs to be redefined with a new focus at both the supra-national and local levels which are gaining influence. Globalization does not automatically equate to the replacement of national welfare states by unregulated markets and private provision. Comparative analysis of how urban and regional planning systems and practices have been adjusted in different European welfare states is a rich field to research these matters, as reflected in the proliferation of recent

Table 2.2 Changes brought about by globalization to space, place and territory

	Space	Place	Territory
Physical	Information Communications Technology changes the nature of existing relationships across space and between time and space.	New forms of cultural expression in physical built environment, including global cultures of consumption.	Formation of new economic and social groups dilutes the significance of previous boundaries. International migration pressures.
Economic	New international division of labour develops. Restructuring of industrialisation and agriculture creates different opportunities (and crises).	Flows and networks become as important as places, but institutions embedded in places become more important. Place-marketing develops to capture global flows.	New zones of global economic integration develop separately from territories. (Re)-emergence of regions and networks of cities as key economic drivers.
Legal/ political		Previous governing systems' legitimacy queried. Institutional thickness a factor in managing change.	Change of traditional government units and functions. De-regulation and neo-liberal policies. Partnerships and privatisation alter the territorial base for service delivery.
Socio-cultural		Increasing diversity of cultures in specific places and across space.	Change from government to governance.

publications (e.g. Healey *et al.*, 1997; Danson, Halkier and Cameron, 2000; Madanipour, 2001; Cars *et al.*, 2002).

What is remarkable is that we seem surprised that these changes are taking place. Thinking globally, similar changes have been very much in evidence in the past 50 years in the poorer countries of 'the South'. It is only as countries in the globally dominant 'North' face changes to their hegemonic post-war political, economic, social and cultural values that this has stimulated in-depth inquiry into the relationships built in to their planning systems. In fact it is surprising that political regimes, economic structures and social patterns in the North have stayed relatively static for so long, as indeed they are essentially relationally determined and the underlying trends have not stopped changing.

The relevance of these analytical concepts for spatial planning

What does all this have to do with planning? Land use or physical planning, the antecedents of spatial planning as we consider it early in the twenty-first century, has some 100 years of existence as a 'technical' discipline. Throughout most of that period it has been fundamentally a tool of governments; most professional planners have worked for local authorities or regional/provincial or central governments, and statute has dominated practice. Elected governments constituted the democratic legitimacy for the powers embedded in 'technical' expertise. However, governments' 'power over' has now given way to 'power to', and metamorphosed into 'governance'.[2] Governments recognize that they can no longer operate in isolation, but need to forge relationships with civil society and the private sector to manage change. This dramatic change in polity is forcing changes in planning.

Two developments in the UK illustrate this tension. In England the Ministry responsible for planning announced its intention to 'change the culture' of planning (ODPM, 2001), so that it becomes not only a more strategic means of promoting development, but also takes on the ethos of 'customer care', the norm in a consumerist society. The Ministry (ODPM, 2002) characterized the culture of planning as 'reactive and defensive'. In contrast it sought a culture that would 'improve the experience of planning, for those affected by its decisions, whether businesses, community groups, individual members of the community or planning professionals'. At the heart of these changes are concerns to make the planning system more 'business-friendly' but also to improve its integration with other forms of public policy *and* to enhance the scope for public involvement. There will be Regional Spatial Strategies and Local Development Frameworks (note the absence of the word 'plans'). The Local Development Framework not only links into the Regional Spatial Strategy, but is also a means of delivering the Community Strategy, which is a statutory document that sets out the broad, corporate vision for a local authority's area.

The Royal Town Planning Institute has also embraced the need to change. It has adopted a 'New Vision' (RTPI, 2002), characterized in the catchphrase: 'Mediation of space, making of place', and undertaken a fundamental reform of its requirements for education and membership (RTPI, 2003). The New Vision argues that effective planning cannot be delivered through governmental activity alone, and instead requires working with a variety of organizations. It calls for a view of planning that involves more than statutory systems. It sees professional planners as facilitators of, rather than as having a monopoly of, the activity of planning.

Planning regulates land use and physical development for political, economic and socio-cultural objectives, with changing emphases concerning the latter two objectives depending on the political context. Although essentially dealing with the physical, it is in fact the political and economic objectives that have tended to dominate, generally acting as the filter for socio-cultural objectives. This was possible in a fairly stable governance regime where a public set of conceptions was established corporately after the Second World War and then adhered to with a greater or lesser degree of flexibility – i.e. territorial identity was quite stable within dominant nation-states. In parallel, conceptions of place identity were fairly static and planners felt they could understand and predict these, thus enabling them to act for the 'public good', as advisors to elected representative politicians. However, as society has become more diverse and governance systems also mutate in the face of rapid economic change, the relatively static processes of planning are becoming fast outdated. This is happening in relation to the territorial basis for authority that underpins planning systems; the economic imperatives which influence the system at a macro- and micro-level; and the socio-cultural values which the system purports to permit expression of in physical terms.

It can be argued that the public lost faith in planning long before the economic actors and politicians did so. Indeed, it is probably the politicians who are the main supporters of innovations in planning systems today (albeit these are often put forward by planners), as this represents another component in their 'toolbox' of responsibilities and powers of governance. In Chapters 6 and 7 we argue that it is usually for this reason that innovation in planning has received political support, as although innovatory methods of engaging stakeholders in planning have existed for at least the past 30 years, it is the political and economic need to use these that has led to major innovations in planning processes being implemented, and thus it is the territorial identity context which tends to channel expression of place identity.

If we concentrate on planning in the post-1945 context in Europe, this was initially closely tied to the creation of the welfare nation-states in the recently defined or defended territories. While planning existed as a statutory practice in some countries before then, such practice had been largely local and permissive. With the welfare nation-states, the aspiration was for a form of planning that was comprehensive, consistent and an important component of a socialized reconstruction programme. Here, as noted above, it was possible for a specialist professional group of planners (the spatial experts) to develop a role of acting in the 'public interest', assuming that their rational scientific training allowed them to determine the spatial and physical development aspects of this on behalf of the public. In this they were backed, with varying forms of orientation, by the political authorities, for whom land use and regional economic planning was a relatively new tool, closely allied to the creation of a new governance regime: the welfare state.

In this post-war period many national identities were strong, as were national governments within their areas of well-defined territorial authority; indeed one effect of the Second World War was to settle by 'fiat' some of Europe's contested territorial boundaries. Territorial identity as such was usually unquestioned or unquestionable, except by colonized groups. Despite the recent turbulence of war (or perhaps because of it), society was quite strongly structured and place identities were strongly defined, whether at the sub-national level or local level. Micro-economic factors had been a major influence in the development of the modern industrial economy and were still of great importance – regional planning was in fact an attempt by governments to manipulate micro-economic factors of place and space.

This planning approach was increasingly challenged as the state's authoritative economic power was weakened at a micro- and macro-level in the late 1960s and early 1970s. This was also the period of restructuring in the face of worldwide economic depression and a period of rapid evolution of social structure and of cultural change, leading to a questioning of the fairly static perceptions of the 'public interest' by major elements of the public. Planning was thus challenged in this period with countervailing tendencies to a more strategic level of planning, given the reduction in the state's power as an economic actor, but also to integrate more emphasis on the need to determine public interests through participatory techniques (e.g. the Skeffington Report in Britain). In practice, however, the first tendency dominated as political regimes became more neo-liberal, and planners increasingly were seen as being allied to the state's facilitation of private economic interests. As noted in the previous chapter, this period of planning has subsequently and more recently been challenged as macro-economic realities and socio-cultural attitudes have continued to change.

The neo-liberal emphasis on the primacy of self-interested individuals making their own decisions has been countered by a renewal of calls for more participatory, or collaborative, planning. The notion of people sharing space, and having to find new forms of governance to reach mutual understandings of place, has been central to this line of argument. Perceptions of place identity, and – importantly – participation in the reformulation of macro-level territorial power and associated territorial identities, have thus been promoted by those who wish to contest the neo-liberal dismemberment of the welfare state. Privatism cannot be overturned by nostalgia for the community solidarity that was tempered by the collective hardships of war, a situation where people together had to face the ultimate 'other'. Nor can any alchemy reproduce that 1950s 'golden age of the professional', when experts were trusted to know best.

Rather there has to be some form of rapprochement with the ways that neo-liberalism and globalization have structured today's reality. This involves identification, assimilation and reconstitution of important elements from con-sumerism – market research, branding, new product design and launches, market segmentation, strategies to secure customer loyalty – as new practices to create, co-exist and maybe even integrate identities. This process is very much still ongoing, and this book hopes to contribute to the debate on the future role of planning with regard to both place identity and territorial identity, as it appears to the authors that considerable innovation in terms of recognition of place identity is in fact being manipulated to assist in the definition of new territorial identities and the structure of governance within these. There would also appear to be a new 'window of opportu-nity', even an imperative, to change the nature of the planning system fundamentally with the conjuncture of political, economic and social change.

As such, can we assume that the objectives of planning are 'up for grabs' as much as the system itself? This is a moot point, as much recent theoretical develop-ment has challenged the socio-cultural basis which is embedded in the procedures and power relationships which are integral to government actions such as planning in at least the post-war period. We would argue that it is not planning as a concept that needs radical revision, but the function of planning in relation to society, the state and the economy – especially the 'market' economy with limited state intervention.

Our position is that planning for too long has ignored the socio-cultural aspects of place in relation to the economic aspects of space as well as the authoritative aspects of territory, and this needs to be redressed in planning in future if it is to play a more widely accepted social role. Others agree with this position; for example, Forester (1989, 1993, 1999), Healey (1992, 1997, 2001) and Vigar et al. (2000), amongst oth-ers, have developed approaches to planning that address socio-cultural aspects through what they respectively call 'communicative' and 'collaborative' planning, which is based on the search for consensus through rational argumentation in decision-making arenas. However, we would argue that to advocate more 'discursive' or 'participatory' approaches per se will not change anything unless there is a correspond-ing change in the relationships of planning with governance of territory and in the regulation and promotion of economic activity at macro- and micro-economic levels.[3]

To elucidate this in plain terms, planning can be seen to have three principal fields of action:

*   defining and achieving the dominant governing group's goals (including atti-tudes to forms of democratic engagement);
*   stimulating and/or regulating private activity – individual and collective (i.e. from attitudes to land rights through to attitudes to corporate lobbies); and
*   responding to (both channelling and affecting) socio-cultural pressures/values.

These fields of action derive from the nature of the relationships between the state, the economy (especially the market) and society, as illustrated in Figure 2.1. The interface between these three fields is necessarily an uncomfortable position to occupy. Put in a form that any planner will recognize, it means that politicians, developers and environmental activists are all likely (and sometimes simultaneously) to point the finger of blame at planning when their aspirations are not realized. Part of a professional planner's self-awareness and skill lies in understanding and negotiating such conflicts. However, there are limits to this artistry. There has been a tendency to equate planning with a 'mediating role' between conflicting interests. This blurs important premises in the practice of mediation which are unlikely to be replicated fully for a planner employed by a government department – see the next chapter for more on how mediation affects planning.

As we have argued elsewhere (School of the Built Environment et al., 2003), planning practice in public agencies can take on many of the approaches of mediation, and independent planners can be effective mediators. However, planners are not the only mediating option. The role of planners in operating between politicians' priorities, the development market and socio-cultural pressures is unlikely to be neutral, although most planners will attempt to act in what they consider a 'balanced' way. Spatial planning has essentially developed as a function of state regulation on other sectors, with varying degrees of mediation, and hence planning systems are imbued with 'governing logic' and conducted through a procedural and legal-based meta-language.

The fact that this requires specialist resources and knowledge to counter (e.g. the hiring of their own planning consultants and lawyers) – such as the private sector and other lobbyist groups can muster – has led to greater distancing from direct socio-cultural inputs. In other words, whether consciously or not, much planning practice has been exclusionary: a dance between planners (and related professionals) representing government, and planners (and related professionals) representing

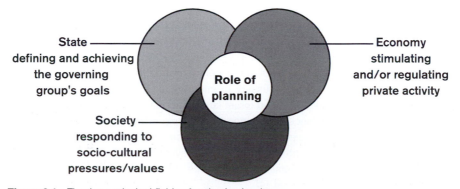

Figure 2.1   The three principal fields of action in planning

developers, in a process that appears opaque to other members of society. Where a discretionary system of development control operates and there are no third party rights of appeal (and both are the case in the UK), alienation by the lack of transparency can breed suspicion amongst the public and undermine the legitimacy of the planning system.

The challenge for planning is to develop new forms of interaction between the above three fields of action that more fully respond to new contexts which fully integrate these. Given the dominance of the state and the market to date, this will require significant redressing of imbalances in relation to socio-cultural inputs in future. For example, there is a long tradition of 'public participation' in planning, but it has typically remained subservient to the logic of government, in that it is usually packaged into a set of stages often spread over several years and unravelling at the pace decided by the planning authority, and at the end of it all an adversarial inquiry, where the main players are employed by government or by land and property owners, is still likely to be the main means of resolving issues.

In societies that have thoroughly imbibed consumerism and are simultaneously confronted by deconstructions and reconstructions of place identities, this will no longer work. Our proposition is that planning systems, and practitioners operating within them, will be pressed to move beyond the traditional structures and statutory confines, and to invent new ways of engaging diverse communities in narratives of place identity. The second part of the book will explore this idea in different practice contexts.

To summarize the main changes in the planning system since its heyday in the post-1945 welfare state, and to advance general propositions that can be used to focus the study of practice in Part 2, we can use the analytical framework established above in Boxes 2.1 and 2.2.

Box 2.1 Space, place and territory in planning in the post-war welfare state

Space
The state significantly increased its role in providing infrastructure (water, electricity and transport) as part of post-war rebuilding. These were delivered by public bodies seeking to ensure that all areas had the benefit of the same standard of provision, thereby evening out spatial differences in competitive advantage. Comprehensive spatial planning was seen as necessary to integrate these as well as protect key resources, especially agricultural and forest land. Regional policy sought to disperse investment to achieve 'balance' and decongest existing urban areas. This led to significant legal/political changes in terms of land use development rights with the creation or substantial strengthening of statutory systems of planning and control. These were predicated on assumed shared values of three aims: containment, redevelopment, and planned dispersal.

Place
Regional and local land use planning were serious attempts to control the micro-eco-nomics of places within a Keynesian macro-economic environment. Planning was part of the general modernization project to create better living environments for the majority. However, the legal/political environment was relatively closed, depending on the forms of representative democracy, with a strong role for professional planners with the technical skills to make the aspirations of governments a reality. A variety of planned interventions – 'growth poles', city centre rebuilding, new industrial estates, new towns, ring roads, etc. – were led by government investment with the intention of creating modern places of functional efficiency and broad social equity. However, the 'character' of places was protected through, for instance, green belts and the listing of historic buildings and monuments.

Territory
Territorial integrity was a major force, and little questioned at first, so that planning was typically defined by national legislation but often a function of historic local administrative units that bore less and less relation to functional realities as mobility and dispersal increased. This led logically to concerns for larger, more efficient terri-torial units and promotion of ideas for regional-scale planning. While local territory increasingly became a friction to be overcome (e.g. to accommodate overspill hous-ing), socio-cultural identification with local territories with claims to historic authenticity was relatively strong.

Box 2.2 Space, place and territory in planning in the light of recent effects of globalization

Space
The globalization of competition and consumerism exposes everywhere to similar pres-sures to manipulate space so as to cut costs, grow markets and reduce state regulation of space while increasing private control and consumption of space. The deregulation of many functions has led to state roles of co-ordination and integration of the spatial aspects of decisions of a much wider group of actors, mainly (but not exclu-sively) private sector, rather than the planning of direct state provision of infrastructure. New technologies facilitate new spatial divisions of labour, and make flows and net-works (and access/denial of access to them) increasingly significant. Many of these are trans-national and/or involve quasi-state entities in funding or regulation. Utility net-works in particular are capital intensive, long-term investments, and when privately provided will be made in locations that are likely to remain or become competitive and viable. Similarly, fiscally challenged governments will find it difficult to sustain invest-ment in facilities at locations that hold few prospects of significant cost recovery. Thus economics and technology together change the functional geometry of space, and force fundamental changes in planning. It changes from being a local process monop-olized by government and dealing with the seemingly fixed and distinct entities of 'town and country' to becoming 'spatial planning' operating at whatever scale is appropriate, and not necessarily confined to a statutory concern with land use.

Place

Many of the assumptions about place are affected as micro-economic opportunities change. Local economic development becomes much more important, but also much more competitive, leading to place-marketing. Places' identities are affected not only by changing socio-cultural patterns – e.g. family units, globalized culture – but also by labour migration. Places become more culturally diverse and this finds physical expression. Physical impacts of globalization can be reactive (e.g. disinvestment leading to degradation of the traditional fabric of production, whether factories or farms) or proactive (place-marketing, tourism, landmark architecture, etc. to shape a new landscape of consumption). Such changes directly challenge, and even deconstruct, narratives of place identity based on claims to historical authenticity. As differences in productivity are ironed out, and economies of scope replace economies of scale, the pursuit of competitive advantage results in a revival of interest in design, paralleled by strong emphasis on conservation of natural and cultural heritage. Global brands (e.g. in sportswear and fast food) and global concerns (e.g. sustainability) are increasingly significant in shaping places. Rural and urban areas are all affected, albeit in different ways, and the relationships between them change so that the traditional dichotomy of place identity between 'urban' and 'rural' becomes increasingly outmoded.

Territory

As the state reduces its direct provision role, and as private and other actors are not bound by the territories previously established, territorial edges become much more porous and create many challenges of planning as a state-mediated activity. The increasing importance of trans-national economic actors is mirrored, although weakly as yet, in the increasing importance of supra-national government systems to control new flows, e.g. the EU. This leads to networks and institutional capacities also growing in importance. Supra-national and trans-national planning begins to develop – e.g. the European Spatial Development Perspective and Interreg projects – and globally agreed commitments (e.g. to sustainable development) affect planning practices. The role of the nation-state in planning changes as does that at local level (more competitive) and regional level (competition, but also collaboration). However, because locality is threatened by global changes it is also a basis for resistance and ongoing social organization.

Given the above trends in the relations between space, place and territory, and the role planning is playing in this, two major questions arise:

1.   Is planning lagging behind the contextual changes?
2.   Who is driving the changing planning agenda?

In this book, we suggest that planning practice is lagging behind and needs to have a clearer vision of its role in the changing context, but that there also needs to be a rebuilding of an understanding of this role that connects concerns over process and decision-making with concerns regarding the changes in space, place and territory.

In other words, those who contribute to planning through academic and theoretical work need to get over the problems that came from the separation of planning theory into the two strands of procedural and substantive, and that left procedural theory 'contextless' while also disconnecting analysis of spatial change from the governance context. In 1989 Beauregard accused planning theorists of

> pursuing theoretical projects for their own sake. Collectively they lost the object, the city, that had given planning its legitimacy. Their new objects – the planning process, policy making, and so on – were only tangentially the objects of practitioners; they were procedurally relevant, but not substantively so (in Campbell and Fainstein (eds), 2003: 118).

There still needs to be an endeavour to connect procedural concerns about governance and participation to the spatial context of the restructuring wrought by the latest phase of globalization. Theory is needed that better integrates the socio-cultural realities as well as the politico-economic realities that face governing authorities, economic actors, social groups and individuals in this period of change. We believe that the concepts of place and territorial identity can be useful as analytical tools in this process, as we hope to demonstrate through several of the later chapters in a way that can engage with and inform contemporary planning practice. More specifically, the next chapter looks at how different socio-cultural groups can engage with the planning system.

CHAPTER 3

PLACE IDENTITY AND PARTICIPATION
HARRY SMITH

INTRODUCTION

In Chapter 1 we raised questions about who was constructing narratives of place identity through the planning system and also outside of it. We asked whether the discourse structures of statutory planning were by their nature exclusionary of some voices and understandings of place. We called for dialogues between policy-making elites and the public over matters of place identity. In Chapter 2 we recognized the breakdown of the redistributive mechanisms of 'traditional' European welfare states under the forces of economic and political restructuring and globalization. We further noted the contestation from below of the identity structures of nation-states, and the potential significance of participatory forms of spatial planning as discourses for the construction of new narratives of place identity. This chapter therefore examines the role of participation in planning, drawing on the concepts described in the previous two chapters. Our aim is to extend and connect the political economy viewpoint that has underpinned our analysis to encompass an understanding of how and why participation in planning has developed in the way that it has, and to set a context within which examples of participation in the construction of place identity can be approached in later chapters.

A POLITICAL ECONOMY OF PARTICIPATION IN PLANNING

Referring to the previous two chapters, it is our view that the (re)-integration of a political economy perspective in planning can be achieved within an institutionalist approach, i.e. retaining insights gained through the mainly sociological institutionalism of Healey (1999, 2001), Vigar et al. (2000), but adding to these analyses further reflections such as those developed by historical and rational choice institutionalisms, as labelled by Hall and Taylor (1996). These take into account power asymmetries associated with the operation and development of institutions and 'path dependence' (historical institutionalism), and the political and economic 'calculations' that influence interactions between actors and the existence of institutions (rational choice institutionalism). Rather than embracing the neo-liberal basis or the narrow view of human behaviour of rational choice theory, however, it is a question of using political economy analytical methods to redress the limited role that is given to structure, as opposed to agency, in communicative and collaborative approaches to planning theory. With this in mind, we return to the concepts of space, place and territory set out in the previous chapter and rehearse how the three fields of action in planning established in Chapter 2 might relate to these with reference to the UK planning system.

The theoretical underpinnings of planning can be examined under the light of three broad 'paradigms' that emerged during the twentieth century (see Table 3.1). These paradigms or conceptions of planning are not incompatible theoretical positions in the Kuhnian sense (see Taylor, 1999), but rather reflect approaches to planning that deeply affected planning theory, education and practice, successively adding new aspects rather than fully replacing previous approaches. They still co-exist, rather than constituting a deterministic chronological progression. For example, many aspects of the 'blueprint' approach have been rehabilitated through the practice of master-planning. Similarly across Europe planning is often split as a profession between a geographical/economic/environmental base (which is most evident at regional scale) and the physical and technical disciplines of architecture and engineering, which are most rooted in (but by no means confined to) planning practice at more local scales. Each of the three paradigms has implications for how participation in planning is conceptualized and implemented, as is seen in this chapter.

Table 3.1 The three paradigms of planning

	Nature of planning	Planning techniques	Predominance in planning	Division of power	Assumed nature of relations	Underlying philosophy
First paradigm	Fixed vision of future (designed 'blueprint')	Master plans, zoning	State planners	Government dominated	Common consensus exists	Rationalism
Second paradigm	Flexible vision and specific action ('systems')	Structure plans, action plans, special development areas	Public–private partnerships	Government with private sector	Common consensus has to be built	Rationalism
Third paradigm	No fixed vision	Above techniques with participatory planning	Negotiation forums	Government, private sector and civil society	Conflict needs negotiation	Relativism

Source: Jenkins and Smith, 2001: 25

Planning in the first paradigm was based on a 'command and control' approach that relied on the production of 'blueprints', and was an activity undertaken mainly by 'architect–planners' (see also Box 2.1). The second paradigm emerged from a critique of the 'blueprint' approach, advocating instead an understanding of urban environments as systems rather than as large designed objects, and an approach based on rational decision-making in which process was paramount (see Jenkins and Smith, 2001; Taylor, 1999). Planning in the first and second paradigms had a strong focus on space, evident in titles such as Ravetz's (1986) *The Government of Space: Town Planning in Modern Society*. The Euclidean approach to planning, in Friedmann's (1998) terms, was linked to a view of the state as guiding urban change in a static world to which universalist principles and standards were applied. Political and economic power was constructed around national identity, and this percolated through the planning system, which was established in the UK, for example, as a nationwide legal framework in which development rights were nationalized, as were many of the means of production at the time. While national-ized sectors of production and distribution became areas for political contestation in the years that followed (e.g. the steel industry, or the railways), planning as a part of the legacy of early post-war social democracy remained deeply embedded in an extending welfare state. Thus, a system to regulate private activity in relation to land use and development was based on the power held by the central government (to legislate) and by local government (to implement), legitimized by the mechanisms of formal representative democracy (with a strong role for corporate groups such as organized labour and business).

The spirit of rebuilding a nation in which the seminal planning legislation was enacted carried on into the 1950s and 1960s, a period during which space and terri-tory were the dominant guiding concepts in planning, as seen in the development of national transport infrastructure (roads and motorways) and the strategic location of new towns. The vision of the UK as a country with universal access to services and unlimited and 'democratic' mobility through the use of the car was well exemplified in the planning of Milton Keynes, the last example of state-led master-planning and imple-mentation of the era in the UK. During these decades planning narratives of place identity looked to the future and idealized urban forms as a counterpoint to what Keeble (1964: 99) called 'the vagaries and disadvantages of unplanned growth'.

From the late 1960s place identity became contested at various interfaces between planning and society. Discontent developed over comprehensive redevel-opment and conditions in some of the new housing estates. The problems went to the core of the failure of the welfare nation-state. By manipulating its system of subsi-dies for social housing to stimulate a demand for system building, the UK government from the late 1950s hoped to reduce production times, improve productivity, lower costs and hence produce more houses more quickly and cheaply. Industrialized mass

production of housing required large and assured markets. Though the local authorities commissioned and then owned the flats, they were mainly provided in 'package
deal' contracts of hundreds or thousands at a time by building companies. It was
these imperatives, rather than the perceptions and views of residents that so dramatically restructured working-class neighbourhoods and their place identity.

The technical expertise of planners in matters of land use and physical construction left them ill-equipped to understand, let alone anticipate and manage, the
economic and socio-cultural aspects of the planned transformations of places. A
contemporary quotation paints a lurid picture and demonstrates the extent and
rapidity of the disintegration of traditional place identities:

> Life in the new urban deserts is rapidly becoming unbearable for those who
> remain. Half-demolished houses and broken drains harbour rats, which make
> their way into still occupied dwellings. The small number of residents leaves
> many areas unsupervized and hence subject to vandalism and crime, for which
> the empty dwellings are ideal. Bricks are thrown through windows by children
> who find the crumbling ruins a dangerous playground. The wide open spaces
> have been colonized by gypsies and tinkers, many of whom are running scrap
> metal businesses …. The cleared spaces also double as public lavatories and
> scrap heaps for old cars and rubbish …: (Stones, 1972: 108).

As comprehensive redevelopment was stalled through a combination of fiscal crisis
and public disaffection, economic restructuring shredded the assumptions on which
planning practice was conducted. The naivety that had underpinned this paradigm
is well captured by a report on inner Birmingham by a leading firm of UK planning
consultants:

> Unemployment was seen as a purely regional phenomenon and the problems of
> the inner city were seen simply as a backlog of unfit housing which could be
> remedied by new construction in 10 years or so, and there was little, if any,
> awareness of the complex economic and social issues of the inner city. Last, but
> not least, no constraints on public expenditure were foreseen right up to 1973
> (Llewellyn Davies and Partners, 1977: 284–5).

The depth and intensity of the crisis prompted a defence of place and 'community'
against space and territory. In cities across Western Europe there were struggles for
housing modernization rather than demolition, protests against roads or the lack of
democratic accountability of commercial property developers and the use of planning
powers to assemble sites for such development. Just as significant were the everyday life practices through which people rejected new and unpopular social housing
constructions. The idea that some areas of social housing were now 'difficult to let'
would have been unthinkable in the 1950s, but emerged in the 1960s and was well

established by the 1970s. Civic amenity organizations burgeoned as familiar town-scapes, important bearers of place identity, were bulldozed. Such struggles prompted an academic literature that was critical of the extent to which planners' visions were both unmanageable and out of tune with the attachment to place of many working-class residents, especially those who had lived in an area all their lives (Ambrose and Colenutt, 1975; Davies, 1972; Dennis, 1970; Muchnick, 1970).

One example of the new places that the redevelopment programme created is Castlemilk. It was one of the public sector housing estates built in the fresh air and green fields on the edge of Glasgow in the 1950s. The new council houses on the 332-hectare site were mainly in three- and four-storey tenement style blocks. Such was the pressure for houses, they came bereft of almost all other facilities. By the start of the 1970s there were some 37,000 people living in Castlemilk, but the disturbing levels of 'moonlight flits' and applications for transfer were symptoms of dissatisfaction and social disruption. By the early 1980s Castlemilk's population had dropped to 29,000, and by 1991 it was 18,000 and there was a major regeneration programme in operation. Similar stories could be told in many British cities.

Public participation was one of the strategies through which these conflicts were negotiated, a process with the rather misleading promise of re-securing consent for progress (Dennis, 1972). In the UK, new mechanisms to allow some degree of citizen participation in planning were recommended in the 'Skeffington Report' in 1969. The recommendations included not only enhanced involvement of the public in the formulation of planning policies and proposals at specified stages within the decision-making process, but also the fostering of community forums that would provide a continuing basis for civic input, and the appointment of community development officers to reach out to the 'non-joiners'. Following this report, new planning legislation that came into effect in the early 1970s made statutory requirements regarding minimum publicity and consultation periods at specified stages in both plan-making and development control processes. Such legislation amounted to a set of procedural requirements, but did not provide a strong support for deeper citizen involvement, let alone a redistribution of power. Rather, Skeffington's recommendation of community forums and community development officers was ignored, and traditional institutions of representative democracy were not fundamentally challenged.

Thus participation became part of the existing planning discourse rather than constituting a new form of discourse. Outside statutory planning, community architecture (Wates and Knevitt, 1987) and 'planning for real' (see www.nifonline.org.uk) were other attempts to involve people respectively in designing the buildings they would live in or use as a community facility, and in establishing priorities for neighbourhood improvement. However, such approaches and techniques have tended to be one-off opportunities for the communities involved, and have focused on the neighbourhood scale, where place plays a key role, and any attempts at institutionalization have led to their absorption and disappearance. In the UK, experimentation with participation at more strategic and territorial levels has been limited and confined to the statutory channels established in the 1970s legislation.

This legislation was once described to the author as 'a charter for busybodies'. Indeed, citizen participation in planning as practised in the UK has become almost exclusively focused on neighbours' objections to planning applications, and objections from lobbying groups to proposals either in draft development plans or for major developments. There are two key types of lobbying group that make extensive use of the narrowly established channels for participation: developers and house-builders, usually seeking designation of land for development; and environmental and amenity groups, usually seeking the protection of the natural environment and built heritage. Both have access to expert advice, which is necessary to engage with the complicated and legalistic procedures of the system. Rather than opening up the opportunity for a more broadly participatory approach to planning and redressing inequalities of power, in practice the UK system has created opportunities for groups that are already powerful either financially or in terms of expertise and influence. To understand more of how this happened we need to look further at the evolution of social democracy.

FROM CLASS TO CONSUMERISM

The 'stagflation' of the mid 1970s resulted in cataclysmic economic and political defeats for social democracy. Fiscal crises undermined the capacity of the state to deliver universal services and globalization gave capital the power to escape from and punish redistributory regimes. In Britain under Thatcherism, defeats were inflicted on industrial militancy and on left-wing local authorities pursuing an alternative economic strategy geared to spending to 'improve services and create jobs'. The new structures and incentives, the new discourses of consumerism, the fragmentation between those in work and those outside work, all combined to break class as a practical means of political action. Politically this accommodation was signalled by the 'new realism' amongst the Left after the Conservatives' victory in the 1987 general election.

Place itself was restructured through this process. Place identity defined by traditional industry became an anachronism or even a barrier to reintegration into the new consumer economy. Place identity as a component of solidarity, a shared and enduring experience transmitted from generation to generation in a myriad of forms and institutions – physical buildings and streets, a common workplace or local shops, long-term neighbours and local family ties – was challenged by the space of flows, mobility and choice. As we have already noted, these changes began before the 1970s – for example between 1961 and 1971 the population of London Boroughs and the main English metropolitan cities fell by almost 900,000, and between 1959 and 1975 over a million manufacturing jobs were lost in London and the main conurbations in Great Britain (Fothergill and Gudgin, 1982). However, the economic transformation also had political drivers that ensured significant changes in place identities in the face of local resistance. In the coalfields the defeat of the 1984–5 miners' strike led to closures which eroded the rationale of place identity. In urban policy the flagship Thatcherite intervention through the London Docklands Development Corporation fundamentally changed the identity of the area, through a mechanism that was designed to avoid community participation.

None of this is to say that place identities were exclusively rooted in class, extractive and manufacturing industry, and nineteenth-century workers' housing. Nor is it to argue that place identities were frozen in time from some early industrial origin until the 1960s. By its nature urban change is ongoing, and as we argued in Chapter 1, there are likely to be multiple identities in and of a place. Farming communities on urban fringes were urbanized, the state imposed new towns in the countryside, people moved within and between cities, regions, countries. Rather our proposition is that the economic restructuring and de-industrialization, accompanied by the political conflict between ideologies of individualism and of collectivism, had profound impacts on places, their identity and the relation between people and the state, not least in respect of planning.

How did these changes impact on participation in planning? The first shock waves of restructuring created a period of stasis. Redevelopment led by councils and following comprehensive development plans was halted. Planning became obsolete. Outdated documents reserved land for industry that would never return, controls were elaborated to regulate non-existent development pressures from the market. A new, more market-savvy discourse structure developed – 'regeneration' – parallel to, but distinct from, 'planning'. Bereft of the capacity to deliver positive redistributive place-based outcomes, planning became synonymous with bureaucratic control operated on an arbitrary or political basis rather than as an expression of professional expertise. This transition was of fundamental importance to the theory and practice of participation.

The political challenge to social democracy from the New Right was deeply based in market ideology and its supportive bodies of social science theory. Thornley (1991), for example, reviewed this ground. We will simply highlight the implications for participation. The starting point is public choice theory (Buchanan and Tullock, 1962; Buchanan, 1975, 1977, 1986; Brennan and Buchanan, 1985; Poulton and Begg, 1988). This seeks to apply the underpinning ideas of neo-classical economics to issues of public goods and services. Thus it is individuals, not social groups, that engage in political choices, and they do so as consumers and taxpayers. The central question then is how can local politics and government be made responsive to something akin to 'consumer sovereignty'? The answer is that local government units need to be small, so that it is easy for consumers to relocate to a polity that maximizes their preferences. The idea of large regional councils forcing through redistributory policies is not something that a rational consumer at risk of being adversely affected by such redistribution would 'buy'. Crucially, each individual is the best judge of their own needs and priorities, and so mechanisms such as participation are essentially bogus. They become seen as exercises controlled by officials to elicit collective endorsement to collective outcomes.

So what form of planning would consumers choose if they had the choice? The answer given is one that protects their interests as property owners from possible externalities; one that provides certainty and confidence through a contractual relationship and in an efficient and least cost manner. To secure this form of planning requires strong central action to prevent the inherent empire-building of local politicians and bureaucrats. The rule of law is fundamental to this. The duties and the limits on governments need to be legally prescribed, so that consumers have recourse to the courts to prevent illegitimate and illegal actions – whether social democratic aspirations to 'tax and spend' or recourse to non-material considerations in determining a planning application. Translate these ideas into practice and you have a narrow, statutorily defined form of plan-led development control system subject to strong central control on decision criteria, and with league tables of performance so that consumers can make proper decisions about the quality of the service that they are paying for through taxes.

Thus planning has been encased in a discourse structure that has emphasized procedures and individual rights rather than collective understanding of, debate about and capacity to influence place identity. Of course this structure is both a product of power relations and a framework within which power can be exercised and contested. It is a structure that largely excludes those who are not property owners – planning controls have been substantially irrelevant in areas of social housing, for example. Participation in planning has therefore become 'ossified' into a series of procedures that local authorities observe, and certain interest groups monopolize – procedures that, in the case of development planning, are normally set in motion by the planning authority. Participatory procedures were put under pressure due to increasing priority being given to efficiency targets and prompt delivery of planning decisions. However, the idea of participation as a real shift in power, and the idea of planning as a means of reproducing place identity, endure and legitimize the use of the planning system to contest development.

In summary, from the mid 1970s there was a rampant fiscal crisis that fundamentally undermined the capacity of welfare states to deliver the kind of places to which voters aspired. The collectivist social democratic ideals were fractured along with the strong state mechanisms (including representative democracy) for their delivery. This was not an even process across Europe, and arguably was evident sooner, deeper and longer in the UK than in continental countries, where written constitutions and proportional representation and the social agenda of Christian Democracy were frictions. However, through globalization, fiscal crises and neo-liberalism constitute a major challenge to the planning discourse everywhere. Nevertheless, the end of class politics does not mean that the market alone shapes place identities and territory. Politics has changed but still exists. The 1980s were a long time ago, even if their legacy lingers. How and why is participation being reconstituted as a means to construct new narratives of place identity?

PLACE IDENTITY AND PARTICIPATION: THE THIRD WAY

The economic and political triumph of neo-liberalism since the 1980s, sustained by global institutions and corporations, has structured the ideological parameters and practical decision space of social democratic politics. One resolution of the tensions has been the emergence of 'Third Way' politics that work with market mechanisms while still espousing some welfarist and/or environmentalist aspirations. The reconstruction of the Labour Party into New Labour in the UK during the 1990s is perhaps the paradigmatic example. However, European social democracy in its different national manifestations has a long history of negotiation and consensus-seeking, partly linked to political systems based on proportional representation that tend to generate coalition governments.

The class base of social democracy as political ideology and practice was not simply defeated by unemployment, sales of social housing, faltering council finances or electoral failures. Rather it was actively challenged and undermined by the politics of place identity. For instance in the UK it was the votes of Scottish Nationalist MPs that ensured the defeat of Britain's minority Labour Government in 1979, paving the way for the Conservatives' historic victory, just as it was British nationalism of the 'Falklands factor' that cemented Mrs Thatcher's hold on power in 1983, a prospect that had looked far from certain a year earlier. However, these expressions of territorially based place identity are not the only forms of politics that deconstruct class as a basis for identity and action. Gender and ethnicity have become increasingly significant as underpinning identities as society has changed, paid work has become more evenly shared between men and women and global migrations have become multi-directional. However, it is perhaps the pervasiveness of consumerism as the defining mode of everyday life that has most fundamentally shaped the new politics and attitudes towards participation and place identity.

Social democratic welfare states were the embodiment of many aspects of Fordism – large organizations delivering standardized products and services to a mass market. The emergence of niche markets and flexible production were both cause and effect of consumer choice, and the feminization of labour markets. In this world, it is not only the personal that is political, but the political is personal. Issues are disconnected – you can pick and mix, opt in or opt out. The new politics is a politics of fluidity and diversity. It is scarcely surprising if traditional political structures – parties, elections and local councils based on representative democracy – seem unable to offer much market appeal. They were fashioned in a different world from the one in which everyday life now operates.

The Third Way is an attempt to reconnect vestiges of social democracy – its ideology and welfarist intent – to this new reality. It means acceptance of the market – not only as the organizing basis for production, but as the very heart of the governance process. It recognizes the limitations of state action but also the need to fill the gaps between atomized competing companies and individual consumers. In the Third Way opposites can be combined (competitiveness and cohesion, sustainable development) and boundaries can be straddled (public-private-community partnerships, trans-national spatial planning projects). Charisma, innovation, institutional thickness can forge new spaces for action. There are limits but they are more to do with vision and managerial capacity than with the old structures of labour and capital as antagonistic interests. The key question is 'what works?' Modernization of governance and public services becomes the core of the Third Way as a political project.

The modernization agenda retains the mechanisms of the market: league tables, privatization, contractors, etc. However, it adds the politics and the information that market processes themselves are unlikely to elicit. Focus groups are reeds in the shifting winds of fragmented, identity-based opinion. Voting in supermarkets, cabinet government, elections of charismatic non-traditional politicians as mayors are further attempts to connect politics and the consumers of politics. These changes are of fundamental importance to planning, participation and place identity. They redefine the nature of technical expertise – the rationale for the planner's professional role. Under social democratic welfarism, planners were technical experts who knew the best solutions for delivery of agreed 'public interest' outcomes. Under the New Right, planners were bureaucratic administrators expected to follow procedures in an efficient and consistent manner. The Third Way emphasizes managerialism, the capacity to deliver what customers really want (not what professionals assume they want) for fewer resources, by effective integration across different service delivery areas. A capacity to combine understanding of the aspirations and expectations of diverse stakeholders with innovation in the design and delivery of services in a flexible manner is the essence of the new form of professionalism in public service.

The Third Way thus recognizes the need for new governance structures, both to accommodate change and to set incentives for further change. The traditions of party loyalty derived from class, that bolstered and stabilized the old representative democracy, have crumbled. Politicians are vulnerable in ways unimaginable in the era of welfarism. Electorates are unreliable and disinterested; they are socialized to expect charisma and celebrity from those who strut the public stage, not back-room machinations and the procedural wrangling that are the heart of the political engine. Thus the Third Way demands a new type of politics and a new type of politician. Fashion, the new idea, becomes a constituent of power itself, giving a 'market edge' over political competitors. Similarly the capacity to integrate diverse identity group-ings and to mobilize them behind some vision is a key to electoral success.

Of course politicians have always depended on votes, made promises for elec-toral gain, and espoused ideology. These truisms should not obscure the very fundamental changes that have taken place in the nature of political processes, and the implications they have for participation in planning for place identity. It is no coin-cidence that participation under strong state welfarism was prone to tokenism. Officials and elected members had powers they were unlikely to concede; they knew best. Plans were made, the public were consulted, and the plans were defended. Under the New Right also, albeit from a different ideological base, there was little scope for participation to be construed as a new legitimate base for policy-making. The rule of law, guaranteed by central state action, ensured that the mobilization of vocal local minorities could not hijack decisions, or disrupt the 'level playing field' for market competition. Of course, individual politicians or even councils might seek to support protestors, pointing the finger of blame to central government for locally unpopular policies such as house-building in country towns and villages. Rather our point, from a political economy perspective, is to stress the structures within which agencies act, and on that basis we conclude that participation was likely to end in incorporation of dissent, or manipulation and frustration.

The Third Way is different. Just as customers do have power in markets and producers seek to manipulate their preferences, so in the public arena participants also have power that politicians will seek to mould and capitalize upon. Participation can be a new channel for political action, bypassing the clogged arteries of tradi-tional representative democracy. Participation can reconnect politicians and public, and can give politicians profile and visibility – and that all-important, but often elu-sive, broader legitimacy. While the welfare state offered standard services to all, the Third Way needs to target and innovate, and build partnerships with a range of stakeholders. Things have to be made to happen, they will not happen by them-selves. Active decisions have to be made, rather than standards routinely operated. Therefore it would be wrong to be dismissive of participation today as inevitably a one-sided and tokenistic exercise of power, characterized as 'Decide, Announce,

Defend' by Blakeney (1997). Rather we see it potentially as a channel through which new power relations are negotiated with diverse social groups. It is not just consent that is required, but active and deliberate engagement of stakeholders, since the state by itself is unable to deliver.

SOME INDICATORS OF CHANGE

As class and party loyalty wither and globalization reconstructs place, place identity also becomes an important arena for the negotiation of consent and partnership. Refocusing of planning and participation on the qualities of place and place identity is a logical outcome of this new politics. Thus there has been a major drive towards the development of an urban design approach through the Urban Task Force in England, which portrayed urban design not only as contributing to 'liveability' (a paradigmatic Third Way concept) but also to competitiveness, as manifest in titles such as *The Value of Urban Design* (CABE/DETR, 2001). The emphasis on who decides on the qualities of place is less marked in these publications, with limited evidence as yet of what Friedmann (1998) terms 'post-Euclidean' planning, where planners work for agents of civil society, focusing on specific project undertakings. Rather than an opening up of planning processes to civil society in the broader sense, what is apparent is that the private sector has increased its participation in planning processes, particularly through public–private partnerships, and the voluntary sector has become more adept at influencing planning through lobbying and the use of the statutory representation mechanisms.

Sub-national territory in the UK was redefined in the 1990s, with devolved governments in Scotland and Wales, as well as with the establishment of regional development agencies in England for the purpose of regional economic development. Under the New Right the statutory planning system became more centralized,[1] with the narrowing down of the role of planning within a highly sectoralized approach to public policy, and the reliance on policy measurement through performance criteria militating against more fluid relationships at the local level (Healey, 2001). As Vigar *et al.* (2000: 274) argue, this detaches sites and projects from their local situation and 'provides the flexibility for business and political elites to pursue their particular agendas'. Reforms in English planning legislation brought forward by the New Labour government (ODPM, 2001, 2002) seek to speed up decisions and make planning more market-friendly while also putting a new emphasis on community involvement and on strategic planning at a regional scale. The continuities and discontinuities between the New Right and the Third Way are evident in these changes.

This major overhaul of the planning system, which does away with development plans in favour of local development frameworks, in principle heralds a key role for citizens through the preparation of community statements. Such increased community involvement has led the government to commission research on the new role that planners could take on as 'mediators' of planning. Such mediation is seen as necessary at all levels, from dealing with planning applications (Welbank, Davies and Haywood, 2000) to facilitating the preparation of strategic development frameworks. The conceptualization of the planner's role as a mediator may recognize the necessity of negotiation when consensus is not achievable. Reform of the Scottish planning system was preceded by a review of the strategic planning framework (Scottish Executive, 2002a), and by a wide consultation on public involvement in planning (Scottish Executive, 2002b). In parallel with this consultation, research was undertaken on the wider public's perception of the opportunities for involvement in planning in Scotland.[2] This research revealed the widespread alienation of the public in relation to government, which affects planning as it is de facto perceived as a government activity (Jenkins, Kirk and Smith, 2002).

The possibility exists that limited redistribution of power can be enacted at certain levels, to preserve the status quo at other levels. Increasing participation in planning (and possibly more generally in governance), at the community and local levels through a shift from representative to participatory democracy, could be used to focus citizen interest and engagement around the 'places' where they live, rather than on the more strategic level, which is controlled by emerging new powers at regional and supranational level. In some USA cities, for example, power has been devolved from the urban level to that of neighbourhoods, and has increasingly shifted from state agencies to private institutions that control governing coalitions, in which state agencies act as facilitators. This devolution to neighbourhood level has created a new site of negotiation and 'struggle' affecting the future of the city as a whole (McCann, 2001). Links exist between spatial scale of planning and institutional involvement. A key challenge for participatory processes at higher spatial scales is how to ensure appropriate representation, how to minimize exclusion.

The resurgence of interest in spatial strategy-making at sub-national level in Europe provides some examples of negotiation and mediation between parties at metropolitan and regional level, where strategic planning through collaboration between existing institutions has been a response to the lack of a single statutory administrative body covering the metropolitan area or region (Healey et al., 1997; Baker, 2001; Campbell et al., 2001; Herrschel and Newman, 2002). Jouve (2001), for example, provides an account of a collaborative, community-led approach to strategic decision-making in the Lyons conurbation in France. This case highlights the multiplication of decision-making arenas in two ways: (1) spatially, with different types of initiative (territorial planning, economic planning, etc.) having different territorial definitions; and (2) sectorally, with increasing fragmentation of interests placing demands on the local political system. The former requires co-ordination between different 'planning territories', the latter requires mediation between political and business sectors. The Joint Structure Plan for Glasgow and the Clyde Valley illustrates the need for mediation between local planning authorities when collaborating on the production of a joint overarching planning framework (Goodstadt, 2001).

THEORIZING PARTICIPATION

As outlined above, the idea of public participation in planning emerged in the 1960s, and was subsumed in the development of the second paradigm of planning, though it was based on the critique of the planner as 'expert', whether this was a designer (first paradigm) or a systems analyst (second paradigm). Spurred on by the results of implemented plans that were regarded by the wider public and critics as destructive of existing urban environments (typically comprehensive redevelopment and road schemes), 'expert' planning judgements were questioned and seen to be in essence 'value judgements' (Taylor, 1999). This recognition of planning as a value-laden and political activity led to calls for higher public input to define planning goals. Some authors were particularly concerned about the representation of the views of disadvantaged groups, and argued for an 'advocacy' role for planners (Davidoff, 1965). In general, the outcome of this critique was a new conceptualization of the planner as a 'facilitator' who identified and mediated between different interest groups affected by planning decisions, still in search of protecting the 'public interest'. The search for procedural mechanisms to allow the public to have its say led to further theorizing.

An early and often quoted contribution to the debate on public participation in planning was Arnstein's 'ladder of participation'. Arnstein (1969) analysed citizen involvement in decision-making in social urban programmes in the USA from the point of view of the redistribution of power. On this basis, she characterized a series of levels of 'devolution' of power to citizens, represented as rungs on a ladder. These ranged from manipulation, at the bottom end of the ladder, where participation was used as a means of manipulating public opinion, to citizen control, at the top, where decisions were taken by the citizens themselves. Arnstein (1969) contended that most of the implemented participation mechanisms that she studied did not belong to the categories at the top of the ladder, i.e. they did not involve redistribution of power, and therefore maintained the status quo.

Creating opportunities for participation in planning was not only the result of a recognition of the political nature of planning decisions, but also an opening for competitive bargaining between parties with differing interests, as illustrated in the predominance of lobbying groups noted above. However, the third paradigm in planning (Table 3.1; see also Box 2.2), based on Habermas' theory of communicative action, attempts to go beyond such competitive bargaining by arguing for a planning process that is based on collaborative consensus-building (Forester, 1987, 1989, 1993, 1999; Healey, 1993, 1996, 1997; Innes, 1995; Innes and Booher, 1999a, 1999b). Such consensus-building would require a 'facilitator' planner who fosters meaningful dialogue between the parties, slowly achieving shared values and visions, and, ideally, agreed planning decisions. This view assumes good will and an openness to sharing or redistributing power that often does not exist in practice (Tewdwr-Jones and Allmendinger, 1998). It is thus an arguably desirable model, but one that understates the *realpolitik* of many planning decisions, where huge interests can be at stake, and negotiating positions can be defended to extreme lengths (as protracted planning inquiries illustrate).

Habermas' (1979) work, the inspiration for communicative planning theory, is critical theory: the ideal speech situation based on comprehensibility, truth, sincerity and legitimacy is unlikely to be realized in societies based on inequality and domination that will 'systematically distort' communication. However, the prescriptive and optimistic interpretation of these ideas as a basis for planning tends to deflect the focus away from political economy, and towards fetishizing participatory processes per se. In other words, there is a risk that discursive participatory processes are seen as 'good things' in their own right, regardless of outcomes. Similarly, the extent to which participatory structures themselves embed power relations that privilege particular political skills and actions (listening, argument, negotiation, etc.) can be too easily overlooked, and risks hegemonizing such discourse systems. Processes are the bearers of structures and uncritical prescriptions of participation as central aspects of governance are likely to reinforce the capacity of the articulate and relatively privileged to shape outcomes.

In our view, communicative planning theory remains vulnerable to the criticism levelled at earlier procedural planning theories: it is contextless and severs process from the spatial substance of planning. We have already sought to show that the participatory turn in planning has its roots in a fundamental change in the capacity of states to deliver universal welfare services and in the restructuring of politics associated with these 'new times'. Similarly, at a professional level, communicative planning theory has been a necessary attempt to reconstruct and legitimate a credible professional role for planners in opposition to that prescribed by the New Right. Awareness of these contexts can strengthen rather than negate the development of communicative planning theory. Indeed, the aspirations at the core of the theory – for planning as an interpersonal and inclusive activity seeking consensus as a basis for action – are, as we have sought to show, necessary core components of Third Way politics and the modernization of social democracy.

Similarly we feel that the theory needs to be connected to an understanding of spatial change. Much of the current writing on communicative planning theory could equally well apply as prescription to any form of public decision-making in a pluralistic society characterized by diversity and difference. At different spatial scales the range and weight of represented interested parties is likely to vary, with implications for institutional contexts. Key to successful articulation of decision-making at these different scales is mediation between decisions and strategies emerging from the community and local scale, and policy directions produced at a more strategic or regional level. Negotiation and mediation happen not only at each spatial level, but also between spatial levels. Some of the cases analysed in the next part of this book help understand how this is taking place in particular contexts in countries around the North Sea. When pondering participation and place we need to reassert the importance of the old questions from political economy – who gets what, and why?

CONCLUSION

In conclusion, we contend that much of the innovation concerning the role of discursive negotiation in planning is an expression of the new politics of the Third Way, which, in turn, attempts the difficult task of integrating traditional values from social democracy with the political realities of consumerism and globalization. We do not see participation as an abstract ideal, a 'good thing' in its own right. Nor do we see it as inevitably a shallow pretence, through which officialdom goes through the motions of consulting while retaining its own agenda. Of course participation will be manipulated and contested; our point is that the new governance has to take such risks because the old ways – representative democracy reproduced by ideologies appealing to class – are now bankrupt. In societies of difference and multiple identities, where consumerism structures everyday life, governance has to become experimental and has to engage with diversity if it is to retain legitimacy. Without a clear political economic analysis, many of these participatory and place identity initiatives are likely to have an adverse effect on the way that planning redistributes resources, opportunities and the capacity of place identity to express memories of past solidarity. However, on the other hand, we consider that opportunities exist to widen the conceptual fields of spatial planning beyond the nation-state in territorial terms, and at the same time to incorporate and strengthen socio-culturally embedded place identities, and that participatory approaches to planning can be means to advance these projects.

PART 2

RESEARCH INTO PRACTICE

CHAPTER 4

BACKGROUND TO PLACE IDENTITY, PARTICIPATION AND PLANNING IN EUROPE
CLIFF HAGUE AND PAUL JENKINS

The trans-national emergence of spatial planning within Europe illustrates the themes of this book. This opening chapter to the second section therefore analyses European spatial planning as a necessary context for the investigation of planning practices in the four European countries that are the core of our text. Planning has been predominantly a local practice shaped by national legislation, or state/province legislation in federal systems like those in the USA or Australia. The EU case is exceptionally interesting since it is perhaps the first time that a trans-national political agent has grappled with planning. As global trading blocks develop further it may set a precedent – or it may remain (or even be stifled by) the specifically European development path that created this departure. There is no legal competence permitting the EU to act on planning matters, rather the concept of subsidiarity applies. This means that matters should be devolved to the lowest level of spatial administration where they can be effectively carried out. Therefore the approach that has emerged represents a consensus amongst all the member states within the EU. In this, as in other areas of political life, things are not always as they appear. Change and conflict compel new compromises that themselves embed ambiguities about intentions and effects.

One reason why a pan-European perspective has come to the fore in planning is because fashioning a new identity for Europe is integral to the creation of the single European market, and the moves towards political and economic union within the European territory. The twentieth-century identity of Europe as a hotchpotch of fractious nation-states and confrontational ideologies had to be replaced by some radically different way of seeing the continent, its nations, regions and peoples. The change is simultaneously a formal political project, the product of innovative institutional action, and an aggregate outcome of the behaviours of firms and civil society. Thus in this crude and preliminary way we can begin to deconstruct the processes, structures and agencies through which narratives of place identity are developed and contested.

A brief review of the emergence of spatial planning as an integrative European concept will take our tentative arguments a stage further. The geography of the EU is characterized by long distances, major physical barriers to surface movement, and huge disparities in population densities, not to mention national boundaries, some of which remain contested by groups within those states. Where and what is its 'identity'? If an identity is to be revealed, and even more so if an identity is to be constructed and communicated, it is necessary to establish some key features of the whole entity. A European identity requires some picture and information of Europe as a whole, as a geographical space. From that building block it becomes easier to steer and mobilize commitment to Europe as a place, something that is understood, familiar and carries meanings. This may sound a rather mechanistic argument, but one should not underestimate the legacy of the Enlightenment within European thinking, with its core beliefs in the capacity of rational human action to effect progressive change.

After the passing of the Single European Act in 1987, spatial planning as part of European identity construction began in earnest. The Act committed all EU members to removing all barriers to the free movement of labour and capital within the EU. Thus it conjured into being a European economic space, replacing traditional mental maps of a continent divided by national boundaries. One of the fundamental goals of the EU is economic and social cohesion and balanced development. A number of official studies from the early 1990s onwards (see Box 4.1) recognized that the Single Market and EU policies for sectors such as agriculture, transport, technology and environment were likely to have significant impacts on the dynamic

Box 4.1 Key steps towards the European Spatial Development Perspective (ESDP)

Europe 2000: Outlook for the Development of the Community's Territory (1991)
This report was prepared by the Regional Policy Directorate of the European Commission and its consultants. It analysed pressures on Europe's territory arising from socio-economic developments as well as from national and regional and Community interventions. It divided the Community into eight trans-national regions and identified two core regions: Northwest Europe and the 'North of the South', i.e. Northeast Spain to Northern Italy/Southern Germany. The last chapter, 'Policy implications', called for concerted attention to the balanced and harmonious development of the Community's territory.

Europe 2000+: Co-operation for the Spatial Development of Europe (1994)
This follow-up study warned of the risk of widening disparities between regions. It began to evaluate the effect of some key EU policies on spatial development, and further promoted the need for trans-national planning and a broad European planning framework.

Principles for a European Spatial Development Policy (1994)
This document was tabled at the Informal Council of Ministers responsible for Spatial Planning meeting in Leipzig in September 1994. It was agreed by the Committee on Spatial Development. Economic and social cohesion, sustainable development and reinforcing the cohesion of the European continent were 'fundamental goals'. It sought a polycentric system, as balanced as possible, discouraging excessive concentration around some large centres and the marginalization of peripheral areas. It also stressed the need for 'spatial coherence' of sector policies.

use of the new European economic space and the location of development. Of course, these were not the only ideas about the New Europe. However, they were significant in grasping that space and territory would intrude on any new European identity, and so needed to be woven into discourses, metaphors, policies and actions.

Shaw and Nadin (2000, 238–9) pointed to the link between economic inter-dependence and trans-national collaboration on spatial planning. They summarized some key spatial trends within Europe: increased concentration of economic activity and an enhanced role of global and regional cities within a pattern of intensified competition between cities; economic polarization within cities; social exclusion; and negative environmental impacts from urban development. As they observed: 'Spatial planning and state regulation within the member states attempts to play a significant role in addressing these trends' (Shaw and Nadin, 2000: 239).

Faludi and Zonnveld (1997) and Faludi and Waterhout (2002) provided an extended analysis of the politics and institutions involved in producing the European Spatial Development Perspective. They described the compromises that were made to maintain consensus, the differential enthusiasms for, and interpretations of, what a European approach to spatial planning and development should entail. The key players in the drama are politicians, especially the planning ministers of the member states who together constituted the Committee on Spatial Development, officials from their ministries, and members of the European Commission, particularly those in DGXVI, the regional policy directorate. None of this is particularly surprising but it does emphasize that narratives of place identity do not arise 'spontaneously'. Human agents operating within institutions with political or technocratic power are crucial in drafting the script for place identity. Language and spatial imagery are at the heart of this process of authoring identity.

In 1989 the French planning agency DATAR identified the *dorsale*, which quickly became known as the 'Blue Banana'. This European megalopolis accounted for only 18 per cent of the territory in the 14 countries (the then 12 members plus Austria and Switzerland) but 47 per cent of urban agglomerations over 200,000, and currently produces about half of the European Union's GDP. A report (Kunzmann and Wegener, 1991) commissioned by DGXVI, countered the *dorsale* with the metaphor of a 'European Bunch of Grapes'. This sought 'to represent the polycentric structure of the urban system in Europe and the fundamental *similarity in diversity* of the interests and concerns of its member cities' (Kunzmann and Wegener, 1991: 63). These characterizations of European space can appear almost comical and self-mocking. Faludi and Waterhout relate how the 'Blue Banana' was accidentally, even humorously, christened. However, the capacity to create and communicate a spatial image of place identity connecting the present to the future is the quintessence of spatial planning. The orderly city (the engineered alternative implanted through colonialism as an antidote to the 'chaos' of organic native settlements) was but one earlier example of the same spell-making. The garden city, the city beautiful, the containment/redevelopment/dispersal package after the Second World War, and the 1960s 'growth pole' are others. Where such visions are absent, incomprehensible, suppressed or lacking in practical credibility, planning is only minimal regulation of development, as prescribed by public choice theory (see previous chapter).

The logic of this argument is that the emergence of European spatial planning as an attempt to move beyond the cataloguing and potential harmonization of the various legislative systems is fundamentally social democratic in its politics. We contend that it is, but with the important caveat, trailed above, that things are not usually what they seem. The economic and political triumph of neo-liberalism since the 1980s, sustained by global institutions and corporations, has structured the ideological parameters and practical decision space of social democratic politics. One resolution of the tensions has been the emergence of 'Third Way' politics, as discussed in Chapter 3. Across the EU, with the exception of the UK, restructuring of nation-states from welfare to entrepreneurial politics supporting post-Fordist capital accumulation (Harvey, 1989) was generally a slow process. However, by the new millennium it was substantially complete, and in the turmoil came a shift from traditional politics based on class to a new politics based on identity. The foundations of identities can be diverse and overlapping: gender, ethnicity, sexuality, nationality, or simple consumerist lifestyle (e.g. 'motorists' or 'country sports enthusiasts'). Some are place-related, some are not. The key point is that shifting, inter-twining and even negotiable identities are now a central part of the post-Cold War political process in Europe.

Giannakourou (1996) asked what the conceptual and ideological identity of a European spatial planning policy could be under a market system. The narratives of European place identity, and of spatial planning as a means to deliver it, are primarily by-products of the social democratic attempt to embrace, but move on from, neo-liberal globalization. Spatial planning is a step towards entrepreneurial politics, but one mediated by histories, cultures and institutions. Compromise, ambiguity, negotiation and new imagery are necessarily at the core of this enterprise. So how has this new 'Third Way' social democracy, overlain by different national traditions, cultures and interests, conceived Europe and an agenda for European planning?

The European Spatial Development Perspective (ESDP) was a landmark document. Its sub-title is 'Towards balanced and sustainable development of the European territory'. It was adopted in 1999 by the Committee on Spatial Development. The ESDP was not a masterplan (Faludi and Waterhout, 2002). Rather, it discussed trends, opportunities and challenges including spatial development in the accession countries. It recognized that not all regions and local communities are 'automatically converging to a regionally balanced territory in the

wake of economic and monetary union' (Faludi and Waterhout, 2002: 19). It therefore proposed 'spatial development guidelines' to be taken into account in 'spatially
significant sectoral policies at Community, national, regional and local levels' (Faludi
and Waterhout, 2002: 19). The key aims of the ESDP were:

- *Enhancing competitiveness* – The EU has only one 'zone of global economic
  integration': the 'pentagon' defined by London, Paris, Milan, Munich and
  Hamburg. The USA has four high income/good infrastructure global economic
  zones, and similar zones, some trans-national, are emerging in Asia.
- *Territorial cohesion and parity of access to infrastructure* – The traditional
  response has been to connect the peripheral regions to the core. The ESDP
  sought to move beyond the core–periphery European identity through development of a polycentric and balanced urban system, based on a partnership
  between urban and rural areas.
- *Sustainable development* – which was particularly seen in terms of environmental aspects and the development and conservation of the natural and
  cultural heritage.

The ESDP strongly endorsed the idea of polycentric spatial development, as the
way to ensure regionally balanced growth and sustainable development. It means
connecting a number of places so that they form a network. By operating together
they achieve a new critical mass that can sustain and grow businesses, services and
facilities. Polycentric development means forging new connections by overcoming
historical barriers, such as those caused by national boundaries, local rivalries or
distance/poor communications. Polycentric development at a European scale
implies a dynamic twenty-first-century geography in which, for example, cities and
regions that were marginalized on national peripheries are now united across fading
boundaries to forge new development trajectories. Old ports gain new hinterlands
and become Euro-gateways. The gaze shifts from parochial rivalry to regional integration into a networked Europe. The map of this new Europe will show a
polycentric pattern of spatial development, with several inter-connected zones of
major growth, each carving its own niche in the European and global space
economies (Hague and Kirk, 2003).

Closely related to polycentric development in the ESDP and the emergent
European spatial planning discourse is the idea of new urban–rural relations. This is
seen particularly as a means of coping with structural change in rural areas. The
polycentric urban system can provide hubs and links for such rural areas, and in particular access to larger labour markets and to services.

> Towns in rural regions ... have an important function as engines of growth for
> regional economic development. In sparsely settled rural areas only towns can

offer certain standards in the supply of infrastructure and services and attract economic activities. In these areas towns are particularly important in the preservation of the settlement structure and the cultural landscape (CEC, 1999: 25).

As Richardson and Jensen (2000) noted, and as Faludi and Waterhout (2002) described in some depth, the ESDP was the outcome of multiple interests and power struggles. Richardson and Jensen (2000: 508–9) pointed to:

- Conflicts between EU institutions – the Commission, the Council of Ministers, the European Parliament, the Committee of the Regions, etc.
- Conflicts within EU institutions – between commissioners, directorates, member states, regions.
- Interests and lobbies seeking to influence the direction of EU integration – e.g. environmental and industrial lobbies.
- Contesting interests within each area of sectoral policy – e.g. agriculture, transport, environmental policy, etc.

Two things stand out. First, the fashioning of the ESDP was undertaken by a policy elite. There was some consultation but it was within quite restricted political and professional boundaries. Thus the attempt to transform European space into European place – i.e. to convert an abstract economic/geographic entity into popular comprehension and reality – and to erect the institutional superstructure for spatial planning has primarily been a mission undertaken by those with political and/or bureaucratic power. Secondly, the sheer complexity of the tensions, together with the need to reach agreement and thus complete a process that had spanned almost a decade, ensured that the story of the development of European space would be laced with ambiguities and elisions. These will be explored in more detail in Chapter 5. To set down a marker, and to alert readers to some of the practical implications of the conflicts embedded in the new European place narrative, we would point to the real policy choices that will have to be made between sustaining the global competitiveness of the 'Pentagon', and spreading the benefits of growth more evenly across Europe. Where should the key nodes and interchanges on fast train routes be located, and which areas will have lines running through them, but no direct access to the network? Where will new housing be located in the context of the 'new urban–rural relations' that the ESDP advocates?

The prime instrument available to the EU to apply the ESDP was the Community Initiative Programme known as Interreg IIC. Launched in 1996, it defined seven Euro-regions and sought to advance trans-national co-operation in spatial planning within these. The programme produced a number of outputs that developed and applied concepts from the ESDP, in line with the principles of subsidiarity. These set an important backdrop for further projects under the successor Programme Interreg III. One

Interreg IIC project, concerned with achieving 'Quality by Identity', underpins the research for this book. It aimed to 'influence the spatial development of each region based on a stronger local identity'. This reflected, at the level of the regions, the ESDP concern to achieve balanced and sustainable spatial development which is seen as connecting economy, society and environment (see CEC, 1999: 10, Figure 5).

Interreg IIC also facilitated the preparation of 'spatial visions'. The Baltic States had already collaborated to produce their *Vision and Strategies around the Baltic Sea 2010* (Group of Focal Points, 1994). A brief examination of spatial visions for the North West Metropolitan Area (NWMA) and for the North Sea Region (NSR) further illustrates the process of constructing narratives of European space, tensions within and between those narratives, and the language, techniques and institutions that underpin this new form of planning discourse. While both spatial visions start from, and endorse, the ESDP principles, there are significant differences between them, which derive from the nature of their existing urban systems. The spatial vision for the NWMA is set out in a schematic map, whereas NorVision, rather like the ESDP, relies on listing desirable strategies without prioritizing them or exploring possible tensions (see Figures 4.1 and 4.2).

Box 4.2 Summary of *A Spatial Vision for North-West Europe*

A Spatial Vision for North-West Europe: Building Co-operation involved partners from seven countries in the North West Metropolitan Area. The area is characterized by strong metropolitan centres based on services operating in global markets. The vision argues that cities like London, Frankfurt, Paris and Amsterdam need to co-operate to promote their financial functions as 'an integrated entity'. The four busiest international airports in the world are here, and regional airports are growing fast. These and the ports are key gateways and there are major nodes on the high-speed rail network. Demands on the natural environment and on energy supply are unsustainable, and areas of high quality countryside and tranquil retreats are under intense pressure. There is rural decline in the periphery.

The vision is expressed in schematic maps. The hubs with global economic functions and super-connectivity are in the highly congested and pressured Central Zone. The vision sees these areas maintaining global competitiveness and internal and external accessibility, while achieving urban containment and reducing pressures on the environment. Polycentricity is invoked to this end, as a way of fostering clusters of cities in, or connected to, the global zone. Eastern Ireland, Wales, Central Scotland and much of England are in the Island Zone, where the major problem to be overcome is the weak transport linkages to the global cities and gateways. Further north and west is the Open Zone of quality environments but out-migration. Here the development strategy advocated is to consolidate regional towns and base development on indigenous resources. The final zone – south and east from the Saarland – is the 'green heart', where agricultural change can be balanced by recreation and tourism opportunities.

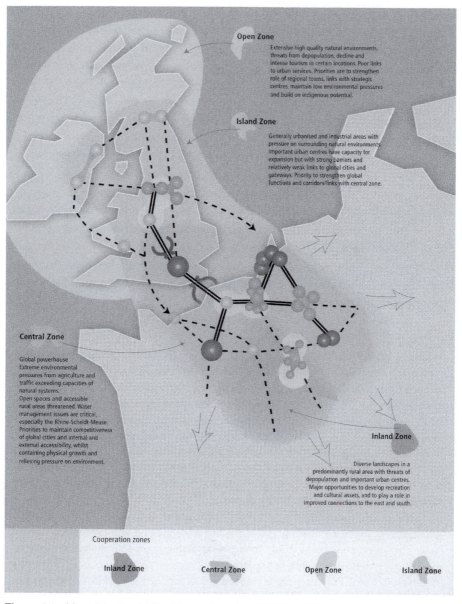

Open Zone

Extensive high quality natural environments, threats from depopulation, decline and intense tourism in certain locations. Poor links to urban services. Priorities are to strengthen role of regional towns, links with strategic centres, maintain low environmental pressures and build on indigenous potential.

Island Zone

Generally urbanised and industrial areas with pressure on surrounding natural environments. Important urban centres have capacity for expansion but with strong barriers and relatively weak links to global cities and gateways. Priority to strengthen global functions and corridors/links with central zone.

Central Zone

Global powerhouse Extreme environmental pressures from agriculture and traffic exceeding capacities of natural systems. Open spaces and accessible rural areas threatened. Water management issues are critical, especially the Rhine-Scheldt-Meuse. Priorities to maintain competitiveness of global cities and internal and external accessibility, whilst containing physical growth and relieving pressure on environment.

Inland Zone

Diverse landscapes in a predominantly rural area with threats of depopulation and important urban centres. Major opportunities to develop recreation and cultural assets, and to play a role in improved connections to the east and south.

Cooperation zones

Inland Zone   Central Zone   Open Zone   Island Zone

Figure 4.1   Map of the North West Metropolitan Area spatial vision

The NWMA is the core of the 'Pentagon', and its wealth is built on the global role of its strong metropolitan centres. While there are some areas of rural decline, and significant differences within the NWMA are recognized, in the main the urban-rural relationship is defined by urban growth pressures. In this context polycentricity is mainly interpreted as co-operation and integration of the big cities,

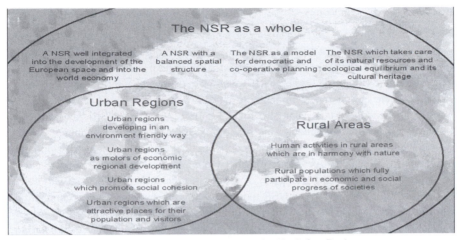

The NSR as a whole

A NSR well integrated into the development of the European space and into the world economy

A NSR with a balanced spatial structure

The NSR as a model for democratic and co-operative planning

The NSR which takes care of its natural resources and ecological equilibrium and its cultural heritage

Urban Regions

Urban regions developing in an environment friendly way

Urban regions as motors of economic regional development

Urban regions which promote social cohesion

Urban regions which are attractive places for their population and visitors

Rural Areas

Human activities in rural areas which are in harmony with nature

Rural populations which fully participate in economic and social progress of societies

Figure 4.2   Summary diagram of the spatial vision for the North Sea Region

to enhance their global role. The report recognizes that 'The effect of market forces in concentrating international economic and communications functions in only a few centres is very strong' (Spatial Vision Group and consultant team, 2000: 35). Trans-national transport corridors and the fostering of 'counterweight global gateways and economic centres' are sought. NorVision for the North Sea Region (NSR), the trans-national region in which the NoordXXI 'Quality by Identity' Interreg IIC project was set, has to address a different set of circumstances. Concerns with peripheral rural areas are given notably more weight, and while the language is much the same as in the spatial vision for the NWMA, sustainable development and environmental conservation feature more strongly. Crucially the NSR as constituted under Interreg II did not contain real metropolitan centres other than Hamburg and Oslo, neither of which is the kind of world city that London or Paris is. In addition the formidable barrier of the North Sea and the lack of hub airports mean that trans-national networks have not been so developed as in the NWMA. Not surprisingly, NorVision stresses inter-regional connections and secondary networks, and hopes that national and regional infrastructure providers will be responsive to such needs.

Thus space is being reworked into place at a trans-national level, through the attempt to identify, define and represent new Euro-regions and sub-regions. Spatial visions are themselves new types of policy instruments created directly as a means to contribute to the new narratives of place. However, spatial planning practice across the EU remains framed within distinctive national legislative codes that operate within distinctive political and economic systems. Together these stake out the 'path dependency' of any local practice, and further complicate the institutional barriers that must be negotiated if a narrative of European

Box 4.3 Summary of NorVision

NorVision: A Spatial Perspective for the North Sea Region was prepared by local and national government officials from the particiapating countries, aided by a consultant. It is intended to set the context for spatial planning, and particularly Interreg III projects in the North Sea Region (NSR). Sustainable development is at the centre of the approach. Overall the approach is process-driven, with an audit of basic values and trends leading to ten 'vision statements' (four for the whole NSR, four for urban regions and two for rural areas), aims, strategies and recommended actions.

It recognizes that the NSR is polycentric but not a functional network, since the numerous regional centres tend to connect more intensively with their national capitals (all of which, with the exception of Oslo, are outside the NSR) than with each other. Similarly the ports in the NSR tend to rely on transhipment via intercontinental ports outside the NSR. The NSR, as defined for Interreg II, contains one major national agglomeration – that based on Hamburg – and some half dozen urban agglomerations of regional importance. Parts of the NSR, e.g. Denmark, have a dense network of small and medium sized towns, which have been an important focus for local trade and services. The extent of sparsely settled rural areas is an important feature. The vision notes that balance is often equated with a polycentric system of metropolitan regions, of city clusters and city networks. However, it stresses that in peripheral regions that do not have such polycentric systems, rural urban centres have a key role to play in providing access to jobs and services. The task then is to ensure that sector policies contribute to spatial balance. To this end there is emphasis on the need to improve internal transport links, not least on the importance of ferries and bus services in rural areas, matters that are largely determined by regional or national agencies and companies, and not at an international level.

place identity sustained through spatial planning is to be propagated successfully. Globalization and harmonization are concepts that trip off the tongue, but the national scale of place identity and its institutional support mechanisms are more resilient than some would suggest. Thus to understand the practice within the NoordXXI project it is necessary to understand the very different contexts that currently structure planning activity in the Netherlands, Norway, Sweden and Scotland.

EUROPEAN PLANNING CONTEXT

To understand the context for different forms of innovatory collaboration/participation in planning across the various countries, an understanding of the legal, political and governance context is required. This part of the chapter briefly explains this prior to the discussion of case studies in more detail in the subsequent chapters.

LEGAL, POLITICAL AND ADMINISTRATIVE SYSTEMS

Newman and Thornley (1996) identified four distinct 'legal–institutional families' in Western Europe:[1]

- The *British* system, which is based on Common Law in England (and hence historically also in Wales and Ireland to a great extent), but modified in Scotland, and founded on *precedent*. In this system there is no national constitution and central government dominates, with local government seen largely as a service-providing agency, dependent for power and finance on central government. Central to local government transfers are hence important, and large units have been developed for efficient service delivery.

- The *Napoleonic* system, which is based on abstract legal norms prescribing possible issues in advance through *codification*. The development of this system historically was strongly tied in to the principles of the Enlightenment and a rational approach to social life. It covers, with national differences: France, Belgium, the Netherlands, Luxembourg, Italy, Spain and Portugal. Major differences within this system include Spain and Belgium's strong regional autonomy, which de facto happens also in Italy. The administrative system is based on the *kommune* at local level, with many small *kommunes*, related originally to the local organizational structure of the church. However, strong central government control is exerted through the codified system and integration of tiers of government, for example through the centrally appointed prefects at regional level who appoint local mayors. Historically there has been a more centralized expression of this system in southern nation-states which were formed later and have had long periods of dictatorships (especially Portugal and Spain).

- The *Germanic* system, which is based on the Napoleonic but with very distinctive features, and covers Germany, Switzerland and Austria. Here there are clearly differentiated powers at regional level in a *federal* constitution with subordinate counties and *kommunes*, although historically some free cities have combined powers and Austria in general has weaker powers at local level.

- The *Scandinavian* system, which is influenced by the Napoleonic code and Germanic legal institutional systems, but developed with the *pragmatic* outlook of the British. This system covers Norway, Denmark, Sweden and Finland and is characterized through strong regional expression of central government. However, local level *kommunes* remain relatively strong, although latterly there has been a tendency to reorganize these into larger units for efficiency reasons.

There are thus differences and similarities in the four legal–institutional systems that underpin the planning systems in the four countries studied in the research which this book draws on: the Netherlands, Norway, Scotland and Sweden. These include three examples of the four above families, each with distinctive features, even if within the same legal–institutional family. However, the legal basis for land use planning (as well as building control) is highly consolidated in the four countries (albeit supplemented with other laws on specific issues). As such they are distinct from southern European countries, which have a large number of laws affecting spatial planning, and also from the federal states of Germany and Austria – as well as Belgium and Spain – which have more complex legal frameworks for planning. This is further reflected in the political and institutional structure, which is also a contextual aspect of great importance for planning systems.

While the EU includes unitary, federalized and regionalized nation-states, the four countries studied are all unitary in basic government structure, with power residing primarily at central government level, although with different degrees of delegation of this to regional and/or local authority levels. Decentralization of roles and responsibilities is especially strong within Europe in the Netherlands and Nordic countries, with the provincial tier of government playing an important role in the Netherlands, and local authorities playing a more important role in Sweden and Norway. In Scotland, as in the rest of the UK, there is a marked contrast, with power being highly centralized. This distinction is also true for the basic political system, where each country has a national parliament elected on a four or five year term, but with varying degrees of proportional representation, which is the main process in the Netherlands, Sweden and Norway. This electoral system was only introduced in Scotland in 1999 for the election of the newly created Scottish Parliament, where it is combined with the more usual UK 'first-past-the-post' system.

Proportional representation is also used to elect provincial/county governments in the former three countries. In Scotland there is only one tier of local government, and in rural areas the units are large, covering areas not dissimilar to a province/county. Scottish local authorities are elected by a 'first-past-the-post' system, though this is likely to change in future.

The legal–institutional and political basis within each country is related to the administrative structure, and indeed to the overall demographic structure of the country (see also Table 4.1):

- *The Netherlands*
  The Netherlands has a population of around 15 million, 90 per cent being urban. It is divided administratively into 12 provinces with an average size of some 1.2 million inhabitants. There are 647 local authorities (*gemeentes*) with an average population of about 23,000.
- *Norway*
  Norway has a population of around 4.4 million, 75 per cent being urban. It is divided administratively into 19 counties with an average size of some

Table 4.1 Demographics and administrative structure in the NoordXXI countries

	National	Regional		Local	
	Average population	No. of authorities	Average population	No. of authorities	Average population
Netherlands	15 million	12	1,200,000	647	23,000
Norway	4.4 million	19	230,000	435	10,000
Scotland	5 million	–	–	32	163,000
Sweden	8.6 million	24	350,000	288	30,000

Source: Jenkins, Kirk and Smith, 2001

230,000 inhabitants, although ranging in size from 75,000 to 500,000. There are 435 *kommunes* at local authority level with an average population of about 10,000, but wide variation, with one-third having less than 3,000.

- *Scotland*

  Scotland has a population of around 5 million, 81 per cent being urban. There are no regions as such, although until local government reorganization in 1996, Scotland was divided into nine regional councils with an average of some 575,000 inhabitants. Currently Scotland has 32 local authorities with an average population size of about 163,000.

- *Sweden*

  Sweden has a population of around 8.6 million, 83 per cent being urban. It is divided administratively into 24 counties with an average size of some 350,000 inhabitants. There are 288 *kommunes* at local authority level with an average population of about 30,000 (but varying between 3,000 and 66,000).

As can be seen, despite a degree of similarity in unitary government structure, the different legal–institutional families are expressed in markedly different administrative units – numbers and size – making up the nation-states, which themselves differ in size, although all are relatively small demographically compared to the largest European nation-states (i.e. Germany, France and Italy with between 58 and 80 million each). These different legal, political and administrative structures are also expressed in the nature of the planning mechanisms, as can be seen in the following section.

PLANNING SYSTEMS AND INSTITUTIONS

As noted in the EU compendium of spatial planning systems and policies (CEC, 1997), in broad terms four categories of spatial planning have been identified in Western Europe:

- the regional economic approach, where spatial planning is closely associated with socio-economic planning and central government plays an important role (e.g. France, and to a lesser extent Portugal);
- the comprehensive integrated approach, where a systematic formal hierarchy of plans from national to local level act as a focus for spatial co-ordination (e.g. the Netherlands and Scandinavian countries), this usually being associated with extensive planning institutions and public sector investment;
- the land use management approach, where spatial planning is not closely associated with other forms of planning or government activity, and where this is locally managed, albeit under national guidelines (e.g. UK and Scotland);
- the urbanism tradition, which is more oriented to urban design, and where rigid zoning and building control is used to regulate development (e.g. southern European countries, although France also incorporates this tradition).

In addition there are four broad categories of planning instruments:

- national policy instruments, such as national spatial plans, planning guidance and sectoral plans/guidance;
- future land use/development strategies, usually for regions (administrative or functional);
- 'framework' plans identifying broad patterns of land use;
- regulatory plans to control and/or promote development, often for small areas.

All European countries have planning instruments and mechanisms which fit within these four categories in one way or another, although their nature and function varies considerably.

Thus, as with legal–institutional families, the four countries studied have similarities and differences. The Netherlands is the only country with comprehensive national spatial plans, although Norway, Scotland and Sweden have general policy guidance and sectoral policy/guidance at national level. All four countries, however, have regional level strategic spatial planning instruments, with these being prepared either by regional government (the Netherlands, Norway and Sweden) or by regional groupings of local governments (Norway, Scotland and Sweden). In addition, while these plans are linked to sectoral plans as well as to plans for functional regions, this is not the case in Scotland, where there is not such a degree of spatial planning integration. Generally speaking these strategic plans are not legally binding.[2]

At the 'framework' and local spatial planning level, various planning instruments are used, with both being an essential part of regulation, although the legally binding nature differs. In general, framework plans cover whole local authority areas (and sometimes a number of local authorities) and provide broad guidance on land use change to guide detailed plans, which are often for only parts of the local authority area. Framework plans are generally legally binding once approved, as are local detailed plans – except in Scotland where, as in the rest of the UK, plans are used within the discretionary system, although they are important factors influencing decision-making.[3] Table 4.2 summarizes the various spatial plans and regulatory instruments and their relevant levels, and Table 4.3

Table 4.2 Types of spatial plans and regulatory instruments

		Netherlands	Norway	Scotland	Sweden
National	spatial plan	National Spatial Plan			
	policy guidance	Policy Guidelines	Policy Guidelines	Policy Guidelines	Policy Guidelines
	sectoral plans/ guidance	National Sectoral Structure Plans			
Regional	development strategy	Regional Policy	Regional Development*		Regional Economic Plan*
	strategic land use	Provincial Structure Plans*	County Plan**	Structure Plan	Regional Spatial Plan**
Local	strategic land use	City Region Plans, Structure Plans	Master Plan		Structure Plan
	local land use plans	Local Land Use Plan	Land Development Plans	Local Plan	Detailed Development Plan
	other regulatory instruments		Building Development Plans	Simplified Planning Zones/ Development Control	Area Regulations, Land Sub-division Plans
Notes		*Spatial, Water, Transport and Environment Plans, or Plan for the Environs	*Developed by the regional representative of central government **Developed by the county		*Developed by the regional representative of central government **Developed by the county

Source: Jenkins, Kirk and Smith, 2001

Table 4.3 Institutions involved in spatial planning

	Netherlands	Norway	Scotland	Sweden
National government	Minister of Housing, Spatial Planning and the Environment	Minister for the Environment	Minister for the Environment and Transport	Minister for the Environment
	National Spatial Planning Commission	Building and Housing Department *		
	National Spatial Planning Agency		Scottish Executive Development Department	National Board of Housing, Building and Planning
	Advisory Council for Spatial Planning			
Provincial government	Provincial Minister for Spatial Planning*	County Executive		Regional Planning Body
	Provincial Spatial Planning Agency			
	Provincial Spatial Planning Commission			
Local government	Municipal Spatial Planning Department	Municipal Executive	Local Authority Planning Committee*	Municipal Building Committee*
	Planning Department*	Municipal Planner**	Planning Department*	Municipal Planner
*Other major participants institutions***	National strategic		National strategic institutions (listed)	National strategic institutions**
			Other lobbying institutions	Other lobbying institutions
	Town, village and neighbourhood		Community Councils	Tenants and labour organizations

Continued

	Netherlands	Norway	Scotland	Sweden
Notes	*or equivalent **various receive state support	*in Ministry of Local Government and Labour **where this exists	*or equivalent	*or equivalent **including National Associations of County Councils and Municipalities

Source: Jenkins, Kirk and Smith, 2001

shows the government organizations with a major participation in spatial planning issues across these four countries.

Regional level (where this exists) and local level government bodies usually constitute executives and/or a specialized sub-committee to deal with spatial planning issues, although all have some level of delegation of responsibility to officials. Only in Scotland is there statutory requirement for consultation, where this includes local area community councils. However, in all countries a wide degree of consultation with organized groups takes place, including a wide range of voluntary bodies – especially in the Netherlands, where town and village councils participate. As noted below, despite the statutory requirements for public consultation in Scotland and the UK, this has not generally been seen as successful in terms of broad inclusion.

REPRESENTATION IN SPATIAL PLANNING

Concerning the legal basis for consultation in planning, this is typically formalized in statutory procedures in the northern European countries – i.e. over and above the normal representative political process. The nature of public consultation is, however, usually seen as separate to that of other interested parties and comes later in the process. Consultation prior to firm proposals being developed is thus often only with official organizations, voluntary or not. That said, however, public consultation processes are under review in various countries with a view to reducing costly inquiries and lengthy appeals, while increasing transparency and public participation.

In the Netherlands, whether at provincial or local level, the public may be informed prior to proposals being confirmed, but this is not mandatory. After publication of firm proposals public consultation is undertaken (an eight week period for regional plans, a four week period for local plans) with opportunity to object. For legally binding local land use plans, objectors may request a hearing to explain the objections directly to the local authority. After formal adoption of the local land use plan this is submitted to the provincial government for approval and displayed for a further four weeks, during which limited objections can be made (new objections being limited to changes in the plan). After approval, appeals to the Council of State are possible only on matters originally subject to objection.

In Norway the kommune is required to seek co-operation with public authorities, private organizations, private landowners and tenants who will have an interest in any plan, notifying these by letter when planning is started and when the draft plan is available. The completed local plan must be made available for public inspection with a reasonable time for comments, which the kommune must take into consideration. The kommune has the power to approve local plans within the framework of national and regional goals and guidelines. If there are significant objections the plan needs to go to the Ministry of the Environment. There is a similar process for county plans.

In Sweden, there is wide organizational consultation on initial proposals for both the master plans and local land use plans with between three and twelve weeks further public consultation after firm proposals are developed, depending on the plan type. After formal approval, while the local land use plans can still be challenged, challenge of the master plans is only possible on procedural grounds. If representations on the local land use plans are not taken into consideration, the objector has the right of appeal to higher authorities which can annul the approval.

In Scotland the public may be informed prior to proposals for the local plan, however this is rare and public consultation usually only takes place during a six week period after first draft proposals are published. If major objections are made, an inquiry can be held (unless all objectors agree it is not needed). The inquiry is held before an independent 'inspector' appointed by national government who records the evidence presented and prepares a report, but the final decision rests with the plan-making authority (although it can be overruled by national government). A further six week consultation period is allowed if major changes are made to the plan. After approval challenge is only possible on procedural grounds. The process for consultation for a structure plans is similar; however, the important difference is that the Scottish Ministers have sole right to determine whether an examination in public is to be held, and they can require changes before they approve the plan.

The legal role of other (statutory) consultees is limited in the Netherlands, Norway and Sweden but specified in Scotland; however, wide consultation takes place in these countries despite this not being a legal requirement, as traditions of horizontal integration are stronger than in Scotland. Scotland on the other hand has specifically constituted community councils, which have no formal planning powers but have a statutory right to consultation on planning issues (since 1996).

Concerning participation in planning of other voluntary bodies, in the Netherlands the planning authorities include a range of voluntary bodies in the planning process as a matter of course, including town and village councils. These do not necessarily get involved in Norway and Sweden, despite a very wide range of well-supported voluntary bodies existing.[4] It would appear that in the Scandinavian countries adequate representation takes place through the formal consultation process (see below).

In Scotland and the UK there is a perception that the formal process is by no means inclusive and hence there have been a number of innovations aimed at involving the broader public in planning. This is parallel, but not formally linked, to a renewed effort at central and local government level to engage the broader public in governance – called Community Planning. The general alienation of the broad public that has built up over a long period, however, makes this a difficult task. Thus despite statutory requirements vis-à-vis public consultation, the general public feels alienated from the spatial planning process and has become reactive, as elaborated below.

SOCIO-CULTURAL ASPECTS

Socio-cultural aspects are perhaps the hardest to determine in the form of short-term research which this chapter draws on, but underlying mental attitudes and values are of fundamental importance for governance systems. These are often built up over very long periods of time, and many of these values are not explicit as others are embedded within society and social learning processes. As such, in the context of this chapter, they will not be discussed in any detail, but a few general observations can be made.

One of these is that all the countries involved in the research developed welfare states of differing natures after the Second World War. The nature of the welfare state developed depended no doubt on circumstances such as the demographic spread, level of economic development, and political parties in power duing the main post-war period. This is even more noticeable now as the 'traditional' basis for the welfare state has been much eroded across all the countries with different reactions to this. However, the nature of the relatively strong welfare states developed permitted a significant growth of – and gave purposefulness to – post-war government policies and relations of governance. This permitted both the elevation in importance and the legal–institutional consolidation of spatial planning as a proactive function of government. However, although to a greater or lesser extent each of the countries studied developed corporatist forms of governance within the welfare state context, the nature of these and the perception of the role of the individual within these differed.

Typically more top-down structured forms of negotiation between corporatist groups became institutionalized in the Netherlands and UK/Scotland, whereas more bottom-up participation in governance was incorporated in Sweden, and particularly Norway, with its strong tradition of 'smallholder politics'. This underpins the balance in perception in each country between what is appropriate for representative politics and what is appropriate for direct participatory politics, and is closely related to the size of administrative units. In general, it would be true to say that individuals tend to feel they have more of a direct role in participation in at least local political issues in Norway and Sweden, than in Scotland or the Netherlands, although in the latter there is much greater scope and encouragement for non-statutory participation. In many ways these differences manifest themselves in the degree of engagement in associational forms, but not in the nature of engagement in spatial planning.

Thus, for example, in Sweden and Norway there is a relatively high degree of participation in voluntary activities and associations, but limited direct participation in spatial planning, which at the local level is mainly concerned with development of individual plots of land, and so is seen as an individual matter rather than as a focus for community involvement. In general, the tendency in governance seems to be to rely on the representative system which most people seem to feel they can influence, if desired, through formal political and corporate channels. In other words, people (still) feel more engaged in, and act through, the formal political processes that have been set up during the post-war period. The smaller units of authority, with relatively stronger powers and resources, and strong traditions of proportional representation, would seem to support this position. It may also be due partly to relatively higher degrees of social and economic homogeneity – at least compared to other parts of Europe. The increasing effect of urbanization and the growing importance of environmental issues are leading to a change in this position regarding spatial planning, with a tendency to more strategic planning and a popular realization that individual activity needs to be regulated in the public interest.

In the Netherlands, to some extent in contrast, there seems to be a much greater public acceptance of the need for spatial planning. This can probably be related to the dense nature of settlement over many centuries and the need for a high degree of public water management to secure geographic integrity and safety. To what extent the traditions of public negotiation of the 'polder model' underpin the arguably more developed spatial planning traditions, and their broad public acceptance, would be hard to determine, but generally there seems to be a higher degree of public acceptance of the formal governance processes, again including proportional representation and strong corporate negotiation processes. However, as in Sweden and Norway, there seems to be evidence of growing proactive individual and group participation in political processes, often on non-party issues.

Scotland differs from these models in that, as in the rest of the UK, there is a tendency for alienation and antagonism towards the planning system and growing apathy towards involvement in public affairs. It can be argued that the top-down nature of the legal–institutional system, and the restricted nature of the party political system and 'first-past-the-post' electoral system, as well as the excessive reliance on limited corporatist forms of governance in the past and the impact of the 'democratic deficit' of 1979–97, have led to this situation. Arguably the discretionary nature of the spatial planning system and the relatively high degree of professionalization of planning have reinforced the position of those with professional (legal and technical) resources in comparison with the individual or social group. In Scotland the historical wide variations between the landowning class, the industrial and bureaucratic class, and the rural and urban working class have also exacerbated this. Thus, despite statutory procedures for public partici-pation in spatial planning – which are not paralleled in the other three countries studied – there is extremely limited understanding of, or desire to participate proactively in, planning, and this often leads to reactive conflictual situations (Jenkins, Kirk and Smith, 2002). National government is concerned with this situ-ation and has launched a number of initiatives to counteract this tendency (e.g. Scottish Executive Development Department, 2002b), but whether these will entail any structural change and thus be fundamentally more effective is unlikely.

CONCLUSION

In this chapter we have seen how European integration, itself a response to global competition, has led to a need to create discourse structures that facilitate some narrative of European place identity. However, that is a negotiated and contingent process, which can be disaggregated to Euro-regions and sub-regions, as in the spatial visions for the North Sea Region and the North West Metropolitan Area. At these scales the drivers of the narratives are almost exclusively the political and bureaucratic elite. However, to encapsulate them under a single heading seriously understates the multiplicity of institutional, national, regional, ideological, cultural, lin-guistic and professional (not to mention personal, this remains a relatively small circle of people) differences that fragment this grouping.

In addition, the spatial visions largely have an enabling role and their translation into practice (i.e. the interpretation of Euro-policy on the ground) is strongly mediated by nation-states, their legislative and administrative traditions and the endeavours and whims of local planners and politicians – together with their local residents. As the second part of the chapter demonstrates, these are quite different in legal–constitu-tional traditions, planning systems, institutions and instruments, and participatory mechanisms as well as the socio-cultural orientation to participation. Thus there exists a range of nationally constituted planning discourses, all with roots in welfare states that have been restructuring. Meanwhile, investment in the land development process proceeds through a range of other public institutions and private firms that remain blissfully ignorant of 'spatial planning', 'polycentric development', the aspiration to fash-ion a 'new urban-rural relationship' or the desire for 'parity of access to transport and infrastructure'. As such, what is happening on the ground? The following chapters begin to explore this through case studies developed within the NoordXXI Project at various scales, from the macro-region to the small local authority.

CHAPTER 5

REGIONAL CHANGE AND PLACE IDENTITY
CLIFF HAGUE

This chapter explores processes of change and narratives of regional identity that have been constructed within the spatial planning discourse. The discussion encompasses European trans-national regions, administrative regions within nation-states, city-regions and rural sub-regions. Thus the chapter is comparative with respect to spatial scale but also internationally. The aim is to analyse how different regions are changing and what place identities are being constructed through spatial planning in response to those changes. In this way, the chapter applies the concepts from the first part of the book to practical examples, with the NoordXXI Interreg project and data collected within it providing the base for the analysis.

The inspiration behind the NoordXXI project was the idea that the authentic identity of rural areas around growing cities could constitute a radical solution to spatial development problems. The partner regions in the project faced a range of challenges that stemmed from the restructuring of activities and places. Agricultural landscapes and small towns, the physical basis of rural regional identity, were undergoing qualitative, discontinuous change. Farming was giving way to agri-business in pursuit of greater efficiency and optimal returns. Continued protectionism and state subsidies through the Common Agricultural Policy – the antithesis of globalization – were under political threat. Traditional manufacturing enterprises had closed: there was a need to find new ways of sustaining incomes and stimulating investment. Commuting to adjacent urban areas was replacing the traditional local economy. Intensification of this dormitory role was a 'present trends' scenario and the NoordXXI project was premised on the belief that there were other alternatives.

The NoordXXI project was put together by politicians and officials from these regions who were united by the belief that their nearby urban centres dominated spatial planning and economic development in the urban fringe and surrounding rural regions. The partners felt that orthodox planning had not engaged adequately with the needs and potential of these hinterlands. Thus NoordXXI reflected and tested, at the level of the partner regions, the European Spatial Development Perspective (ESDP) concern to achieve balanced and sustainable spatial development, which is seen as connecting economy, society and environment (see CEC, 1999:10). Table 5.1 identifies the partners and summarizes their relation to their dominant cities.

Like the ESDP, the NoordXXI project was seeking to enhance competitiveness in a way that would increase cohesion and protect the natural environment

Table 5.1 The NoordXXI regions and their urban–rural context

Country	NoordXXI Region	Regional relation to a large city
Netherlands	'North of the Netherlands' – the provinces of Groningen, Frisia and Drenthe	Traditionally an agricultural region, based on the city of Groningen, these provinces are seeking sustainable economic growth that maintains their natural and environmental qualities. While beyond commuting range to the Randstad, the main urban core in the Netherlands, Randstad-style urbanization was the orthodox growth model to which the North sought to provide an alternative.
Netherlands	Landstad Deventer, part of the province of Overijssel	Based on the city of Deventer, Landstad Deventer is a concept that seeks to forge positive links between the 'stad' of Deventer, and the surrounding 'land' or countryside.
Norway	Buskerud County	One of eight counties that make up the Østlandet, based on Oslo. Half of Norway's population is in Østlandet. The southern part of Buskerud is within commuting distance of Oslo.
Norway	Østfold County	Another Østlandet county, south-east of Oslo. Much of Østfold is within commuting distance of Norway's capital.
Sweden	Västra Götaland	The region includes the city of Gothenburg, all of its commuter hinterland, and rural areas beyond commuting range.
UK	Aberdeenshire	Aberdeenshire encompasses the commuter hinterland of Aberdeen, but again some areas beyond commuting range.
UK	East Lothian	East Lothian shares a boundary with Edinburgh, but is not the only authority within the commuter hinterland of the Scottish capital.

and cultural heritage. In economic terms it sought to build upon practices and theories about resource-based local economic development that generally related to more remote areas. Maskell *et al.* (1998) argued that such localized capabilities depend on the built structures and natural resources of the region, local knowledge and skills, and the region's institutional legacy. In reviewing the literature on the links between place and competitiveness (e.g. Porter, 1990; Krugman, 1991) they recognized that 'backwardness', often associated with rural areas, can be an advantage in situations of rapid structural change. In other words, regions unencumbered by the structures and institutions of the 'last round of investment' may be able to achieve innovative development. Such arguments underpinned the economic possibilities of 'quality by identity'.

Of course, as noted in Chapters 1 and 2, identity is first and foremost a cultural construct before it is an economic resource, and as such identities are likely to be ambiguous and contested. Traditional rural identity − defined in part from the social and economic order of the countryside − has been subject to critique. In the age of modernity the countryside was seen as backwards; more recently postmodernity celebrates the diversity of the city and the scope it offers for freedom of choice, while exposing the fake pastoralism of marketed rurality. Identity is also a political construct and − as we have already argued − is central to the politics of fashioning and legitimizing the EU. The overall aim of the Interreg programme is that 'national borders should not be a barrier to the balanced sustainable development and integration of the European territory' (CEC, 2001: 4). To achieve this, some sense of territorial and place identity crossing national boundaries needs to be present or to be created. This imperative implies some simultaneous contestation, or at least significant adaptation, of narratives of identity based on nation-states. Thus our analysis of new discourses of planning that seek regional change and place identity begins at the level of the European Interreg region within which the NoordXXI project was created.

THE NORTH SEA REGION

As explained in Chapter 4, the North Sea Region (NSR) was defined and constructed by the European Commission to foster co-operation in spatial planning under Interreg and thus contribute towards the implementation of the ESDP. Other regions identified and organized by the Commission were the North West European Metropolitan Area, the Baltic Sea Region and the Central European, Danubian and Southeast European Space, South Western Europe and the Mediterranean and Latin Alps (see Figure 5.1).

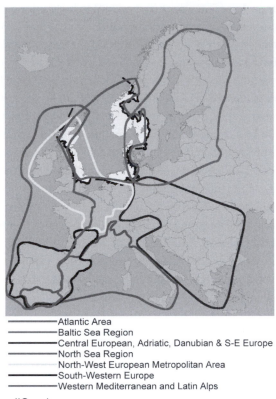

————————Atlantic Area
————————Baltic Sea Region
————————Central European, Adriatic, Danubian & S-E Europe
————————North Sea Region
————————North-West European Metropolitan Area
————————South-Western Europe
————————Western Mediterranean and Latin Alps

Figure 5.1 Interreg IIC regions

These are all huge trans-national areas. They represent a significant spatial intervention seeking to advance the competitiveness and cohesion of the territory of the
EU in the context of international competition and the accession of countries from
Central and Eastern Europe. Of the 15 member states plus Norway, only four
(Belgium, Luxembourg, Finland and Greece), were completely and exclusively in
one of the trans-national regions. The boundaries of some of these mega-regions
overlap, reflecting a pragmatic recognition that these are not unambiguous entities.

Similarly the areas included in the NSR were extended between Interreg II and
Interreg III, through the addition of further areas within Denmark, Germany, the
Netherlands, and Essex in England (see Figures 5.2 and 5.3). In addition, the
Flemish region of Belgium became part of the NSR at this stage. The effect was to
add some urban 'weight' to a somewhat tenuous functional construct, not least in
terms of aspirations to create dynamic zones of global integration. All of this demonstrates that the new trans-national constructs of territory are led from above and are
substantially administrative in their rationale, but also, in a post-modern way, have
somewhat porous edges.

Notwithstanding the bold administrative vision that conjured these new territorial units, there are obstacles to creating corresponding identities. The NSR of
Interreg II, within which the NoordXXI project operated, included only one national
capital, Oslo. Thus intra-national linkages focused on capital city hubs formed networks beyond the NSR, and these connections were stronger than the main
trans-national links contained within the NSR. Edinburgh to London, compared with
Edinburgh to Gothenburg, would be one example.

The North Sea, the definitive base for this new Euro-regional territorial identity,
is actually a major physical barrier that divides rather than unites those living around
it. There are some historical cultural ties courtesy of the Viking diaspora, but these
are not strong beyond Scandinavia. There are also significant differences in population density between the sparsely populated rural and island communities, mainly in
the north, and the urbanized zones further south. Sogn/Fjordane in Norway has only
six inhabitants per square kilometre, and the figure in the Scottish Highlands is only
eight. These areas would seem to have little in common with the big city of Hamburg
with its 2,250 inhabitants per square kilometre (Vision Working Group, 2000: 18).

Figure 5.2   Map of Interreg IIC North Sea Region

Figure 5.3   Map of Interreg IIIB North Sea Region

Such contrasts imply that any notion of a shared identity could prove fragile, and that place narratives at the scale of the Euro-region may be weak and competing.

The development of trans-European transport networks has so far probably exacerbated rather than overcome those problems of core and periphery. Time–distance has been reduced in core areas, e.g. through high-speed train networks; but this has had the effect of increasing relative journey times across and around the North Sea. Low population densities and significant distances between the larger cities will continue to hamper the emergence of integrated polycentric trans-national regions in this part of Europe. It has been argued that an 'integration zone' requires a densely populated region such as the Rhine–Meuse–Scheldt delta, where almost 40 million people live in an area of scarcely 300 km in diameter (Ministry of Housing, Spatial Planning and the Environment, 2000: 129–30). The Interreg II North Sea Region is simply not like that. Thus the challenge of enhancing competitiveness and cohesion and strengthening integration round the North Sea has to be faced in a realistic and sustainable manner, and territorial identity is unlikely to be built on the kind of development interconnectedness that underpins the North West European Metropolitan Area, for example.

In European terms the NSR is significant for its natural resources, rather than as a potential space for polycentric urban growth. This is an energy-rich part of Europe. The oil reserves in the North Sea have made Norway one of the wealthiest

countries in the world in relation to its population numbers. At the turn of the millennium the North Sea was yielding six million barrels of oil every day (CEC, 2001: 27).
Gas production from below the North Sea is also important. Denmark has the highest production of energy from wind power of all EU countries, while hydro-electricity
has been important in Norway and Sweden, and is also a source of energy in
Scotland.

The region also contains landscapes and ecological areas of European significance: the estuaries, and the Wadden Sea that stretches from the Netherlands to
Denmark, are of special value; there are significant woodland resources in Scotland,
Sweden and Norway; there are a range of cultural landscapes and World Heritage
Sites. These fragile resources need to be managed. Such assets have potential for
tourism, though climate, high costs of living and poor transport links constrain the
potential for mass tourism on the Mediterranean model.

As a territory, the NSR has some major inherent contradictions. Norway is
essential to make the region a geographical entity, yet the Norwegians have twice
decided in referenda not to join the EU. The NSR is a wealthy part of Europe, but its
economic scale and energy-based affluence do not fit the ESDP notion that the
'Pentagon' is the development model to be replicated through a polycentric development of global economic integration zones. Meanwhile, the North Sea's
peripherality, and especially the extreme peripherality of its northern areas, will be a
growing problem as accession countries to the east join the EU, and traditional economic activities such as fishing and farming contract. Arguably national (and
increasingly private) control of energy exploitation means that the energy base of the
region is under-developed both as a narrative of place identity and as a concern for
European spatial planning.

The spatial vision prepared for the North Sea Region rightly recognized that 'the
NSR is not commonly perceived as an area of particular internal cohesion' (Vision
Working Group, 2000: 4). This was attributed to integration into the wider European
space and the lack of major urban and administrative centres. Nevertheless, NorVision
explicitly searched for a common identity. Table 5.2 summarizes the components of
that identity.

This listing of points can only form a rudimentary narrative of place identity. It is
not even clear that all of the items contribute positively to a shared sense of North
Sea identity. For example, strong regional identities may overshadow or exclude the
formation of a North Sea identity, while few will glory in identification with the climate!
Fishing and farming are perhaps the most persuasive and evocative strands in the
place narrative, the ones most deeply rooted in social and economic practices, but
these sectors are undergoing restructuring and decline. Aspirations to build a North
Sea place identity as a base for a new territorial identity do not mean that such an
identity has substance in practical, everyday life. NorVision recognized the difficulties

Table 5.2 North Sea Region: common identity

• North Sea climate leading to specific forms of development. • Traditional (diminishing) orientation towards maritime economy. • Joint responsibility for valuable 'wet nature'. • Closeness of cultures and traditions across the North Sea. • Co-existence of remoter areas having unique valuable characteristics, with urban centres and highly advanced economies. • No dominating mega-urban agglomeration with NSR. • Strong identity of the regions. • Traditional orientation towards areas outside the region. • Long standing urban cultural tradition. • Valuable heritage of towns and cities. • Attractive cultural landscapes.

Source: Vision Working Group, 2000: 4

in applying the ESDP to this peripheral region. Poor internal transport links are barriers to integration but require national, not trans-national solutions. The situation in the partner regions of NoordXXI exemplifies this reality, as the next section shows.

PARTNERS IN A COMMON TERRITORY?

TRANSPORT

In the North of the Netherlands the main transport corridor links are the motorways A6 and A7 that connect the Randstad to Germany via Emmen and Groningen respectively. There is a possibility that the Dutch government will support a light rail connection between Amsterdam, Groningen and Hamburg, but it would not be ready until 2015. In Landstad Deventer the connections are also east–west. The upgrading of track will improve Amsterdam–Berlin rail services through Deventer, but the fast trains will not stop there. The North of the Netherlands was described by Nijkamp (1998: 45) as being part of the intermediary area between the core 'European Banana' and the 'Boomerang area' consisting of cities in central and eastern Europe including Gdansk, Berlin, Prague and Budapest. Neither connects to the North Sea Region of Interreg II, though the area around Hamburg was added for Interreg III. Future options discussed by Nijkamp included the North of the Netherlands being a transport corridor between these two conceptual Euro-regions; an outpost for extension of the Randstad; a gateway to central, eastern and northern Europe; or a modern 'green technology area'. The location and transport corridors stake out Euro-scale connections (see Figure 5.4). However, if the future of the North is seen only within the nation-state of the Netherlands, then 'an extension of the Randstad', with urbanization on the model of the west of the country, would be the most likely scenario.

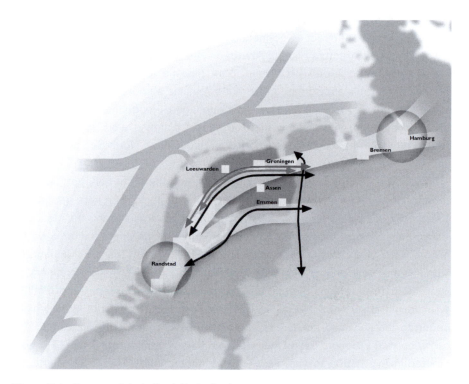

Figure 5.4 Transport links in North Netherlands

In Scotland there has been research and debate into the idea that the Glasgow–Edinburgh belt might be a polycentric urban region. Bailey and Turok (2001) showed that central Scotland has a topography and label as 'the Central Belt' that differentiates it from other parts of Scotland and from other urban regions. However, if central Scotland were seen as a useful unit for spatial planning it would probably include East Lothian, but not Aberdeen or its rural hinterland. There has been no discussion of a polycentric east coast growth region running from Aberdeenshire to the Borders and encompassing the NoordXXI partner regions of Aberdeenshire and East Lothian.

The relatively poor transport infrastructure, particularly the rail links north from Edinburgh and the road links south, are again cause and effect of this lacuna. There are no fast road connections from Edinburgh through East Lothian to the Northeast of England, though the A1 route is now being upgraded. There is a fast rail route to England that passes through East Lothian, though few of the trains stop there. Aberdeen is some 2 hours 30 minutes travel by road or rail to the north of Edinburgh.

The airport and harbour at Aberdeen are important links to the rest of the UK and to Europe. It is oil, the most global of industries, which makes the strongest connections between Aberdeen and the non-UK parts of the North Sea Region. For example, there are direct air connections between Aberdeen and Stavanger in Norway. The Draft Structure Plan for Aberdeen and Aberdeenshire encouraged the relevant agencies to improve rail, road, port, pipeline and airport infrastructure. Similarly Edinburgh's airport has grown but it remains a spoke not a hub, and the only direct flights into Scandinavia are to Copenhagen, though there are also direct links to Amsterdam. In summary, there is spatial planning work to be done to strengthen the integration of these Scottish partners into a North Sea territory and identity.

There is a Scandinavian identity, of course, and there the transport linkages also help. However, in respect of NoordXXI partner regions, even here geographical distances combine to impose substantial blockages to achieving the ideal of a dynamic trans-national region able to complement, but also offer an alternative to, the core area of European economic space. The Nordic Triangle Multi-modal Corridor is the only priority project in the Trans-European Transport Network to benefit the partner regions directly (see Figure 5.5). Thus Buskerud and Østfold are linked into major road and rail systems that connect the west of Norway with Sweden to the east and south (the latter linking them to Västra Götaland). The recently opened Oslofjord tunnel has improved these connections. 'Scan Link' was promoted in the 1980s to improve the Oslo–Gothenburg–Europe connections. The plan was to establish a double track railway line and to upgrade the E6 road to motorway. To date the double track railway only extends as far south as Moss in Østfold. The Gothenburg port receives one-third of all Swedish cargo by sea, and 60 per cent of all cargo by containers. Thus Gothenburg is an international gateway on a scale unmatched by any of the other partners. It is also accessible to the Oresund fixed link between Malmö and Copenhagen, a definitive trans-national connection of the new Europe.

SENSE OF IDENTITY

In the course of the research we asked members of community councils in East Lothian and in Aberdeenshire whether they felt any sense of identity with the North Sea Region and the countries around the North Sea, such as Norway, Sweden or the Netherlands. Nobody whom we interviewed did. Some felt that those working in the oil industry might feel some affinity. Another community councillor from Aberdeenshire hypothesized that fishing communities in his Mearns area might sense links. However, he qualified this by adding that 'Mearns people are quite inward-looking, perhaps too much so. It's interesting that there are no Mearns 'twin-towns' in Scandinavia; they all seem to be in France.'

From all of the above, it is very clear that the building of an identity for the North Sea Region is still at an early stage. This is recognized in the Interreg programme,

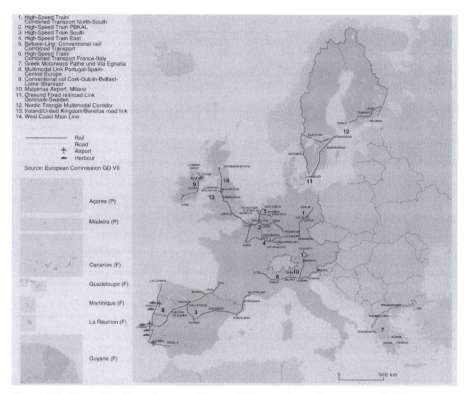

1. High-Speed Train/
   Combined Transport North-South
2. High-Speed Train PBKAL
3. High-Speed Train South
4. High-Speed Train East
5. Betuwe-Line; Conventional rail/
   Combined Transport
6. High-Speed Train/
   Combined Transport France-Italy
7. Greek Motorways Pathe und Via Egnatia
8. Multimodal Link Portugal-Spain-
   Central Europe
9. Conventional rail Cork-Dublin-Belfast-
   Larne-Stranraer
10. Malpensa Airport, Milano
11. Øresund Fixed rail/road Link
    Denmark-Sweden
12. Nordic Triangle Multimodal Corridor
13. Ireland/United Kingdom/Benelux road link
14. West Coast Main Line

——— Rail
——— Road
⊥ Airport
⸺ Harbour

Source: European Commission GD VII

Figure 5.5 Map of the Trans-European Transport Networks in the European Spatial Development Perspective

which notes that 'The region shares the North Sea as a common resource and has historic links binding the area together. It is still too early to talk of the North Sea Region as a fixed structure but as a region it is certainly developing' (CEC, 2001: 31). The approach to developing a North Sea Region has in reality been top down and somewhat technocratic, e.g. through the emphasis given to spatial planning and the preparation of a spatial vision. A simple exercise was carried out with participants in the NoordXXI meeting in Hjortviken in October 2000. They were asked to write down four key words that defined for them each of the partner regions, and to indicate whether they had visited the region in question. Not surprisingly, this revealed much stronger perceptions about regions that people had actually visited for one of the meetings during the project than for those they had never visited. This shows that direct involvement of people in European networking is vital to building the knowledge and identity that is a necessary, but not sufficient, condition to achieve territorial cohesion and some shared sense of place identity.

Will globalization assist the attempts to build an identity for the North Sea Region? NorVision described the NSR as benefiting from, and being challenged by, global trends, while noting that the challenges are 'not very different from those of other regions in Europe, nor will be the solution approaches' (Vision Working Group, 2000: 27). This rather implies that the global forces are neutral in their impact on the identity of the NSR. However, while globalization will reduce the friction of national borders, there is every likelihood that it will increase the dominance of the 'Pentagon' at the heart of Europe, rather than strengthen peripheral networks such as those in the NSR. The ESDP, Interreg and NorVision are interventions consciously seeking a development strategy that is an alternative to this scenario, but transforming such ideals into practices will not be easy. Kunzmann (1996) argued that large scale spatial planning has only a slim chance of influencing location decisions by capital within a market economy. However, spatial planning can be a potent means of developing spatial images that can have a guiding effect on political decision-making. At the moment such spatial images are lacking for the North Sea Region and for the kind of intra-regional patterns that could be considered to contribute to sustainable development.

NEW URBAN–RURAL RELATIONS: GLOBAL PRESSURES

This book argues that concerns to reassert, reinvent or even invent narratives of place identity are shaped by pressures exerted on places through globalization. The ESDP catalogued a number of European trends and issues while recognizing that there are variations in their intensity and incidence. These included:

*   decline in population, migratory movements and aging of the population profile;
*   smaller households and increased demand for housing;
*   unemployment, with substantial disparities between different regions;
*   shift from manufacturing to services, and the shift of production by large companies from urban to rural areas;
*   attraction of direct foreign investment but marginalization of regions not prepared for competition;
*   growth of telecommunications and information technologies;
*   urban development, agricultural change, tourism and infrastructure have all contributed to loss of habitats, and put pressure on the quality of the landscape;
*   need to reduce CO_2 emissions.

These pressures are intertwined with spatial change. In particular the ESDP noted that 'development pressure on areas surrounding cities has become a problem. It is therefore necessary to work together to find sustainable solutions for planning and managing urban growth' (CEC, 1999: 65–6). Rural–urban relationships in densely populated regions were seen as particularly problematic, and a threat to rural character. In less densely populated rural areas shifts in agriculture and forestry, and problems of out-migration, undermine the viability of services. However, 'the natural and cultural heritage of these endangered rural areas are key assets which can form the basis of economic and social regeneration initiatives, based on sustainable tourism and recreation, amongst other things' (CEC, 1999: 66–7). The NoordXXI project sought to tackle these spatial planning problems through 'quality by identity'. Thus rural-based planning for place identity would supersede the urban-centred planning that expected hinterlands to absorb poor quality spill-over development from the larger urban settlements, thus extending car-based commuting and eroding the character of natural and cultural land-scapes. So how have the broad European trends identified by the ESDP impacted at the level of the NoordXXI partner regions?

DEMOGRAPHIC CHANGE

The partner regions faced the challenge of accommodating increased numbers of households due to the trend towards smaller households and the migration of people from the large cities and from some more remote rural areas into the accessible zones within commuting distance of cities. However, there was a range of demographic situations. In Buskerud, for example, there was a huge contrast between the urbanized and industrialized area around Drammen (a town of 54,000), and the 44 per cent of the area of the region that is over 900 metres above sea level, and where average densities are only 3 persons per square kilometre. Table 5.3 shows that the project encompassed a number of regions or sub-regions where population growth had been running at around 0.5 per cent or more per year, but also that in some more remote rural areas growth had been weak, or even negative. Such variations pose challenges in terms of territorial cohesion.

EMPLOYMENT

Change in primary industries has fundamental implications for the identity of these regions. Although all the partner regions could be described as 'rural' or at least had substantial tracts of rural land, everywhere agriculture accounted for only a small percentage of the employment, and the number of jobs in agriculture had declined. In the North of the Netherlands, for example, van der Aa and Huigen (2000a: 9) report that agriculture is losing its significance, and declining in number of jobs and in its share of total income, though there is still an organic connection between the villages and the countryside. In Landstad Deventer employment in agriculture decreased about 20 per cent between 1988 and 1998, a rate in line with the national average, and reflecting overseas competition and strict environmental laws, though the land area devoted to agriculture had not diminished (van der Aa and Huigen, 2000b). Though the Hallingdal area of Buskerud still had the primary sector

Table 5.3 Population change in the NoordXXI regions 1980–99

Region/Sub-region	Population change 1980–99 (%)
North of the Netherlands	
• North Drenthe Province	15.6
• Groningen Province	0.7
Landstad Deventer	
• Deventer	10.0
Buskerud	10.4
• Drammen region	14.8
• Midt-fylket region	0.8
Østfold	6.4
• Moss region	10.8
• Halden region	0.7
Västra Götaland	7.0
• Gothenburg area	11.8
• Skaraborg area	0.3
Aberdeenshire (1991–2001 projected)	4.6
• Kincardine and Mearns	7.1
• Banff and Buchan	−2.7
East Lothian (1981–96)	11.0

Source: Baseline Study, NoordXXI Project

as its main base, employment in the sector had declined by 35 per cent over a 12 year period. In Västra Götaland, the Skaraborg and Fyrbodal sub-regions, at 4 per cent and 3 per cent respectively, both exceeded the Swedish average of 2 per cent employment in agriculture, forestry and fishing. Nevertheless, the absolute numbers remained low and the proportionate level of decrease of jobs in this sector was high (a 43 per cent loss across Västra Götaland between 1990 and 1998). Fishing and farming in Aberdeenshire were traditional industries of national importance within Scotland. Peterhead is Europe's premier white fish landing port. However, long-term changes in these industries have been exacerbated by the UK's BSE crisis in 2001, reform of the Common Agricultural Policy and changes in fishing quotas. Further decline in employment is predicted.

There have also been important declines in the manufacturing sector in some of the towns in the partner regions. Such changes again impact directly on place identity. Drammen was perhaps the best example, with 5,000 jobs lost in building and construction, manufacturing and port-related activities over five years. Østfold is a region with a strong manufacturing tradition. It had also experienced restructuring and job loss, with employment in manufacturing reduced from 29,000 in 1983 to 23,000 in 1998, a rate of loss greater than the Norwegian average. The traditional industries in Deventer (metal and meat processing) had also restructured and downsized.

While the broad structural shift towards service-based employment was evident everywhere, unemployment rates were quite varied. Västra Götaland's unemployment rate was 10.4 per cent in 1998. In contrast, in Østfold in 1999 unemployment was only 3.1 per cent, and in Buskerud 2.2 per cent, a figure similar to the 2 per cent recorded in Aberdeenshire in 1998 (though pockets of 10 per cent unemployment can be found throughout the region). In East Lothian unemployment had fallen from 8.1 per cent in 1993 to 3.4 per cent in 1999. The differences between the different partners reflect a mix of national and local factors. The economic cycle has been slightly different, with Sweden coming out of the 1990s recession later than the others. However, access to the labour market of the adjacent large city was certainly a factor in constraining unemployment levels in the Norwegian and Scottish regions. Thus in Scotland, at a time when annual inflation was around 1.8 per cent, pay increased on average by 2.8 per cent in 2000, with the average wage being £379 per week. However, in Aberdeenshire the average rise was 8.2 per cent, the highest in Scotland, and the average weekly wage was £445. The rate of increase in Aberdeen City in the same year was 3.2 per cent. 'In the Lothians wage levels also rose sharply, reflecting Edinburgh's pay boom' (Jamieson and Gray, 2001). Decline of traditional industries may erode place identity, and commuting trips may be seen by planners as unsustainable, but everyday practice of households has made these areas affluent dormitories. The service employment opportunities in large cities now dominate the competitiveness dimension of urban–rural relations.

LABOUR MARKET

The issue of car-based commuting was common to all the partners. It was not possible to get directly comparable data, but car-based commuting was distinctly higher in the Norwegian counties than in their Scottish or Dutch equivalents. This may reflect the more dispersed development pattern in Norway and be interpreted as showing that the more contained urban forms in Scotland and the Netherlands are more sustainable. However, there could be other explanations – e.g. higher disposable incomes in the Norwegian counties. The situation in Deventer highlights some issues on commuting. Between 40 and 50 per cent of the labour force that works in Deventer commutes in from surrounding smaller municipalities. Most travel by car – 71 per cent – with 25 per cent using bikes and the other 4 per cent public transport. Car-based commuting is attractive because there is relatively little congestion, certainly when compared to the Randstad. Thus the 'rural' quality of the sub-region makes it attractive for car-based commuting, and so erodes its 'rural' identity.

COMMERCE

Retailing and other services are also being restructured. The growth of large stores in, or on the edge of, large urban areas is undermining more local shopping provision through the process of market competition. Commuting is also likely to encourage a pattern where shopping is done close to the workplace or on the route between workplace and home, rather than in the village or town where people live. Against this, increases in households following new housing development in small settlements may secure some of the existing shopping facilities. Van der Aa and Huigen (2000a) noted that retail provision has been a major issue in discussion about the liveability of villages since the 1970s, though in practice it is hard for policy-makers to achieve direct influence over such commercial provision. Across the Netherlands as a whole there is on average one shop per 138 people, but in the northern provinces of Groningen, Frisia and Drenthe the figures are 142, 143 and 147 respectively, with lower population densities further extending the average spatial accessibility to a shop. This is one of the most densely populated rural areas in Europe, so the problem of maintaining viable local shops is smaller than in the most rural parts of the other NoordXXI regions. Van der Aa and Huigen (2000a: 23) concluded that:

> A comparison with some other countries, however, learns [sic] that the situation in the Dutch countryside is not that very bad. First, the rate of car-ownership is quite high. Second, there is no real competition between the shops in the small villages versus the huge shopping malls in and at the edge of the nearby cities. The absence of this competition from shopping malls is simply because shopping malls have never become that popular in the Netherlands. And such developments are neither foreseeable in the near future.

In contrast, during the period 1981–98 Aberdeenshire suffered the closure of 188 shops, 32 post offices, 53 petrol stations and 24 banks. Closure of post offices over the past decade is also reported from the North of the Netherlands, though van der Aa and Huigen (2000a) say this is not a problem, because they have often been replaced by smaller post offices in supermarkets and kiosks. The 1998 Aberdeen Shopping Study (GVA Grimley, 1998) noted that the reach of Aberdeen's supermarkets now extends well into Aberdeenshire, and recognized that the lack of services in dormitory towns was a factor in people choosing to shop in the city, which ranks in the top ten UK cities for shopping. There are high levels of leakage from Aberdeenshire to Aberdeen City: about 35 per cent of total available expenditure for convenience goods, and nearly 60 per cent for all types of comparison goods. For dormitory towns like Banchory or Ellon, the leakage to Aberdeen for bulky and convenience goods is typically around the 70 per cent mark. There has been a loss of independent shops in towns and rural areas.

SERVICES

A related problem has been the retention of public services and facilities as fiscal pressures have triggered rationalizations and closures. However, the patterns are not identical across the countries in the North Sea Region, rather they reflect different traditions in local government and the degree of market penetration in welfare provision. In Norway and Sweden the kommune provides libraries and primary schools, which means that these facilities are available on a relatively local basis even in very sparsely populated areas. Indeed in Norway the range of facilities provided by the lowest level of local government is extensive; in addition to primary schools and libraries it includes local health services, water supply, electricity, social housing, cinemas, local roads, recreational facilities, and public transport as well as land use planning. This very decentralized and welfare-based system ensures that municipal offices are located relatively close to the people, even in areas of sparse population. Scotland is at the other extreme. As shown in Chapter 4, the councils are of a much larger scale, and in addition some facilities such as health services, water and electricity are not local government responsibilities, and increasingly are 'marketized' to varying degrees.

East Lothian, with a population of 89,570, has 36 primary schools and 6 secondary schools. Landstad Deventer, with a population of 97,050, has 53 primary schools and 3 secondary schools. Pressure on schools, and hence on local authority expenditure, is one of the consequences of new housing development in East Lothian and in Aberdeenshire. Thus the secondary schools at Ellon (Aberdeenshire) and Haddington (East Lothian) have some of the largest school rolls in Scotland. Here it is increasingly common for the planning authority to ask housing developers to agree to make a financial contribution towards the costs of school provision as part of their planning permission. This form of negotiation did not appear to happen in the other NoordXXI regions.

Van der Aa and Huigen (2000a) described the provision of public facilities in the North of the Netherlands as being very good for a rural area. However, they reported a fall in the number of schools in the three provinces of almost 20 per cent in the period 1991–9, due to rationalizations and expenditure cuts in education. In addition, the number of municipalities has been reduced – from 34 to 12 in Drenthe and from 57 to 25 in Groningen. Overall though, van der Aa and Huigen (2000a: 22) argued that 'there are no real problems for the small villages', in part because of the density of population, but also because they receive special support to maintain the level of services. Similarly in Landstad Deventer, while the city of Deventer is the location of the three secondary schools in the region – the smaller settlements of Olst (9,290) and Bathmen (5,160) each have primary schools, a post office, a library, general practitioners and dentists.

URBAN–RURAL RELATION

The relation between the main regional city and the rural hinterland is problematic. Is the relationship supportive of the hinterland or exploitative of it? In both Dutch

regions the relationship between the urban and rural areas appears to be a complementary one: the urban centres provide the main services, but do not appear to be
undermining service provision (in either the public or the private sector) in their (relatively high density) rural hinterlands. The villages around the towns extend housing
choice and provide a labour force for the economy of the urban centre. Out of town
housing areas are particularly associated with car-based commuting, something
that is being addressed through local planning for the location of new development.
The overall result in the Deventer area was summarized by van der Aa and Huigen
(2000b: 10) as follows:

> ... the economic relation between the rural and the urban areas has changed. In
> previous times, the city was rich, or at least richer than the countryside. However,
> it is now the other way around (Metz, 2000: 6), as the rich, young families are
> leaving the city and the poor, elderly and immigrants are staying behind in the
> city. Nonetheless, it should be noted that the inhabitants of the small villages do
> still feel connected to the city. It is the place where they go to school, where
> they work and do their shopping.

In the Scandinavian regions the urban–rural relationship was more complicated.
While regional growth in the North of the Netherlands or Deventer, both distant from
the Randstad, constitutes decentralization at the national scale, the Norwegian partner regions' proximity to Oslo means growth is part of a process of centralization
nationally. Østrem and Edvardsen (2000a: 5) said that

> The main challenge for Norway, for Østlandet and for Buskerud is the continu-
> ing strong centralisation to Østlandet, and in particular to the capital-region. A
> development in that direction will place major pressure to the lower areas of
> Buskerud, which also represent some of the best agricultural areas and the only
> coastal areas.

Within the Scandinavian partner regions there were also extensive sub-regions
which were sparsely populated and deeply rural in character. There were other sub-
regions where industrial closures had created major setbacks for some of the
kommunes and social groups. Thus the main challenge for Västra Götaland was
seen to be a combination of the threats posed by competition from Oslo, Stockholm
and Copenhagen, together with long-term unemployment and a serious skills mismatch. On the region's periphery, notably in Dalsland and in the northeast of
Skaraborg, as well as in the northeast of Gothenburg, there are concentrations of
the unemployed and unqualified (Østrem and Edvardsen, 2000b).

In East Lothian and Aberdeenshire the relation between the big city and the
rural hinterland has been characterized by the export of people and houses into the
areas around and beyond the edge of the city, while jobs and shopping have grown

in the city. The result has been that new housing development outside the city has imposed costs on the local authority more evidently than it has bestowed benefits. This has been combined with a fiscal squeeze exerted by central government on the local authorities, and the increased marketization of services like health and the post office, a trend evident in all partners but most advanced in Scotland.

CHANGES IN PLACE IDENTITY

Thus the activities, facilities and institutions around which resonant narratives of place identity are likely to be reproduced are being restructured in all the partner regions, though there are some important differences in the details. Do polycentric systems of settlement at the intra-regional level help to sustain services, a rural population and an associated rural identity? The answer would seem to be a tentative 'yes', though population density and institutional structures are important mediating influences. Sustainability of local services seems to depend on settlement patterns, but also on the extent to which the practices of consumerism structure everyday life. Public services, and the shared sense of place identity that they engender, are being pressured by fiscal crises and centralizing tendencies within welfare states.

How have the regions reacted to this array of pressures that derive from broad exogenous processes of restructuring, competition and fiscal shift? To what extent, why and how have narratives of place identity been reproduced, refashioned or invented as a means of managing change? The remainder of this chapter introduces some of the key place narratives associated with spatial planning practice in the partner regions.

CASE STUDIES IN CONSTRUCTING NEW TERRITORIAL IDENTITIES

INTERNATIONAL COMPETITIVENESS: VÄSTRA GÖTALAND

Västra Götaland was only created in 1999, as part of a deliberate Swedish experiment to explore the potential of new regional structures to enhance competitiveness and more effective public service delivery, and to create the institutions for a 'Europe of the Regions'. It has a land area of 26,000 square kilometres and a population of almost 1.5 million (see Figure 5.6). Traditionally, regional identities within Sweden have been closely related to landscape types, with administrative units and local radio sometimes fitting these. The new Västra Götaland encompasses three different traditional landscapes. The intention in casting this large spatial unit was unambiguously to enhance regional competitiveness and to reposition this substantial part of Sweden internationally. The regional development strategy for Västra Götaland (Västra Götaland Region, 1999) is based on a Vision with seven points:

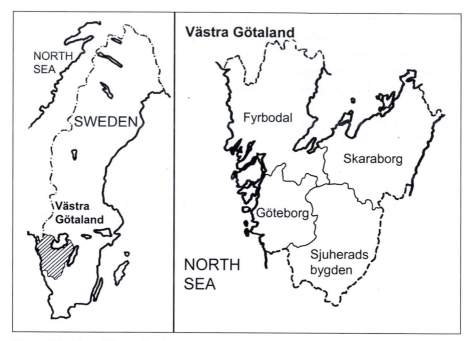

Figure 5.6 Map of Västra Götaland region

- Viable businesses – large and small – that are able to compete on domestic and international markets and a growing potential in all parts of the region.
- Citizens who have jobs and are in good health, are constantly updating their expertise and training, as well as having access to lifetime learning and a rich cultural life.
- There is a clear, positive and driving approach to opportunities and creativity.
- International exchanges and co-operation are highly rated in the region.
- Valuing the use of both male and female resources.
- Valuing the qualifications and experience of ethnic minorities and opposed to segregation and alienation.
- Sustainable growth, i.e. needs are fulfilled without endangering the needs of future generations.

Competitiveness and social inclusion are very evident in this list and in the ten objectives of the strategy. Several of these were explicitly pitched at visibility and performance at European scale – e.g. to have a leading position within Europe as an IT region, to lead in developing resource-saving and environmentally friendly technology in Europe, and to be internationally recognized for and through its networking with regions in other countries. In many respects the vision was aspatial – creating a brand rather than building on place identity. However, one of the objectives sought to increase Västra Götaland's advantage over other regions as the leading cultural region in Sweden, noting that its cultural heritage and history give the region identity and distinctive character (Västra Götaland Region, 1999).

In the course of the research we asked the planners in Västra Götaland if they could define the identity of their region for us. They responded that it has an 'international focus' and is 'characterized by diversity'. The former expresses the aspirations behind the vision, but the idea that identity is based on diversity is intriguingly post-modern. As Chapter 1 showed, identity is conventionally a means of claiming originality or authenticity, of distinguishing between 'us' and 'others'. The planners went on to elaborate this identity in diversity by citing 'hilly landscapes, flatlands, forests, and a variety of urban environments ... A rich pattern of cities, countryside and urban areas with distinct, different characters and cultural characteristics.' (Västra Götaland Regional Executive Board, 1999: 8). This needs to be read alongside the explicit support for ethnic minorities within the vision. Strengthening the identity of the inhabitants of the new region is a central theme in the strategy.

However, the strategy's 'four fundamental pillars' (co-operation, participation, flexibility and a holistic approach) are essentially managerial statements of process severed from place. They seem an unlikely basis for popular mobilization and identification with the new administrative unit. Can a place identity be created for a large, administratively willed and physically diverse regional territorial identity such as this? To do so would require spatial planning to orchestrate the complementarity of the various sub-regions and to demonstrate the added value that can be achieved through integration and co-operation. Spatial concepts could help to articulate the idea that Västra Götaland is indeed a coherent region, secure in its diversity, and with a shared purpose and development trajectory. This is exactly the kind of new urban–rural relation that the ESDP sought: grow Gothenburg as a Scandinavian gateway city in a polycentric region, connect urban and rural, past and future, through a network of innovative towns in a cultural landscape and high quality environment.

DIVERSITY AND COMPETITION: URBAN AND RURAL IN NORWAY

In Norway the county councils (*fylkeskommune*) and the municipalities (*kommunes*) were legally established in 1837. Although there have been accretions of responsibilities over the years, this means that the spatial units of Østfold and Buskerud have remained unchanged, though the nature of urban and rural relationships within and beyond them has changed dramatically. The case for updating Norway's territorial units was considered by the Division of Responsibilities Commission (*Oppgavefordelingsutvalget*). It reported in 2000, and recommended some reduction in the number of counties, reviving the idea of wider regions. The counties around Oslo, the Østlandet counties, already co-operate informally. This can be seen as an anticipation of such thinking – an attempt to strengthen regional competitiveness while avoiding the problems of unbalanced growth.

Given that Østfold and Buskerud are territories demarcated over 150 years ago, it is not surprising to find that today they are characterized by internal sub-regional diversity. Planners from Buskerud County said that

> The County has no particular identity that fits for the whole area, it is rather put together of separate regions which have their own identity. You do not say that you are from Buskerud, you rather say that you are from Numedal, Hallingdal, Drammen and so on.

Buskerud can be divided into two broad parts based on culture, history and landscape. 'The upper part with the valleys of Hallingdal, Sigdal/Eggedal and Numedal' is an area of forests and mountains and powerful rivers. Here the basis of the economy has traditionally been agriculture, hunting, fishing and forestry, though today tourism is of growing importance. The other face of Buskerud is 'the lower parts [which] have, in a Norwegian context, a much smoother surface'. Here the agricultural land is good quality, and there is the industrial tradition of the Drammen valley. However, this sub-region is increasingly characterized by the growth of commuting to Oslo.

Østfold County also has an urban/rural divide. The north and east of the region – Indre Østfold – has a landscape of agriculture and forestry, and any settlements are relatively small. However, the towns in the south and west have been traditional centres of industry, as was Askim in the north. Such towns have developed their own institutions, largely through parochial competition with each other. Thus there are four separate towns on the southern coast, each of which has its own newspaper. This polycentric situation means there is typically competition for major facilities such as hospitals. In addition, mergers of smaller kommunes in these areas, creating larger units based on Sarpsborg and on Fredrikstad, have been controversial (see Figure 5.7).

The strongest interest in local identity amongst the Norwegians came not from the *fylkeskommunes* but from urban kommunes, especially in towns adversely affected by economic restructuring and seeking to overcome the combined effects of job loss and an external image of ugliness and failure. The case of Askim in Østfold is discussed in some detail in Chapter 9. Drammen in Buskerud has a reputation as one of the most air-polluted places in Scandinavia, is a place known through the media for crime, and also has been labelled 'the biggest crossroads in Norway', yet in an attempt at place-marketing, its official website labels the town 'the Venice of Norway' (Carlsson, 2001)! In summary, regional identity in the Norwegian partners appeared to be weak, with the counties seeming to be rather remote administrative bodies. However, economic changes have prompted attempts to redefine territory and identity at the kommune level.

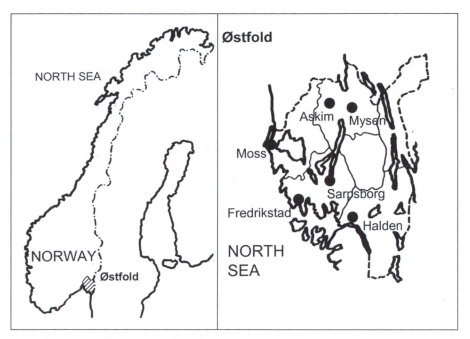

Figure 5.7   Map of Østfold with sub-regions

EAST LOTHIAN – RURAL PLACE OR CONSUMER SPACE?

While the Swedes were creating regional units the Scots were deconstructing theirs. In 1975 local government in Scotland had been reorganized to replace a hotchpotch of historic units with a more rational two-tier structure of regions and districts. In 1996 Scottish local government was comprehensively reorganized once more into a unitary system – in effect the regions were abolished with respect to urban Scotland. Thus East Lothian District Council was formed in 1975, as one of four councils in Lothian Region. Then in 1996 the region disappeared and the (new) East Lothian Council gained responsibility for the full range of local government services. The changes in 1975 were an attempt to create a shared regional territorial identity based across urban and rural areas. However, the regional councils failed to forge a popular sense of place identity over their 20 years' existence. Apart from their own professional employees, few contested their abolition. The roots of the 1996 reorganization were political and fiscal: the Conservatives, who formed the UK government but had lost all power in Scottish local government, wanted to weaken local authorities as institutions of opposition. Furthermore, their New Right ideology prescribed that small authorities give the public choice about which package of services and costs they 'buy into', and so constrain the ability of politicians to effect redistribution through welfare policies. A further aspect of the 1996 changes was that responsibility for water and sewerage was taken out of the realm of local government altogether and passed to 'arm's length' public agencies operating on a cost-recovery basis.

The changes in 1996 negated the notion that there was a shared interest between city-dwellers and surrounding suburbs and rural areas. Under the Conservative Government there was no discourse of strategic spatial planning, no real engagement with the emerging European regionalism. Instead, the gaze was backwards to recreate aspects of the pre-1975 system, although carefully avoiding the fiscal unreality of very small units. The other political parties, who all supported the campaign for a devolved Scottish parliament, pragmatically accepted the need to lose a tier of government to 'make room' for the parliament.

East Lothian's planners were uncertain about identity. 'It is by no means clear if East Lothian has a separate identity', they told us. 'As a unit of local government, its present boundaries have only existed since 1975. Before then the urbanized and industrialized western areas were part of a different unit (Midlothian), while the rural eastern sector, with its attractive villages, was a separate local authority, the County of East Lothian. Commuting to Edinburgh further dilutes residents' identification with East Lothian.' Thus diversity, history and everyday practices of residents were seen to be potent barriers to equating the territorial unit with a place identity. In contrast, in earlier and simpler times, the county planning officer for East Lothian before the 1975 reorganization was elegiac about the then identity: 'Few County Planning Officers have had such a beautiful county in their care as East Lothian – a small county ... east of Edinburgh with a population in 1952 of 52,000 and a landscape and a building tradition of great distinction, which has endeared it to many people' (Tindall, 1998: 1).

Tindall's place narrative of a 'traditional' rural East Lothian is echoed in the work of local historians. For example, Anderson (2000:3), in compiling a book of photos of *Old East Lothian Villages*, opted to consider only those villages that were part of 'the historic county'. The boundaries of that county 'conformed to natural features provided by nature', a land that first appears in written records during the Roman period. Viking bands arrived in East Lothian at an earlier stage of North Sea competition. The current landscape was shaped by innovative farming practices of the eighteenth and nineteenth centuries, with closed fields, farm steadings and several planned model estate communities. Before the 1975 local government reorganization there were seven towns that were self-governing local authorities within the county – the equivalent to Dutch municipalities or Scandinavian kommunes. Anderson (2000:4) excluded photos of these towns from his collection, since they were not villages, though he made an exception for 'the united settlement of Cockenzie and Port Seton', since 'at heart it is still centred on its harbours and retains its village character'.

In Chapter 1 we quoted Duncan and Barnes (1992: 7): 'Places are intertextual sites, because various texts and discursive practices based on previous texts are deeply inscribed in their landscapes and institutions.' Anderson's selection of old photographs and his accompanying narrative is one illustration of this. A focus group with East Lothian residents (Hague and Storey, 2001b) provided further examples. Participants more commonly related to their town or parish than to East Lothian, though identification with East Lothian was stronger than with Lothian or 'near Edinburgh'. 'I say North Berwick and then I'll say the county, East Lothian. I'll bring Edinburgh into it only if I have to', was how one participant put it. Similarly, a community councillor considered her 'local area' to be the local parish centred on the small village of Gifford, where 'There is certainly a sense of local identity'. The identity was 'rural' and she felt that there was a link in identity to East Lothian in that 'it's all quite rural in character'. East Lothian is 'a rural area with towns in it'. A key landmark is Soutra (a hill), which has a clear view to the North Sea and reminds the viewer that they are in a clearly defined region bordering the sea.

Planning policy, as expressed in development plans and through development control, has sought to conserve and reproduce the village/rural character of the east of East Lothian. To achieve this, land for new housing has mainly been allocated in the former mining settlements in the west and development has been constrained and closely controlled in the coastal villages and eastern part that mainly comprised the pre-1975 county. However, house-builders and their customers have inscribed another text on the East Lothian landscape. 'Our main housing design problems arose from speculative builders, who, in the 1960s, turned their attention to the growing prestige and attractions of East Lothian' (Tindall, 1998: 144). The development pressures of the following decades exacerbated these problems and bequeathed on a number of villages developments that in scale, layout and materials substantially disregarded, and hence redefined, village character (see Figures 5.8, 5.9 and 5.10). Rather than responding to local context, the house-building industry in the UK is organized at national level and primarily oriented to the efficient production of suburban houses for which there is a reliable demand. Those operating within the industry face increasing competitive pressure from company headquarters, reflecting the wishes of shareholders, to meet production targets.

A focus group with professional planners working for house-builders exposed some of the contesting narratives about planning and place identity in East Lothian. When challenged about the impact of new housing developments on traditional village identity the response 'If our houses didn't sell, we wouldn't build them' was widely endorsed. Some questioned whether vernacular styles sell, but a more perceptive line of argument was that

> The real issue about vernacular is that on the scale that development must be provided in this aggressive, consumer society, it will become just as monotonous as any other style. Anyway, customers see only their own house, not others.

Figure 5.8 Traditional housing in East Lothian

Figure 5.9 Contemporary housing in East Lothian

Figure 5.10 New housing development in East Lothian

> Personally I feel that if you stick to two-storey, you can clothe it with landscaping
> – that's the best you can do.

It was also argued that 'the supply of traditional materials is simply not there. Also, we should not repeat the past. Scale is the real problem.' Planning restrictions were blamed for excessive scale of development in some villages, by forcing developers 'to pack more in than they want to'. Planning gain agreements (under which developers agree to provide facilities, or finance for them, as part of their planning permission – a response to fiscal pressures in local government) were seen as encouraging local authority planners to favour large-scale developments. However, there was also a consensus that the pressures of the market meant that incremental growth was no longer possible in East Lothian. Thus the practice of spatial planning is not an unconstrained process of challenging or reproducing extant place identities – competition, consumer demand and institutional structures (both within the building industry and within the planning system) significantly mediate outcomes.

'NOTHING ENDURES ... NOTHING BUT THE LAND': WRITING PLACE IDENTITY INTO PLANS IN ABERDEENSHIRE

Perhaps of all the partners it was Aberdeenshire who most engaged with the idea that plans could be structured around a narrative of place identity. Aberdeenshire did not exist as an administrative unit – i.e. did not have a clear territorial identity – between 1975 and 1996. The reintroduction of old names in the 1996 reorganization of Scottish local government was itself an exercise in trying to use place identity, and even local government itself, by looking back to the past, to an age before local government in rural Scotland became politicized and racked by fiscal crises. From 1975 until 1996 there was a Grampian regional council, and three district councils. In effect, the three districts were amalgamated in 1996 to form the new Aberdeenshire and the region was abolished, with the Aberdeen District Council becoming another new unitary authority (see Figure 5.11).

When invited to define its identity, Aberdeenshire's planners said that 'identity and the qualities which define communities are built on the rich heritage and cultural values of the region'. Elements listed included the landscape of the Cairngorms, the rich agricultural lowlands, and a 'long and varied coastline'. Alongside the idea of landscape as the basis of identity they cited 'the work ethic of the labour force' and a spirit of 'entrepreneurship' in an 'outward looking' region.

This sense of a place identity fashioned through an interaction between land and culture was taken forward in the structure plan that was being produced during the period of the NoordXXI project (Aberdeen City Council and Aberdeenshire Council, 2001). This begins with a quotation from Lewis Grassic Gibbon's definitive novel of the area, *Sunset Song*:

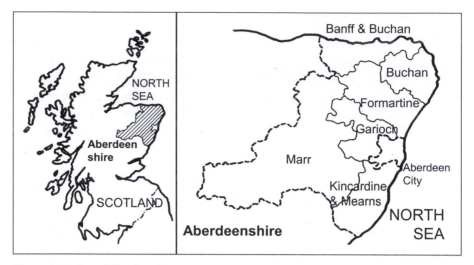

Figure 5.11 Map of Aberdeenshire

> nothing endured at all, nothing but the land she passed across ... the land was
> forever; it moved and changed below you, but was forever; you were close to it
> and it to you, not at a bleak remove it held you and hurted you.

The plan then connects the traumas of rural social change in the early 1900s that
are etched in the novel with today's challenges and the need to plan on the basis of
sustainable development. There may be global change but the land will endure.

The central theme of the plan, 'connecting communities', echoed ESDP concerns for social inclusion and parity of access to infrastructure and services. Similarly
the statement of the vision in the plan begins with an assertion about developing a
'sustainable community' in the North East, and goes on to say: 'This will embrace the
social and cultural identity of the North East in a way that improves its economic competitiveness, and delivers prosperity and a high quality of life for everyone within a
secure and well-managed environment' (Aberdeen City Council and Aberdeenshire
Council, 2001: 6) The name of the plan, *North East Scotland Together*, was itself a
place narrative – making claims on the cohesiveness of the area of the councils of
Aberdeen City and Aberdeenshire, and projecting a common 'North East Scotland'
place identity and conjoined territorial identity. The plan included strong visual images
of landscape and townscape and the juxtaposition of the two.

Place identity also featured in the consolidated local plan produced by
Aberdeenshire. This arose out of the complicated situation where Aberdeenshire
inherited different local plans and planning policies from the three pre-1996 district
councils that formed the new unit. The consolidated plans represented
Aberdeenshire as an area of high-quality natural and built environment that should

be protected. This was reflected, for example, in strong support for Aberdeen's green belt, and resistance to sporadic housing development in the countryside. Distinct 'local' identities were recognized, based on heritage and a sense of community. Local place identity was described as 'what makes an area different or special. The characteristics are not individually unique but go together to make a blend, which identifies one place as distinct from everywhere else' (Aberdeen City Council and Aberdeenshire Council, 2001).

Thus planning in Aberdeenshire has recognized issues of place and territorial identity and the pressures imposed on traditional identities by social and economic change. While there was acknowledgement of the need to adapt and reposition the region, not least as traditional sources of jobs in oil, farming and fishing decline, in the end 'the land will endure'. Research undertaken in the NoordXXI project explored this sense of a traditional place identity. In particular we looked at the place narratives of those involved in enhancing competitiveness and attracting business. Aberdeenshire's Economic Development Department makes strong use of visuals and text projecting the quality of the physical environment. A leaflet headed *Experience Aberdeenshire* has a front and back colour photo of a sandy North Sea beach at low tide with four small figures and a dog below a long low sky (see Figure 5.12). Smaller photos are inset – a cliff coast and a white water stretch of a mountain stream. The text inside is more directly addressed to business, with words and pictures about the oil and fishing industries and the quality of Aberdeenshire's farm produce. Opening the leaflet out to its full A2 size reveals a map that identifies the council's industrial estates and the main harbours, but also golf courses, ski areas and distilleries. Again words and visual images (e.g. stone circles, castles and mountain scenery) define Aberdeenshire as 'a place to enjoy life and succeed in business'. This narrative, in its essentials, is congruent with that in the development plans.

An interview with staff of the local enterprise company also probed the competitiveness dimension of place identity. The importance of the high quality natural resources – oil, fishing, agriculture, timber and scenery – to the North East identity was again noted. There was agreement that the topography is important in all of this, and three distinct sub-regions were identified: the coastline, the mountains and (between these) a rolling agricultural area. Thus overall regional identity is able to encompass significant sub-regional variations. However, the Grampian Enterprise officials also spoke of some of the tensions. Some of the coastal settlements north of Aberdeen were felt to have a negative image as a location for new business, due to social problems and unemployment. Transport networks were felt to influence place identity, with those areas in the Aberdeen commuter zone being increasingly identified with the city. Closely linked was the whole issue of the relation between a regional identity strongly based on landscape and resources, and the need to

Figure 5.12 Cover of the *Experience Aberdeenshire* brochure

accommodate, even enhance, development pressures. Conflict over development, particularly housing development, was common. In addition, those interviewed at Grampian Enterprise felt that there was a gap between the North East's self-identity, and the way outsiders saw the region as being 'remote and peripheral, with poor business accessibility, and off the beaten tourist track'.

NORTHERN SPACE IN GRONINGEN – GREEN ALTERNATIVES TO THE RANDSTAD

The North of the Netherlands was also seen as having an identity strongly rooted in the land. The North of the Netherlands is neither a new creation nor even a formal, legally constituted administrative unit, rather it is the territory covered by the three provinces of Drenthe, Frisia and Groningen (see Figure 5.13). However, it has another reality as a concept that is known and understood within the Netherlands, where the area is the *Noorderruimte*, the 'Northern Space' or 'Northern Area'. An identity goes with that word: historically it has been an identity of the North as an economically backward region with a rural landscape. However, environmentalism,

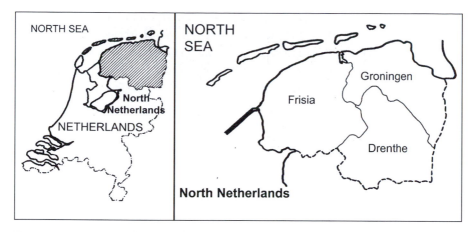

Figure 5.13 Map of North Netherlands

sustainable development, even anti-urbanism have created a conceptual space within which the North of the Netherlands can be re-configured to create a new, more positive identity that re-interprets rurality. This is the identity of a green and prosperous garden region on the periphery, an alternative to the crowding and congestion in the Randstad, the 'other' in this narrative of place identity. Thus the Province of Drenthe stated in a planning document that 'We in the northern part of the Netherlands choose for a policy wherein sustainable economic growth is combined with maintenance of natural, landscape and environmental qualities' (Provincie Drenthe, 1998: 21).

This secure sense of identity may explain why the planners from Groningen Province were the most eloquent and articulate in defining identity when questioned in our research. Again the picture was complex. The planners from this province identified four 'different landscapes' within its overall sense of rurality. The north of the province is the unique landscape of the Wadden Sea. Second is the south west, a sandy area with a creek valley landscape, and again this is an ecologically and topographically distinct area. In the east is the *Westerwolde*, a wooded area. Then to the south east are the *Veenkolonien* ('peat colonies'), again a landscape of international significance. Thus the prime definition of identity by the province's planners was in terms of 'the organic connection between village and landscape ... the "rural identity" ... open space, peacefulness, small villages, beautiful cultural landscapes and nature areas'. However, there is also the city of Groningen, 'the metropolis of the north of the Netherlands', which is surrounded by a large hinterland that looks to the city for shops, jobs, education, etc. (it has a reputation as a 'student city'). Visually the transition from the city to the rural hinterland is 'clear-cut', leaving the villages 'still reasonably uncomplicated' and combining urban and rural lifestyles.

The other Dutch area in the study, Landstad Deventer, is – like the two Scottish authorities and Västra Götaland – a recent, administratively willed regional identity (see Figure 5.14). It is 'a region that was established to develop a spatial and socio-economic path of development for the city of Deventer (including the former municipality of Diepenveen) and its surrounding municipalities of Bathmen and Olst' (van der Aa and Huigen, 2000b: 3). The concept was a response to structural changes that undermined the significance of agriculture in the countryside and the manufacturing sector in the town. There was also increasing pressure for housing development as people moved east from the Randstad. The initiative to create Landstad Deventer came from Overijssel Province and the three municipalities, but also from the Ministry of Agriculture, two water management bodies and a countryside association called *Issala*. It can be seen as an attempt to enhance and recreate identity as part of a new process of governance. Importantly, people in this part of the Netherlands see themselves as different from those in the west, and also have little attachment to the Province of Overijssel, which is not a historical region but an administrative creation combining the older regions of Twente and Salland (Alma, 1999). Integration, efficiency and identity are some of the key objectives of the project. Van der Aa and Huigen (2000b: 3) say:

> Rural residents, immigrants, city-dwellers, designers, autochthons, policy makers, and their organisations were all consulted in answering the main question. It can be stated as follows: 'Is it desirable to develop in the same way as, for example,

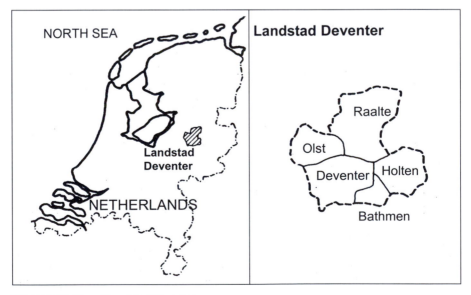

Figure 5.14 Map of Landstad Deventer

Amersfoort – a city about 40 kilometres to the West and of a comparable size – which has seen a tremendous growth in numbers of people, businesses, jobs and traffic?'

The very name *landstad*, combining the meanings of countryside and town, perhaps best translated into English as 'country town', is expressive of a harmonious, mutually complementary urban/rural linkage, and also a prescription of how to achieve that positive relationship. Any identity, while a subjective matter of words, ideas, and feelings, must also have some basis in objective reality. Landstad Deventer is described as 'a region that is characterized by strong economic, functional and cultural links ... It is one region with one labour and housing market ... These intense links are increased by a revival of the inner city and the countryside' (Landstad, 1999: 5). Despite its newness, the country town idea has some roots in a historical narrative of place identity. Alma (1999: 5) notes that traditionally the city has both serviced and used the surrounding countryside, as the city and the countryside prospered through trade in the Hanseatic League, using its position on the River Yssel, a branch of the Rhine.

CONCLUSION

This chapter has shown that all the regions included in this research face broadly similar pressures. The restructuring of agriculture, drain of population from the most remote areas, extended commuting, loss of rural services and pressures to rationalize the territorial units of local and regional government are the common currency of the countryside. Towns that had an industrial base have also suffered from run-down and closures, and are hampered in their regeneration ambitions by negative images and traditional identities. Fiscal pressures are familiar to all the partners. However, there are some differences that we might note. The double reorganization of local government in Scotland, and the abandonment of regional units, combined with the high degree of the run-down of rural services contrasts with all of the continental partners. Similarly there are suggestions that the contained settlements of Scotland and the Netherlands may result in less car use than is the case in Norway, where variants on ribbon development are the normal settlement structure. However, the nature of the research, as a limited exercise carried out under contract, precluded rigorous assessment of these presumptions.

More confident statements can be offered about the attempts to move towards new institutions of governance and related territorial identities. The invention of the North Sea Region and the parameters set by EU regional policy are both examples of this, and also explain to a large extent the experimental creation of the

Västra Götaland region in Sweden. However, none of the other examples shows much responsiveness to this pan-European territorial agenda. Rather, change in macro-regional units either has not happened (Norway, North of the Netherlands) or has been triggered by concerns at a more national or sub-national level. The 1996 local government reorganization in Scotland is particularly interesting in the extent to which it was created out of a New Right ideology fundamentally at odds with the social democratic assumptions that have been so important to the EU. It is no coincidence that the capacity to deliver integrated strategic planning was one of the casualties of that reorganization.

Perhaps one of the clearest themes to emerge from the analysis of place and territorial identities in this chapter is the importance of sub-regions and landscapes. Typically identities appeared stronger and less ambiguous or compromised at sub-regional scale than at the broader scale that matched the formal territorial unit. Similarly settlements, whether villages or towns, seemed to be a stronger focus for identity than larger units. All of this raises serious questions about the attempts to create new territorial identities and associated institutions of governance from above.

Finally, we have noted that a number of narratives of place identity have been constructed as components of the spatial planning process within the partners. Table 5.4 attempts to summarize the main ones. These are not a comprehensive list of place identities within the NoordXXI partners; rather they are, in effect, the place narratives of planners and administrators. They concentrate on the urban–rural relation, and attempt to interpret the spatial planning implications. As the table shows, none of them is unproblematic.

These identities fashioned by planners are not fixed, objective, unambiguous or uncontested. Rather they are ways of suggesting, communicating, and developing spatial planning responses to urban and rural change. They are a necessary means of simplifying, of organizing ideas and understandings about an impossibly complex reality. Such identities embody the interests, prejudices and prescriptions of those who create and/or use them, while suppressing other possible narratives about the same place, so as to facilitate choice of policy and action. As traditional welfare states have wilted under fiscal strain and political challenge, and competition and consumerism have replaced a unified conception of the public interest, a new planning and a new politics of place identity has developed.

Table 5.4 A typology of regional identities constructed by spatial planners

Identity narrative	NoordXXI examples	Spatial planning assumptions, implications and questions
Landstad – the Country Town – where there is a symbiotic urban–rural relationship	Landstad Deventer	The town provides jobs and services to the rural area, which reciprocates by providing the town with land for new development that can create a high-quality living environment in a country setting. This is a sustainable alternative, agreed by a wide range of stakeholders, to growth and congestion that would follow from unplanned enlargement of the town. Is it sustainable if it proves attractive and growth pressures increase? How does it regenerate the declining parts of the town and assist the poor who live there? Does it rely on car-based commuting?
The green rural region where natural heritage and cultural landscapes are protected	North of the Netherlands, but also the valleys and mid-county area of Buskerud; in Østfold the rural parts of Inner Østfold and also Aremark; Bohuslan and Skaraborg in Västra Götaland; the east of East Lothian; the Cairngorms and western Marr, and Banff and Buchan in Aberdeenshire.	Continuity with a rural past and conservation of cultural landscapes, but with some new growth linked to green technology and sustainable tourism. Towns provide education and other services to the region, but do not undermine the villages. Population is sufficiently dense or mobile in rural areas, or policy of self-help is sufficiently committed, to sustain services. Strong landscape conservation, careful design of new urban extensions to retain compact city character and clear urban/rural land use difference. A sustainable counterpoint to urban living, agri-business and homogenization. Is it economically and socially sustainable, and demographically balanced? What is the cost of maintaining village services? Does it depend on weak growth pressures to be implemented?

Continued

Identity narrative	NoordXXI examples	Spatial planning assumptions, implications and questions
A large, dynamic, integrated, competitive and balanced polycentric region based on a big city with an extensive hinterland.	Västra Götaland, and the co-operation of Norwegian counties in Østlandet; Grampian Region 1975–96; Lothian Region 1975–96.	Need to create a regional scale of administration and/or planning to achieve efficiency and to integrate urban and rural areas over a large space. Need to build a sense of identity with the new region. This probably requires some emphasis on European scale and competitiveness, as it is difficult to piece together diverse local identities and experiences. Good internal transport links will also be needed to show benefits and reduce isolation. Positive enhancement of sub-regional identities may be more fruitful than ignoring them or overriding them. Is there a credible shared identity? Does new transport infrastructure threaten existing identities in rural areas?
The green belt that protects countryside from the sprawl of a large city.	Edinburgh Green Belt, Aberdeen Green Belt, Lier and Hole in Buskerud.	Need to contain the outward spread of the big city to ensure protection of landscape and agricultural land, prevent settlement coalition and provide access to the countryside for recreation for urban residents. The effect can include increased land and housing prices, extended commuting, and protection of land on the basis of its location rather than its quality. Is this contributing to sustainability?
The border zone/commuter belt provides space for family housing in villages and small towns away from congestion and dangers of the big city.	West of East Lothian; south and central Aberdeenshire; 'The cities and their surroundings' sub-region of Buskerud and the Horum Peninsula; Moss, Lowe Glomma and accessible parts of Inner Østfold.	Such areas can provide land for new housing which can inject new life into small existing settlements. However, jobs and services are unlikely to follow the housing, and people will commute to the larger city. The form of the development may be corridor-based or focused on infill and town expansion while avoiding coalescence of settlements. How to overcome problems of peak hour congestion and car-based commuting? How to integrate the new development with the old? How to prevent increased leakage in retail spending to the big city?

Continued

Identity narrative	NoordXXI examples	Spatial planning assumptions, implications and questions
Regeneration of small industrial, mining or port towns suffering decline within predominantly rural regions.	Drammen, Askim, Peterhead, coastal towns of Banff and Buchan, Dunbar and Sjuharadsbygden.	These places have potential – a critical mass that can support urban services, a legacy of industrial architecture and culture, a supply of empty buildings and brownfield land. Re-imaging and place marketing can attract service industries and industrial heritage tourism. Communications improvements to increase access to wider labour markets, and to attract commuters by offering cheaper housing than in more attractive or central locations. Regeneration and brownfield development saves the countryside and is sustainable development. Living environment may be poor, land may be contaminated, re-imaging must have credibility (Drammen is not Venice); regeneration of these places may mean unnecessarily extending commuting distances to the main employment centres.

CHAPTER 6

TERRITORIAL AND PLACE IDENTITIES: NEW COLLABORATIONS IN STRATEGIC PLANNING
PAUL JENKINS

While the previous chapter has looked at the role of place identity at the trans-national and sub-national scales in Europe (i.e. within the North Sea Region and the regions involved in the NoordXXI Project), this chapter investigates the relationship between place identity and territorial identity in more detail at a sub-national, or meso-regional level, and how this is affecting planning. Again, the empirical basis for this chapter is primarily work undertaken through the NoordXXI project, one component of which focused on participation across six local authorities in the four participating countries. While the initial intention of this research component was to investigate innovation in public participation in planning as undertaken by some of the project partners, in practice the investigation also discovered considerable innovation in inter-institutional collaboration. In many situations this was in fact probably the dominant factor in creating the 'arena' of participatory activity or negotiation.

Drawing on this material (which was reported in Jenkins, Kirk and Smith, 2001, based on research undertaken during September–October 2000), the chapter focuses on two strategic-level planning case studies: provincial planning in the Netherlands and regional planning in Norway. To a great extent these can be seen as new forms of collaborative action in largely top-down planning, and in this follow on from the regional impacts of ongoing – or sponsored – top-down change at regional level identified in the previous chapter. The chapter also leads on to the study of new forms of collaboration with, and in, bottom-up planning, which is the focus of the following chapter.

It is stressed that some of the conclusions are still tentative, as the processes of change that are examined were still underway at the time of the original study and only partial follow-up has been possible since. It is also important to understand that the processes studied in this chapter include: collaboration between different tiers of governing authorities (i.e. vertical participation); collaboration across different authorities at the same 'level', including across nation-state and sectoral boundaries (i.e. horizontal participation); and participation of very different socio-political actors (e.g. political authorities with social institutions, or with economic actors). These can be seen as three dimensions of participation, as Figure 6.1 illustrates.

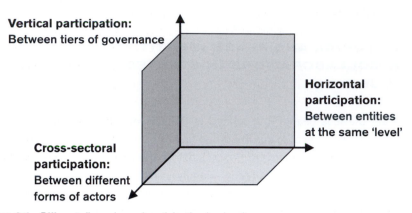

Vertical participation:
Between tiers of governance

Horizontal participation:
Between entities at the same 'level'

Cross-sectoral participation:
Between different forms of actors

Figure 6.1   Different dimensions of participation in planning

THE PLAN FOR THE ENVIRONS (POP PLAN), GRONINGEN, THE NETHERLANDS

INTRODUCTION

As described in the previous chapter, the province of Groningen is situated in the northeast of the Netherlands and has a population of some 550,000 inhabitants. The province is divided into 25 municipalities and the provincial government's influence extends to all aspects of daily life including housing, jobs, recreation, traffic and transport, environment and culture. The provincial council is elected and the council members then choose five or six deputies who form the provincial executive, together with the Queen's commissioner – i.e. the representative of national government at provincial level.

The provincial government in Groningen recently adopted a new approach to provincial level strategic planning, incorporating four previously separate strategic plans. This new Plan for the Environs (otherwise know as the 'POP Plan') has been developed to integrate and replace the Regional Plan 1994, the Environmental Policy Plan 1999–2000, the Water Management Plan 1999–2000 and the Transport Plan 1994. Each of these plans has implications for spatial planning, and the technical rationale behind the proposal for the POP plan was that their separation was not conducive to strategic clarity. Although the province previously drew up these plans independently, in 1994 the plans were drawn up concurrently, albeit still as separate proposals. At that time it was decided that in future the provincial government would prepare one integrated plan for the physical environment: the Provincial Plan for the Environs (POP Plan).

The POP Plan covers living, industry, water management, nature and landscape, and infrastructure. The very scope of the plan allows the province to focus on strategic questions regarding the general character and future direction of the territory, and an equally wide-ranging public participation process was envisaged as integral to plan development. Through involving the general public and specific interest groups in the drafting process, it was thought that the plan would both engender wide ownership and be more likely to be adhered to. A related consideration was the need for a focus on implementation and it was argued that having one integrated plan would strengthen the link between planning and implementation. Thus, by ensuring wide support for the plan, it was anticipated that this would lead to not only greater ownership but also more effective implementation by key stakeholders.

A further political consideration was the need to raise the profile of the province. The provincial level of government has been relatively weak and has had a low profile as perceived by municipalities, trade and industry, interest groups and citizens. The province has thus been perceived to be distant from the general public and to have no direct link to the citizen. Through the POP process, a predominantly new set of provincial politicians sought to present themselves in a new light in shifting from a directing to a more enabling role, providing sound strategic leadership for the region as a whole. The provincial government also sought to use the planning process to have a closer relationship with municipalities. As such, the process of development of the plan, and the wider consultation on this, were seen as enhancing the provincial level's overall profile and powers, and effectively had as much importance as the plan itself.

In addition, the province had been working with its neighbouring provinces of Drenthe and Friesland, in the North of the Netherlands, in setting out a common macro-regional vision called 'Compass for the Future'. Central to this vision was the conviction that the region could only acquire a significant place on the socio-economic map of the Netherlands through co-operation. The 'Compass' plan was thus prepared in anticipation of significant amounts of public funds becoming available from national government. The POP Plan therefore also sought to convert this joint administrative regional vision into directives that could be implemented. In this, increased co-operation and the commitment of local and provincial interests to the regional vision were seen by the partners to be essential.

In summary, the drafting of the POP Plan was seen as an experiment in both process and expected outcome, and it is the former that is primarily examined here. In the past, efforts to promote public participation in the planning process had focused on the provision of information to citizens, but in the POP Plan attention shifted to involving citizens as well as other institutional actors early in the plan process, to allow them to influence the basic concepts. As there was no set process for such a plan, the province could thus develop its own process and methods, although the new plan still had to take into account the existing legislation relating to each of the different plans. Thus, in the development of the POP process in Groningen, both traditional and more innovative mechanisms were utilized.

THE PROCESS: COLLABORATION AND PARTICIPATION IN PLAN DEVELOPMENT

The plan development process can be divided into three phases: an orientation phase, a discussion phase and the plan development phase as described below.

ORIENTATION PHASE

In 1997 the provincial council drew up a 'note of prospects', initially defining its own goals with respect to the POP Plan, and published this as a brochure which addressed the people of Groningen in an effort to initiate a broad and open discussion with key stakeholders. In 1998 a 'campaign plan' was published, establishing some prior conditions for the development process. These included the need for serious engagement in debates with institutions, citizens, interest groups, and especially youth; and that the consultations should involve members of the provincial council. The brochure *Stand up for the future of Groningen* followed, presenting six themes for discussion through six future scenario evenings organized on a regional basis. These attracted wide representation, although it was felt that young people were under-represented. The evenings involved a presentation followed by discussion, for which the provincial politicians were coached not to take a party political view. The key question discussed was: 'how do we take advantage of the spatial–economic organisation of the Netherlands and how do we make the province an attractive place for people and companies who want to settle down in Groningen?'

This stage of the campaign was widely advertised in local newspapers and TV, as well as through a video, a press conference and a radio programme. Other activities included a children's competition, a youth parliament and an Internet website. An informal debate took place within the provincial council based on the results of the public campaign, and members gave their opinion on the future development of Groningen to 2030 at a public session of the council.

An official working party (the 'POP Group') was subsequently set up within the provincial government. Twelve staff were allocated to this, to conduct the POP Plan development process and organize all the necessary activities. They initially set up a 'POP market', an in-house information afternoon which provided clarification of the process and proposals for its continuation. By January 1999, the POP Group had elaborated key 'spearheads' of the plan relating to: water, living, the future of agriculture, mobility, energy and information technology. These were further developed in working groups, which traced problems in the province and proposed solutions, consequences and conflicts. In March 1999, the booklet *Groningers over*

Groningen was published and sent to a wide range of participants, with the results of the first campaign and feedback. The following month the POP Group made a tour of all relevant departments of the provincial government. The results of the working groups and information collected from departments were presented at an in-house meeting resulting in a status report entitled 'How are we now?', which was the basis for the next phase of plan development.

DISCUSSION PHASE

This status report was used as the basis for three workshops in May 1999: one urban, one rural, and one on the vision of Groningen 2030. As part of this process, various experts or 'interested' parties from the provincial administration, other administrative levels, key interest groups and companies were called upon to give their opinion. The results of the workshops were then used to inform the second public campaign, which took place in autumn 1999, and through which the conceptual foundations for the new plan were laid. The results of the workshop discussions were considered by the newly elected provincial council and executive, and a workshop for members of the council was organized inviting them to think about the process itself and the role of the council within it. In this, the province accepted that the first campaign had created an expectation among stakeholders for further participation in the development of the POP Plan. It was thus agreed that the second campaign should continue to encourage stakeholder participation, but should also outline what was expected of them. In July 1999, a second tour of departments was made to assist with the development of a policy framework.

In the second public campaign, the province's intention was to show the public more clearly what happened with their contributions. The provincial government again published a high standard brochure, entitled *Choose for the Future of Groningen ... show your hand*, which set out its proposals for discussion (see Figure 6.2). To illustrate choices already made by the executive, 'Perspectives for 2030' were outlined on a thematic and regional basis. These regional perspectives were translated into a series of tasks, to be elaborated and implemented with the co-operation of 'the region'. As before, an extensive publicity machine was set in motion, including TV and radio slots, two press conferences, an Internet site, and one video prepared by the provincial government and another by a group of citizens. In each sub-region, a group of citizens was invited to picture the 'qualities and possibilities' of their sub-region.

A more explicit attempt to involve young people was made through 'Groningen 2030', with a story-line project (supported by NoordXXI) aimed at secondary school pupils, who were encouraged to develop their own plans. Pupils and teachers received information packs and staff received training in skills required in story-line techniques. The project culminated in a presentation by the pupils in the provincial government (see Figure 6.3).

Figure 6.2   Brochures published during the POP Plan consultation

As in the first campaign, six future scenario evenings were held, with 1,500 people attending, and people could communicate with members of the provincial executive by way of the Internet. In addition, a broader consultation than usual was undertaken involving interest groups, regional councils, water boards and administrative partners. Four regional meetings were organized to discuss the regional perspectives and to consider how to achieve goals by adopting a more integrated approach. The aim of these meetings was to generate support for the regional approach at the subregional level. The second campaign concluded with a debate in the provincial council, on the basis of which the council set up the preparatory procedure for the final drafting of the POP Plan.

Figure 6.3 'Groningen 2030', secondary school pupils' presentation in the provincial government

FINAL PLAN DEVELOPMENT PHASE

In early 2000, in-house meetings in the provincial government were organized to allow departments to comment on the first draft of the POP Plan. Meetings to discuss the plan were also arranged with the provincial council, the provincial executive, and the provincial management. These were followed by official and administrative discussions with the municipalities and water boards in each region, to reach agreement on the regional perspectives and the new regional approach adopted. Comments expressed through this process were taken into consideration in the preparation of the second draft of the plan, and another round of sub-regional meetings was organized. These meetings were open to everyone and once again comments were taken into account in preparing the subsequent official draft. There followed a statutory ten week period during which anyone could submit written comments and, in September 2000, three widely advertised public hearings were held. Comments submitted were collected in a 'Note on Remarks and Comments'. In December 2000, the POP Plan was formally placed on deposit by the provincial executive for three months, during which appeals could be made with respect to policy decisions.

KEY ASPECTS OF THE POP PLAN DEVELOPMENT PROCESS

The original research into the Groningen POP Plan investigated participants' own evaluation of the evolving participatory process (see Jenkins, Kirk and Smith, 2001). The intention of this analysis is different, focusing on how the three elements of *space*, *place* and *territory* were integrated in innovative ways in the plan development process, and on some of the key conditioning factors in this.

The POP Group – as technical drivers of the process – made significant efforts to engage with as far-reaching a set of stakeholders as possible throughout the process, using a wide range of mechanisms. Most of these focused on providing information, although another set of participatory mechanisms focused on collecting feedback through, for example, public meetings and scenario evenings and work-shops. The third set of participatory events was aimed at actors within the provincial government, specific 'interest groups' and sub-regional administrative entities such as municipalities and water boards.

The research showed that, while to a great extent the agenda was pre-set for the first and second sets of events, the latter was of a more open nature that allowed negotiation, albeit more wide-ranging and possibly more intensive than normal. It is not clear to what extent the main scenarios presented in the plan really were outcomes of the process, and to what extent these primarily continued to reflect the input from the specialists.[1] Arguably as much effort (if not direct 'media' costs) went into the third form of participation as into the first two, which were more directed at the public.

Thus, while the process represented a high investment of resources and time of many specialists and politicians to engage with interest groups and the public, there was a strong awareness in provincial government that the provincial council would take the final decisions – although based upon a sound(er) knowledge of what peo-ple in the province and key interest groups thought. The key politicians who backed the process were aware of the risks associated with raised public expectations, and possible frustration if comments were not seen to be taken into account. Indeed, a number of issues were left open for later interpretation. This was of particular interest for other tiers of government, both at national level and local level, for some of whom this could amount to the province absolving itself of its responsibility. Some other institutions expressed doubt that the provincial politicians would adequately confront powerful sectoral interests and take the sometimes hard decisions required. For instance, national government was especially concerned about contentious housing issues where national policy is to concentrate development in key settlements but there is competition between municipalities to attract new housing investment. Also, some smaller advocacy groups, such as environmental NGOs, saw the wider engagement process as creating advantages for more powerful economic interests who seemed happy with their continued ability to influence the process.

The fact that not all key decisions had been taken and not all the implications for subordinate actors had been resolved led the provincial government to con-sider the extension of activity in a continuous development process of the plan. This was to be characterized by co-operation between the province and its sub-regional partners through 'administrative deliberations' to be held in each sub-region twice a year, developing regional programmes in a spirit of mutual co-operation. In addition, there was to be a continuing engagement between the administrative partners and key target groups at sub-regional levels. Here the growing trend to inter-municipal councils is seen as providing a new interface between provincial and local.

Each of the sub-regions in the province had developed a staffed 'Inter-municipal Council', through which municipalities had started working together on a range of different issues. These were used as a mechanism to co-ordinate the views of the municipalities involved in the POP Plan process. This trend towards joint working at the sub-regional level was said to have come from the realization that, as most municipalities are relatively small, through co-operation they can exert more influence on provincial and national government. In the past, it has been the case that the province and municipalities were in competition. The POP process is said to have led to greater co-operation between the two.

In all of this, municipalities were aware that implementation of the POP Plan largely depended on their co-operation, and would therefore require a redefinition of roles for those issues left for local decision-making. The province, however, generally expected that its engagement at sub-regional level would largely be confined to the most likely and urgent projects by theme and region, especially those requiring an integrated approach. National government expressed concern regarding enforcement, claiming that provincial governments had been traditionally weak in the enforcement of their own policy at municipal level.

One of the key objectives of the POP process – to enhance policy integration at the provincial level – was not as straightforward as was first thought. The organization of national policy on a sectoral basis meant that there was no national guidance in place by which to judge the new integrated plan. The integration of the four plans was also only a partial success as it has been almost impossible to fully integrate these for legal reasons, which led to the production of a very complex final document. In addition, national directives relating to environmental planning were not included within the plan as it stood at the time of the research, and this was seen by national government as a serious problem. On the other hand, some municipalities did not consider the plan to be integrated enough and wanted it to include other social issues which are decided at national level. Again, these would be areas with potential for conflict between policies in the plan and national policies.

Overall the objective of raising the province's profile and capacity to exert influence on national policy could lead it into potential conflict with national government. At the time, national government was in the process of preparing a new National Spatial Plan (Fifth Note), which is primarily a physical land use plan. The fact that the POP process started prior to this complicated the process of integrating the POP Plan with the national plan. The province argued that the POP Plan process needed therefore to be seen as a two-way negotiation, and hoped to put pressure on national government to change legislation accordingly. The growing influence of EU directives on national policy with its emphasis on regional policy was seen as a support in this respect, together with the trend towards municipalities to work together in a 'Europe of the

Regions'. It was also suggested that consultation with some national departments was limited, and that overall these had become involved too late.

In general, the POP Plan development process was a well thought-out and structured strategic integrated land use planning exercise with a lot of investment of resources, and innovation, in public participation. That said, its starting point and overarching objective seems to have been a new provincial vision, with an eye on national resources and 'place marketing', rather than starting from a concern to work from the bottom up. In other words, the participatory process was still quite a top-down exercise. An essential aspect of its operationalization was the achievement of a high level of political cohesion at provincial level in a major attempt to align various aspects of planning to the macro-region's advantage, a process which involved creating new space for negotiation with forms of local government. However, national government and some environmental groups have expressed concerns over the capacity to implement and control adequately the outcomes for wide public benefit.

One of the key elements of this level of analysis starts with the genesis of the plan. This was initially driven by two major considerations: the more or less 'technical' rationale of integrating four related plans into one development process, and the macro-regional interests in building on the Compass Plan as a basis for national funding for macro-regional development. It can be said that the initial impetus for the plan's development was fundamentally to reinforce the provincial government's position vis-à-vis accessing welfare state resources and the more efficient co-ordination of sectoral activities at a regional level. The latter interest also related to maximizing the effectiveness of the regional planning process through increasing ownership and commitment from a wide range of stakeholders, including the general public. This led to a wider ranging consultation process than might normally have taken place for any of the four plans alone.[2]

This objective was of a more political nature, although not party political (at least initially). The coming to power of a predominantly new set of politicians in the provincial council, and especially the executive, who saw the opportunity to consolidate the provincial power base in general through a wider participatory process, led to a high political profile for the plan development process. This in turn permitted access to a high level of resources, driving the process through what could have been sectoral resistance within the provincial government, and taking risks in relation to higher and lower tiers of government. In other words, there have been strong political–administrative motivations to underpin the process, including a new emphasis on corporate working at executive level, with less emphasis on a 'culture of control', and more openness to take risks.[3]

Returning to the concepts of space, place and territory, we can see the provincial space being used here as a focus for building a stronger sense of place for the residents through what was both an inward- and outward-looking place-marketing initiative, which was very well organized and resourced. However, looking behind this initiative, it becomes clear that its driving force was essentially a political one. This was related to territorial strengthening – the building of a stronger image, but also of political power and access to national resources – through a process that was seen primarily as negotiating with lower tiers of government through ongoing liaison, albeit within a context of an agreed broad agenda for development which crossed provincial boundaries and was intellectually supported by EU regional development policy. This was being resisted by national government at the time of the plan's finalization. This line of analysis is further developed below, with comparisons to the Buskerud County Plan preparation process in Norway.

CASE STUDY: BUSKERUD COUNTY PLAN, NORWAY

INTRODUCTION

The underlying trend for renegotiation of territorial identity and powers can be seen also in a parallel case study from Norway, concerning the development of the county plan for Buskerud. Buskerud County is located in southern Norway, north west of Oslo, and has a population of 250,000 inhabitants, just over a fifth of which live in the main town of Drammen. The area is predominantly rural, but is under increasing development pressure from Oslo. The Buskerud County Plan preparation process was directly inspired by the Groningen POP Plan process though the NoordXXI project. This is apparent in the emphasis on openness in inviting public debate and in some of the techniques used, which were based on the Groningen experience.[4] However, the process in Buskerud was considerably more compressed in terms of time, and did not involve investment of comparable resources. More importantly for this chapter, it was set within a very different political context.

As noted in Chapter 4, the county plan is a normal part of spatial planning in Norway which the county council must prepare every four years. The main objectives of this level of planning are to:

*   identify the most important priorities in terms of population, industry, communications, nature, cultural heritage and environment;
*   focus on trends of development, challenges and goals based on analysis of needs and possibilities in different parts of the region;
*   provide a long term perspective (10–12 years) and a four year action plan (this is the normal planning perspective at local level as well);
*   give guidelines concerning land use and resources in issues that affect more than one municipality;
*   clarify how municipalities are expected to put national guidelines into practice.

County plans are strategic and indicative but not legally binding. However, if objections were made to a local master plan based on a county plan, the latter would normally take precedence. National planning guidelines specify that it is the county's responsibility to create suitable arenas between authorities, organisations and others that should participate in the process. The Ministry of Environment defines potential participants as the county, municipalities, regional commissioner, other state agencies, industrial organizations, labour unions and voluntary organizations. There are no specific guidelines as to which organizations should be involved, just general advisory guidance that relevant organizations in relation to the actual topics of the plan should be involved as equal partners. In Buskerud, young people and the general public were seen as priority groups to involve, as other organizations had already been involved in both the recent strategic industry plan and the common health and social services plan, which also are a formal part of county level planning.

County plan development has experienced problems in recent years in Norway as, apart from the county plan itself, there are many other plans and processes set up by different departments in the county, with little co-ordination between them. In addition, the county is not seen as a higher tier of government to the municipality and has not been seen as important by the county level representatives of national government, the regional commissioners. Despite wide consultation in the past, the need to focus the county plan has led to queries over 'ownership' of the final product, which led to proposals for a new process in Buskerud, stressing the incorporation of different administrative groups as well as political groups in the plan's development.

This was reflected in the main issues identified as needing to be addressed by the plan: to enhance co-operation; to identify common solutions and their relevance; to clarify the position of political and administrative officials; to clarify the position of participating public authorities and organizations, individuals and groups; and to emphasize participation to promote ownership of the plan and commitment to implementation. The county executive stressed the need for a process that was manageable in terms of financial and staff resources within a realistic time frame. It also stressed the need for integration of plans that had already been approved for industry, health and social services and public transport. In addition, it was intended to integrate the county plan with those prepared at the wider macro-regional and national level.

THE PROCESS: COLLABORATION AND PARTICIPATION IN PLAN DEVELOPMENT

In Buskerud, the intention was to prepare a new county plan to be approved before the end of 2000, although the process only started in January 1999. As in Groningen, the Buskerud process consisted of a number of steps, which can be divided into three distinct phases.

PHASE ONE: WORKING OUT 'BASES FOR RESOLUTION'
The process organizers had a meeting with all municipalities before the process started, with the objective of producing a document of 'challenges and choices', involving politicians as well as 'work and reference groups' from different levels of government under the leadership of the county executive. These were set up to include:

* a County Work Group, consisting of the senior advisor from each department (health, education, regional planning, culture and general staff);
* a County Reference Group, comprising leaders from the same departments as above;
* a State Work Group, consisting of one person from each relevant national agency;[5]
* a State Reference Group, comprising leaders from the above agencies;
* a Municipalities Work Group, consisting of one person from each sub-region selected by the executive committee of the assembly of all chief municipal officers; and
* a Municipalities Reference Group, consisting of the executive committee of the assembly of all chief municipal officers.

Later in the process the following were also formed:

* a Youth Council Work Group, comprising five appointed members from the youth parliament; and
* a Youth Council Reference Group, the youth parliament's executive committee.

The different work groups started by analysing the existing county plan, making suggestions for improvement and proposing key topics to be covered within the plan. These were drafted in a common discussion document for an initial seminar on plan development in March 1999. This seminar was led by planning staff and included speakers from the municipalities and the state. It involved all of the above groups as well as the provincial executive council, and focused on different criteria in preparing a 'successful' county plan and the suggested key topics. The resulting proposals then went to the reference groups and to the executive council for final decision and, by June 1999, the executive council had agreed a document for wider discussion entitled *Outline for the Basis for Resolution*.

It was the executive council that decided on the agenda of issues and the values defining success for the plan process, stressing that the plan was to focus on: issues needing regional co-ordination; ownership of the plan among users; and maximizing implementation of plan proposals. The overall vision for the plan was development that should be sustainable, healthy and especially take into account the challenges children and young people will meet. The emphasis on sustainable

development and children/young people led to a focus on 'education and competence, transportation, land use and resource management and the development of
the place (development of townships and cities)'. In terms of resources, NKr
200,000 (around € 24,800 at the time) had already been allocated to the process,
and the executive council also granted an additional NKr 150,000 (€ 18,500 at the
time) for participation and the provision of information at this stage.

Members of the work groups subsequently reviewed the *Basis for Resolution*
document and outlined a follow-up phase of broader participation activities in a
major 'scenario workshop' at which a regional analysis of Buskerud and two future
scenarios developed by a local academic were presented. All relevant municipalities, state agencies, industrial and labour unions and council representatives were
present. This workshop was accompanied by publication of a brochure which presented 'black or white' or 'provocative' choices and stressed the need for a common
strategy (see Figure 6.4). Two alternative scenarios were presented, one based on
continued expansion along transport routes, and an alternative one which stressed
environment and contra-urbanization. The selected key topics were also presented
with alternatives and strategies of action, and the participants were questioned as to
whether these were the only or appropriate topics. In addition, there was an attempt
to tie these topics to political issues: for example, on knowledge and higher education, it was suggested that Buskerud was one of the poorest counties in Norway
and questions were posed regarding the kind and location of education required to
encourage young people to stay.

The final version of the *Basis for Resolution* document was then printed and
distributed to all municipalities (including libraries) and some 60 other voluntary
organizations throughout the county. These included health and environmental organizations, labour unions, education agencies and organizations involved in children's
activities. This document differed from the previous brochure in that it contained
more facts and questions and also attempted to suggest some solutions and participants' potential contribution to achieving these. While this document circulated, in
November 1999, elections to the provincial council were held, and a training and
briefing programme on the plan development process was organized for new
incoming members.

PHASE TWO: POLITICAL DEBATE

The aim of phase two was to promote and strengthen the concept of the county
plan process itself as a political responsibility. Informal discussions in a series of
'topic groups' and workshops were held from September to December 1999 with
the above work and reference groups to prepare for this. This activity also included
a 'Future Workshop' with the youth council, a joint county council/youth council
seminar, and a brochure focused on the youth parliament. Phase two also included

Figure 6.4 Cover of the Buskerud County Plan consultation brochure

two open public meetings in the two main cities of Drammen and Konigsberg, to which municipalities, council organizations and the general public were invited. Approximately 70–80 people attended these meetings in total. Other smaller local meetings were also held with the municipalities. This process of political debate led to the executive council agreeing on a draft 'hearing document' in March 2000, which was to be the formal consultative plan document.

PHASE THREE: FORMAL HEARING
The formal consultation was constituted, as normally, by a series of regional public hearings which took place from March through to September 2000 (the date of research). After this, the final plan was to be developed by December 2000.

KEY ASPECTS OF THE BUSKERUD COUNTY PLAN DEVELOPMENT PROCESS
In the first instance it is important to reiterate that although the process was inspired by the approach adopted in Groningen, the Buskerud plan process did not have

comparable resources and the time span was considerably shorter. However, both were at an administratively similar level (i.e. regional framework plans) and both were prepared during a period when new politicians at that level were elected. Both also had the express intention of consolidating the regional level of government.

In general, those involved in the Buskerud process felt that this had encouraged broad participation between different levels of government and thus had helped to develop wider ownership of the plan and a more strategic outlook. More specifically, it was felt that the plan process created a channel through which county and municipal government could communicate, and the municipalities and other organizations that had been involved indicated their interest to continue to have an influence. However, this deeper sense of ownership was undermined by changes within the provincial administration which resulted in a number of changes to the plan introduced by the chief executive. In retrospect this may have been a result of the fact that, although plan preparation was supposed to be a political process, it tended to be dominated by officials in the early stages, especially given the election halfway through the process. It also reflected the organizational process through working groups, with politicians involved in reference groups, and thus not so deeply engaged in the process itself. That said, there was some increased co-ordination amongst officials across different departments and with lower tiers of government. However, there was relatively little engagement of the wider public or organizations within the voluntary sector, as in the process there was a strong focus mainly on youth engagement. To some extent this was also affected by the markedly different resources available and the time constraints, leading the primary process organizer to concentrate on specific groups.

Traditionally, the provincial council has had a comparatively weak position in Norway relative to municipal government, having no formal authority over it, and as such one of the key aims of the county plan development process was to promote wider ownership of the plan to ensure its implementation at local level, as well as to promote awareness and address strategic issues. However, during the preparation of the Buskerud plan, the very future of a county level of government in Norway was under national discussion (Bukve, 2000). This both raised uncertainties as to how the plan would be implemented in practice, and focused attention of some of the participants on the issue of co-operation between the different levels of government. Some questioned the value of strategic planning being carried out by the county, as this is not required to directly provide services, and suggested that this strategic overview could be achieved through greater inter-municipality co-operation.

The context of questioning the role of the county led to some extent to a reluctance by the county politicians to be seen to promote the plan too actively, and hence this undermined the political ownership objective of the process organizers.

As a result, while both the politicians and professionals in the various reference and working groups understood their relative roles, the objective of the politicians leading wider discussion throughout sub-regions did not materialize. Thus, although politicians overall felt that the process was worth implementing, they did not prioritize their involvement in this. One of the outcomes of this was the attitude of the incoming chief executive at county level, who more or less unilaterally instigated changes in the plan after the wider consultative process. Restructuring within the internal administration had meant that the chief executive assumed responsibility for the plan from the regional department which had been previously responsible for the process. In this the chief executive may have been mainly concerned with the forthcoming formal consultation process, and with the fact that the structure created for participation would not continue in the formal consultation, which was seen as being a more traditional process for which the county had overall responsibility. This may have been one of the factors which led to the regional state officials to withdraw from the consultative process halfway through, awaiting the formal consultation stage to make their position known.

Hence, as with the Groningen POP plan, there seemed to be some tension between the national state representatives at county level, over the inherent proposed strengthening of the nature and role of the county in strategic planning. This was less evidenced at local authority level however, where there was a continuous negotiation with municipalities. This was facilitated by the executive committee of an organization for all the municipalities within the county which acted as a reference group in the process. In general, municipal respondents were positive about the process and felt that the involvement of these working and reference groups was an improvement on previous practice, although making clear that they were aware of the county's domination of the process. As in Groningen the need to follow up the plan with concrete action was stressed at municipal level, and the danger of raising expectations within the wider public was noted.

CONCLUSION

CONCLUSIONS ON THE GRONINGEN EXPERIENCE

In the Groningen POP plan process, there was a deliberate investment of political power and state resources to: (a) strategically strengthen the province's impact at national and municipal levels through collaborative agreements at a macro-regional level with neighbouring provinces, and more specifically develop more open-ended negotiation processes with sub-regional groups of municipalities; and (b) widen public participation as well as rally wide stakeholder support for a strengthened provincial strategy role through the visioning process.

In other words, using the analytical framework of Chapter 2, there was a deliberate attempt to adjust territorial identity through negotiation. This was both with new intermediate and non-formal levels of government (i.e. above and below provincial level) as well as with a wider group of stakeholders. The negotiation on territorial identity was not focused on new boundary definitions (although the possibility of closer collaboration across provincial and even national boundaries was an element) but primarily a negotiation on the roles and responsibilities that the provincial territory entailed. In other words, the extent of the territory was not queried, but the identity associated with this was.

To be seen as legitimate, this renegotiation of territorial identity required social, economic and political legitimacy. The political legitimacy was to some extent derived from the economic and social support engendered by the plan development process, but also crucially from the wide range of other stakeholders which were involved in the negotiation process – especially the lower tier authorities. However, economic aspects featured heavily in the scenarios which were used to base the negotiation, and economic development was a key feature of the impetus to prepare the new POP Plan (as part of the wider Compass Plan) in the first place, with a wide range of economic actors having opportunity to participate. What is seen as innovative in terms of public participation in the POP Plan development process can thus be seen as aimed at getting a broad social consensus built around the key economic and social development alternatives, as proposed by the province.

This is in no way to be seen as critical of the valid attempts to get the wider public involved in understanding and agreeing to these broad social and economic objectives, but suggests that behind the interest in promoting participation there was a strong political need to create legitimacy for the implicit changes in territorial identity. Arguably, this is the main reason why the process was so well resourced and politically supported. However, while the participatory process can be seen largely to have delivered the necessary level of general legitimacy, and support from lower tiers of government and other major economic actors seems to be in place, this has been due partly to the openness to negotiation itself. It is exactly this aspect which some political and administrative actors are concerned with – mainly national government, but also the water boards and some of the environmental voluntary groups. For these institutions there is a risk in too much negotiation as this can undermine what are seen by them as higher order objectives – i.e. national and environmental ones – which are currently safeguarded mainly at national level.

The determined attempt in Groningen to use place identity as a focal point for discussion and decision-making in relation to broad social and economic development objectives in provincial level strategic planning (i.e. the visioning process), and to use this process to underpin new forms of negotiation of political objectives with regard to territorial identity, has not been totally successful. To what extent the province can get national backing for the POP Plan, and to what extent municipalities see this as continuing to deliver new spaces where they can negotiate their own role, are open questions at the time of writing. This reflects in a general way what is happening in various parts of Europe, as territorial identities are renegotiated in the context of changing economic and social priorities which themselves challenge relatively static governance systems (Danson, Halkier and Cameron, 2000; Le Gales, 2002; Raagma, 2002).

CONCLUSIONS ON THE BUSKERUD EXPERIENCE

The experience of Buskerud backs up this latter claim. Again, in summary we have a regional administration wanting to bolster its position in general – here its very existence was threatened – through using the existing county planning process in innovative ways as a 'space for negotiation'. The fact that a number of mechanisms for public participation were copied from Groningen is fairly irrelevant to the main thrust of the objective. The key aspect is that again visioning around place identity was the focal point for the process, which ostensibly was more about strengthening territorial identity at county level. Again we see that intermediate and informal institutions played a part – the association of municipalities. While no major collaboration across county boundaries was evident, the fact that the role of counties was being questioned probably provided some political context at cross-county level.

As was the case with the Groningen POP Plan, misgivings about the process of negotiation were expressed at national level. However, here it was preoccupation at the role of the officials vis-à-vis the politicians and other stakeholders that seemed to be the main expression of these. This is the main differing feature between the two case studies (other than the national differences expressed in Chapter 4). In Groningen the incoming politicians saw their opportunity to use discussion around place identity as the means to strengthen their territorial identity, and threw their considerable weight behind the plan development process, which had been started mainly by officials. In Buskerud the incoming politicians opted to stand at the sidelines while the officials developed the process, with the intention to come in after the consultation. Although the research was undertaken before the final plan was approved, in general this political ambivalence was probably a major reason why the planning process was not so successful at getting wide support – partly due to the limited resources and lack of clear political backing, and partly due to the fact that the officials tended to dominate the process. The structure of the process also reflects this, as do the mechanisms for participation used and the timescale available.

Thus in Buskerud a different national context probably dictated that the expansion of the territorial identity of the county, while desirable, was not politically the best thing to be promoting at the time, and the resulting 'hands-off' process for the plan development led to a series of difficulties with this. That said, the process was seen by many – especially municipalities and voluntary organizations, as well as some officials – as being worthwhile and something to be built on in the future. The fact that county planning, as strategic for economic development, was subsequently backed by national government, will probably create a more conducive context in future for this also (Amdam, 2001).

OVERALL CONCLUSIONS

These case studies are too limited in scope to provide clear empirical evidence on their own that strategic planning is being used to bolster changing territorial identities across Europe. However, other research also seems to support this (Healey *et al.*, 1997; Cars *et al.*, 2002; Herschel and Newman, 2002; Madanipour, 2001). One of the main conclusions to be drawn here is that while the techniques of wider stakeholder involvement in planning that are currently being developed and implemented in various parts of Europe at strategic planning level are valued for their ability to promote more inclusive forms of governance where the public can be more involved, probably more pertinently these are seen as permitting existing tiers of government to renegotiate their territorial identity. Crucial to this is the strong regional focus of the EU and support this gives to regional tiers of government, as well as to new informal institutional structures, some being intermediate forms of alliances between tiers. Concerning these intermediate forms of negotiation, we can see new forums for these developing, as illustrated in Figure 6.5.

Evidence at the sub-national regional level is the Compass Plan for the three northern provinces of the Netherlands and its relationship to the POP Plan in Groningen. The changing role of the county planning process in Norway also reflects this desire. The micro-regional tendency is related to these tendencies. In Norway, the need for more integration of planning between independent *kommunes* is

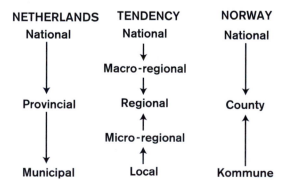

Figure 6.5 New intermediate negotiation forums in the Nertherlands and Norway

increasingly felt in relation to resource allocation and common issues such as environment, transport, urban expansion, etc., whereas in the Netherlands it is perhaps more a reflection of the need to maintain a relatively strong co-ordinated voice within the strengthening arena of provincial government strategy formulation regarding the nation-state – i.e. the meso-regional level.

The other important conclusion to be drawn is in relation to the question: How does this affect our attitudes to planning and the role spatial planning is developing? Here we reiterate the position put forward in Chapter 2, and further developed in Chapter 3: the wider stakeholder participatory planning processes which many governments are investing in are not only a response to changing territorial identities – and above all here the relative increase in the power of city-regions vis-à-vis the nation-state – but also reflect changing governance contexts. While to some extent the former can often be seen as a type of manipulation, there is a tendency to see the latter as generally positive in that, as 'communicative' planners argue, it brings strategic planning closer to the wider public. However, the above case studies show that the arenas and agendas for this new form of planning are still largely set and controlled by the government and bureaucracy (or elites within these).

More to the point, some of the gains made through long-term negotiation within the welfare states may well be eroded in this process, and planning as essentially a redistributive mechanism may be reduced in scope in the face of city region competition – and powerful players within these regions may well have more power to lobby and influence the process than they would have at national level. This may lead to a regional form of nimbyism rather than to a comprehensive negotiated balance between inevitably unequal partners. Here the importance of supra-national governance structures is again clear. The erosion of control at nation-state level leads to the need for greater supra-national levels of regulation and support, and the EU to date has a clear agenda in this regard. As such there is the possibility of more effective strategic planning at regional level which goes beyond nation-state boundaries, but this is still in its infancy. The issue of relevance here is: how is this level of regional strategic planning regulated, as much of the activity is undertaken through new informal mechanisms with intermediate tiers that are often not statutorily constituted? This question could be posed in another way: what happens to bottom-up initiatives in wider stakeholder planning? This is the theme of the next chapter.

CHAPTER 7

LOCAL PARTICIPATION AND PLACE IDENTITY
Karryn Kirk

INTRODUCTION

This book is concerned with how narratives of place identity are constructed and contested in the context of spatial planning – i.e. through practice and participation. In this it inevitably touches on issues generally referred to as 'governance' – i.e. both systems of government and the social and cultural basis for these. This chapter evaluates the potential for building upon local initiatives which have used place identity as a focus, and the extent to which elements of these local discourses have been adopted or have influenced local authority planning as a result. It is based on research in two case studies in the NoordXXI project, the *kommunes* of Tidaholm and Falköping, located within the Västra Götaland region in the south west of Sweden.

We have interpreted planning for place identity as a process of constructing a discourse within which specific place narratives are written (Chapter 1). Local case studies provide a basis to research the detail and to explore how the components of such a place identity discourse are fashioned, developed, used and contested. They allow us to analyse how external structures, different institutions, policy vehicles and different actors define and mould the discourse. Put more simply, the questions are about who uses what initiatives to demarcate the scope and content of policy and action about place identity at a local level, and how this affects – and is affected by – larger scale place identity discourses.

As noted previously, the selection of the case studies was to a great extent driven by the priorities and co-operation of our clients. It is thus not possible to claim that our examples are definitive of practice in Sweden, let alone across the North Sea Region as a whole. Rather, we were presented with two *kommunes* which demonstrated real attempts to go 'beyond traditional spatial and economic development', for investigation of these local innovations in participation. These were places where there had been very serious attempts to engage local people in actions that were strongly premised on a commitment to place identity. Our task in the project was to analyse and evaluate these initiatives. Our aim now is to re-interpret them within a more systematic context of wider research and the themes of this book. To that end we begin with some discussion of how structural economic change impacted on the Swedish welfare state and on approaches to participation in planning.

RENEGOTIATION OF THE SWEDISH PLANNING MODEL

Sweden is particularly interesting as a focus for research on local level participation. A characteristic feature of the Swedish system of government is the high degree of decentralization of responsibility to the municipal level. The large number of *kommunes* covering relatively small populations has meant that there is a culture of informal lobbying but there is much less familiarity with direct grassroots involvement, as noted in Chapter 4. This provides a particularly interesting example of governance at the interface between direct participation and the system of representative democracy at a local level, with the global economic restructuring of a social democratic welfare state.

Newman and Thornley (1996) presented a cogent and provocative review of how the Swedish welfare state, and with it the Swedish planning system and practices, had been restructured in the 1980s and early 1990s. Drawing on Castles (1978) and Heclo and Madsen (1987), they described the 'consensus culture', 'corporate pluralism' and structured consultation process that lay at the heart of the strong welfare state of the 1950s–1970s. They noted how this culture placed importance on 'opportunities for participation' (Newman and Thornley, 1996: 202). However, four devaluations of the currency in the 1970s and 1980s, de-industrialization and an ongoing fiscal crisis in local government led to the historic defeat of the Social Democrats (who had dominated post-1945 Swedish politics) in the 1991 General Election, and ushered in a fundamental reform of the welfare state. The revival of the Social Democrats in 1994, and entry into the EU, could not restore the welfare state of social equality and full employment that had been the definitive expression of the Swedish polity before the era of globalized competition and deregulation. As Newman and Thornley (1996: 203) succinctly noted, 'It could no longer be assumed that the state could deal with all problems.'

Newman and Thornley further showed that centralization of power had been challenged from the 1970s. There was a five-year official inquiry in the late 1980s into power and democracy, which chronicled the passing of an era of urban growth, welfare state expansion, corporatist consensus, universalism, centralism and general trust in authority. Successive legislative changes have led to the *kommunes* gaining greater responsibility, e.g. over care facilities for the elderly and children, education up to upper secondary level, housing policy, physical planning and environmental planning (Westman, 1991). However, strains on the traditional welfare state resulting from a combination of financial pressures, demographic developments and rising expectations have in fact limited the *kommunes*' scope for action (Wetterberg, 1991).

Planning and participation are thus likely to be infused by the wider tensions affecting Swedish local government. In crude terms, under Sweden's 'classic' welfare state, planning had been a technical, rationalistic means for supplying the land and designing the layouts for what was essentially a social housing system. The 1987 Building and Planning Act responded to 1970s criticisms of this rigid master planning approach, and one of the aims was increased public participation in the planning process. Beyond this, the intention of the 1987 legislation was to make planning fully the responsibility of the *kommune*. Central government can only intervene if the national interests safeguarded in the Acts are affected. This is a much more decentralized system than that in the UK, where central government can issue planning policy as and when it sees fit and require local planning authorities to take such central policy into account. However, this empowerment of the planning process at a local level coincided with serious fiscal problems. In addition the land use planning tradition still created barriers to using the planning system as a means for a popular construction of place identity.

Development plans in Sweden are of two types: the comprehensive *oversiktsplan* or 'structure plan' and the more detailed *detaljplan* (see Chapter 4). Both are prepared by the *kommune*. The *oversiktsplan* covers the whole *kommune* area but is not legally binding. It has three main aims:

- to provide a forum/document where the future development of the *kommune* is discussed including visions, development targets and strategies for action;
- to demonstrate agreement between the *kommune* and national government about how to take care of land area of national interest; and
- to act as a comprehensive policy document that will simplify daily decision-making.

One of several more recent amendments has been to change the aims of the *oversiktsplan* from being a mainly land use plan into a more strategic integrated planning document with an increased focus on social aspects and people's living conditions. This is hardly surprising given that the guidelines for its preparation were nested within key legislation intended to implement sustainable development (1987 Natural Resources Act). Amendments to the legislation in 1996 also sought to give more importance to consultation in preparing the *oversiktsplan*. Many *kommunes* therefore had a stronger incentive to revise the *oversiktsplan* and focus more on participation as a means of surveying inhabitants' main concerns and to plan for relevant issues. As such there is potentially more of an emphasis on 'territorial planning', as defined in Chapter 2, in these strategic plans, with land use being one component.

Thus, part of the renegotiation of the Swedish welfare state planning model has been to emphasize decentralization and participation, as well as broader integration of government functions at a strategic level, with the *oversiktsplan* as the key policy vehicle for this. However, Newman and Thornley recognized a counter-tendency also. This they termed 'negotiation planning'. It was developed during, and as a consequence of, the shift towards commercial property development in the 1980s, which forced a more flexible planning regime where developers and their financiers would negotiate with the *kommunes*. Such negotiations were not transparent to the public, and the fiscal crisis within local government, together with the city centre location of major schemes, often meant that the power within the negotiation was tipped in favour of the private sector.

Thus, in summary, Newman and Thornley (1996) argue that while participation appears to be strongly rooted in the planning system, in reality participation can be 'by-passed and manipulated' (1996: 214) in favour of the market. They back this line of argument with three case studies of large development projects, concluding that 'the lack of participation' stands out, as 'the corporate dimension is more important than the participatory one' (1996: 243). This is expressed through 'a close relation-ship between developers and top politicians' (1996: 244), so that this elite formulates development projects that are then strongly promoted as being in the interests of the city. Newman and Thornley concede that their focus on major, con-troversial projects may give an unrepresentative picture of how the system operates, though they hypothesize that such projects are likely to influence the system as a whole.

Arguably, Newman and Thornley understate another important element of Swedish institutional culture. There is a tradition, especially in small towns and the countryside, of involvement in community activities and voluntary community man-agement of shared facilities – e.g. village halls and sports clubs. There is thus a strong institutional base for governance through self-organization within civil society in which place identity and historical continuity are to the fore. This system throws up dedicated volunteers called 'souls on fire' who dynamize local civic engagement. In addition there was a nationwide movement during the 1990s, which translates as 'Let all Sweden live', which aimed to promote rural living and to sustain rural ser-vices. A more recent nationwide process based on wide civic participation has been Local Agenda 21. This is the context for the innovation around local identity in Sweden that this chapter examines.

LOCAL AGENDA 21: AN ALTERNATIVE DISCOURSE

The development planning system is not the only discourse through which narra-tives of place identity can be constructed and woven into policy or everyday life. Sweden is regarded as one of the foremost nations in responding to Local Agenda 21 and is often referred to as a pioneer in the field of environmental policy.[1] The environment has been on the national agenda since the 1960s and Sweden has continued to play an important role in trans-national negotiations. The Brundtland

Report (1987) led to the formulation of Agenda 21 at the Rio Earth Summit in 1992. Agenda 21 committed national governments to the preparation of national sustainable development plans, and envisaged significant local authority-led action at the local level (UNCED, 1992). Crucially, these Local Agenda 21 (LA21) plans rely on active citizen participation and empowerment and their delivery is dependent on engaging the energy and imagination of local people in specific places. Thus the fact that communities were already engaged in environmental activities around rural development in Sweden ensured that the *kommunes* were well placed to respond to LA21.

When the Bruntland Report was produced, momentum for environmental policy in Sweden was high and all political parties accepted the challenge. In promoting LA21, national government emphasized the need for visions of future development and stressed that the *kommune* was the most important level for implementation. However, national government did not specify the content of individual *kommune* LA21 strategies. Nevertheless, the introduction of the Green Code, which became operational in 1999, aimed to 'promote sustainable development such as [that] today's and future generations will be guaranteed a healthy and good environment'. This linked environmental issues and analysis more closely to land use planning than was the case before.

While the term 'sustainable development' is a contested concept, in practice in many countries (including Sweden) it has mainly been claimed by environmentalists, and so the discourses of LA21 tend to favour environmental concerns. So while the new legislative context in Sweden would have seemed to support greater integration between land use planning and other policy areas, in practice there would appear to have been a significant mismatch between visions and actual policies on the ground in important policy areas − national policy in fact has tended to support a narrative which holds that sustainable development can be achieved through narrow environmental and technical solutions as opposed to adopting an integrated approach. More recently, this has been structured in terms of environmental concerns being factored into economic action − ecologically adjusted growth. However, there are examples in some *kommunes* where LA21 groups have been involved in land use issues.

More important perhaps than the content of LA21 visions, LA21 constituted a new discourse about the relationship between local authorities and their citizens, embracing informality and innovation, rather than precedent and statute. By the end of 1996, about half of Sweden's *kommunes* had employed LA21 co-ordinators (Eckerberg and Forsberg, 1998). There were, however, considerable variations in approach. Eckerberg and Forsberg (1998) identify 'pioneer' *kommunes* that tended to be already heavily engaged in local environmental activities, of which 'some projects and policy goals may be seen as early signs of more fundamental changes in local government policies concerning infrastructure, resource use and individual lifestyles' (1998: 337). As with land use planning, cuts in public spending restricted *kommune's* potential to implement LA21 strategies and criticism was directed at national government that few extra resources had been provided to assist local sustainable development activities. A survey carried out by SALA (Svenska Kommunförbundet – Swedish Association of Local Authorities) found that political and financial support at both the national and local level were 'critical bottlenecks' (Eckerberg and Forsberg, 1998).

In general, LA21 has been a parallel activity to land use planning, and while many *kommunes* have introduced new forms of participation through LA21, including neigh-bourhood groups, schools and local businesses in the process (Eckerberg, 2000, 2001), the discourses demarcated through the *oversiktsplan* and the *detaljplan* remain more rationalistic, technocratic and 'comprehensive'. In contrast, the participatory activ-ities around LA21 at local level often have gone much further than those advocated at national level. Thus, in terms of place identity and participation, LA21 and development planning generally continue to constitute two related but distinct discourses.

While the *kommune* is a central institution in both, and national government is also a player, LA21 and 'participation in planning' have some important institutional differences. Not least, we have the hypothesis from Newman and Thornley that the real dynamic in the planning system is away from participation and towards the lan-guage and decision criteria of the market. A key question then is how far LA21 has proved a conduit for the development of place identity narratives (and what is the content of such narratives), and how have the development plans, and the territorial interests with ownership of these, responded?

LOCAL AGENDA 21 IN TIDAHOLM – INITIAL PHASES

Tidaholm, with a population of around 9,000, is the largest settlement in the largely rural *kommune* that bears its name. It is a couple of hours' drive inland from Gothenburg, in the Skaraborg area, where there is a long tradition of farming and forestry. It lies beyond the commuting catchments of big cities, and is surrounded by farmland and recreation areas. The town itself has industrial roots. The Vulcan matchstick factory was established here in 1868 and became the largest match fac-tory in the world, accessing the abundant local supplies of timber and cheap rural labour. Thus Tidaholm grew as an industrial town. Linen and car manufacture (which began in 1903), and the Vulcan plant dominated the life of the settlement and its institutions. The railway arrived in 1876, but has since been closed and now can only be accessed 30 km away. Vulcan still produces in Tidaholm, though the original factory is now a museum telling the story of the town and its industry, and housing a lithographic art workshop (based on the making of the matchbox labels). Thus Tidaholm is still a manufacturing town, but one where the number of manufacturing jobs has been declining, and growth in service employment has been relatively weak. There are empty shops and some empty houses.

It is evident, therefore, that one narrative of place identity here is an industrial history. However, the more problematic Janus face of this identity is the enduring identity as a working-class company town. Tidaholm lacks higher education facilities and specialist services. Work reported on in NoordXXI spoke of youth feeling that the town gave them a bad image, and those who leave to better their education tend not to return. Tidaholm is seen as being 'dead at night', transport links are poor, unemployment high, and the *kommune*'s tax base is declining. Nevertheless, the place narrative Tidaholm presents in its tourist literature is that it is 'a small town idyll' lying in 'a beautiful cultural landscape' between areas of 'nature and fishing' and 'breathtaking beech forests and open fields', where 'Local residents maintain old traditions and history within their community'. How have the discourses of LA21 and the *oversiktsplan* related to these narratives of place identity – or created new ones?

The LA21 process in Tidaholm was researched by Malbert (1998), and this section draws on his work as well as on interviews conducted as part of the NoordXXI project. The LA21 process in Tidaholm grew out of an earlier initiative, the 'Town and Country Project', that began in 1992/3 and ran for about three years (see Box 7.1). This involved a group of council officials and researchers from the Swedish University of Agricultural Sciences in Aalnarp. It sought to investigate feasible strategies for local sustainable development, with the idea that this involves harmonious relationships between the town and the countryside.

The Town and Country Project thus reflected some elements of Sweden's corporate pluralism and structured consultation traditions, but it also reached out to actively engage children in particular. The themes cut across the council's administrative structure, and there were few formal rules and procedures to constrain innovation. Individual 'souls on fire' got involved and had the power to demarcate and drive the agenda. Together the sub-projects contributed to a narrative of place identity based on an ecological, mutually sustaining relationship between town and countryside, a green town of parks and open spaces in which a riverside walk is a learning experience about flora and fauna. This narrative does not seem to have really engaged directly with the narrative that sees the town as stigmatized by class and deprivation, rather the project offered a rural and environment-led alternative to this.

In 1994, a change in political leadership within the *kommune* led to a review of the Town and Country Project. National government had ratified the outcomes of the Rio Summit, and so *kommunes* were expected to add the preparation of LA21 strategies to their existing range of activities. Thus bottom-up participatory projects

Box 7.1 Tidaholm Town and Country Project

The Tidaholm Town and Country Project comprised three sub-projects. One, 'Activating the Grassroots', was directed at schools and sought to develop environmental awareness and knowledge amongst young people. A voluntary 'green network' of interested school leaders, teachers and childcare staff was set up. This triggered numerous activities, many of them very practical – e.g. a recycling house with composting, vegetable production and hens laying eggs. This project allowed children in particular to act in everyday life in a way that built a narrative of place identity of Tidaholm as an environment, a part of an ecological system with the surrounding rural area, while also embedding strong place memories within them through 'learning by doing'. A second sub-project, 'A Liveable Countryside', was mainly undertaken by an expert from the regional district of a national association providing information, advice and education for farmers. It explored the notion of a liveable countryside and town–countryside relations. A third strand was called 'Sustainable Green Structure' and was led by Bjorn Malbert, a planning academic based in Gothenburg. This was mainly a grouping of officials and experts. Its central concern was to develop and apply the concept of the urban green structure – i.e. the interconnected network of gardens, parks, open spaces, green verges and rural fringe. The approach was holistic, encompassing ideas of cultural heritage, but also environmentally friendly sewage treatment, for example.

now fell within the ambit of representative democracy. Tidaholm appointed an LA21 co-ordinator to develop the *kommune*'s LA21 strategy, and the 'Town and Country Project' was formally closed in 1995. There is something essentially contradictory about a UN decision on sustainable local development, ratified by the Swedish government, leading to the closure of a bottom-up project in a small *kommune*. On the other hand, the review led to the elected members taking greater political ownership of the project. Furthermore, the challenge to innovate coincided with a deep fiscal crisis in the Swedish public sector, to which Tidaholm was not immune. This restricted the staff resources that could be invested in the LA21 process but also made innovative actions more imperative, as the traditional approach of increasing budgets to tackle problems was no longer feasible. The LA21 process thus created both opportunities and obstacles for innovative actions on participation and place identity.

Tidaholm's LA21 can be seen as a conscious attempt to move from the officer-led model that characterized the former Town and Country Project to one which had broad political participation and the involvement of other interested parties. In particular there were three organized components in the LA21 work. 'Vision 2010' was produced through five 'ideas' groups, (the council's political leaders, head officials, industry leaders, farmers and a final year class at the secondary school). There were also ten 'thematic groups', each with two politicians and a final year pupil, that

could involve officials or other experts. They produced reports and newspaper arti-
cles. Thirdly, there was the production of a report by the LA21 co-ordinator that
sought to summarize the LA21 work. The report was sent to a network of 17 *byalag*
– rural or village committees – for comment as part of a formal 'hearing process',
and was subsequently redrafted, taking account of comments made. The draft
report was also sent to a range of environmental and voluntary organizations and
local schools. In addition there were a number of what Malbert describes as 'individual innovative initiatives'. These were led by middle management officials of the
kommune who had been involved in the Town and Country Project. Through these
initiatives the officials sought to apply LA21 thinking to their everyday practice.

The LA21 process, and the Town and Country Project from which it was built,
while intermediated by local political and bureaucratic power structures, does
appear to have contained elements that were genuinely participatory. In particular
there was outreach to the senior class in the secondary school, who were involved
by *kommune* officials in the design and conduct of a questionnaire survey targeted
at 1,000 people, about the planning of the parks and woods. There has also been
linkage through schools to engage younger children in studies of their local environments. In addition, through a project led by an adult education provider and night
school classes, 14 of the 17 'rural development groups' in the *kommune* actively
contributed data and ideas about how they wanted their area to be developed and
how services should be organized. Thus, when opportunities were presented, civil
society was active, not passive. Indeed there is evidence that those in the rural
development groups found the experience to be interesting and added to a sense of
group cohesion. Nevertheless, Malbert noted that certain groups had not been
engaged in the Town and Country Project, and that the 'social sector' was not
involved in LA21, perhaps because of its physical and environmental orientation, but
also because of the growing budget problems.

Did the discourse of LA21 in practice in Tidaholm, with its emphasis on local
participation and environmental sustainability, fashion a particular place narrative?
The answer is 'yes', though the roots of the narrative and perhaps its purest expression lay in the Town and Country Project that preceded LA21. For example, seven of
the ten thematic groups were closely related to the Town and Country Project. It is
these and their broad focus that constitute the place narrative (see Box 7.2).

In Box 7.2 the first seven themes listed are those that came from the Town
and Country Project, whereas the last three are those added after the politicians
'took over' and launched the LA21 exercise. Overall the dominant narrative is one
of Tidaholm as a rural and local environment rooted in agricultural tradition and a
care for high environmental quality. It is the green infrastructure and the water systems that ecologically connect town and country, and embody the idea of 'nature'.
However, green space and a town–country linkage also means access for all –

Box 7.2 The LA21 themes in Tidaholm

1. *Health and housing* – an ecological approach to natural as well as human resources.
2. *Rural development* – promote a sustainable and living countryside.
3. *Water* – prohibit polluting substances within the *kommune*'s drainage area.
4. *Waste* – reduce the amount of waste brought to the dumps by one-eighth of the 1990 levels.
5. *Locally grown food production* – produce food as close to the consumer as possible.
6. *The environment/green structure* – increase biological diversity.
7. The agricultural landscape – preserve and develop the existing farming landscape.
8. *Trade and industry* – increase environmental awareness within these groups, and take measures to make environmental considerations profitable.
9. *Energy* – replace electric heating power sources with renewable energy sources, preferably locally produced.
10. *IT* – use information technology to exchange knowledge and to market our assets and resources.

the legacy of an egalitarian welfare state still underpins the vision. The concerns with industry, energy and IT, added by the politicians, extend the theme of the place narrative to more economic concerns.

The research in the NoordXXI project found that the visioning process in these initiatives encouraged wide debate and that the thematic approach enabled participants to take a holistic view which highlighted linkages across sector areas. Another important consideration was that the elected members involved were not tied to party lines so that they could come up with ideas and discuss issues openly, thereby ensuring that all involved worked towards consensus on the 'common good'. It also found that the process generated broad enthusiasm and innovative thinking, but also generated a large volume of information and ideas. Although valuable to policy-makers, the exercise posed considerable problems in terms of information management.

It is often in translating visions into practical actions or implementation that LA21 processes come into disrepute. Visions need to be backed by commitments to finance, human resources, benchmarks of achievement and monitoring systems. Without these, the vision tends to become discredited and initial broad ownership will be eroded. A key consideration, therefore, was the LA21 process's interaction with the political process in ensuring that identified actions become political priorities and that adequate resources are allocated to tasks to enable their implementation. Although the LA21 process in Tidaholm sought to make the links between the participatory and representative process, there was a view amongst some politicians that it had led to the development of unrealistic goals which were overly ambitious and difficult to implement.

New follow-up groups were set up to implement the strategy mirroring the former theme groups but involving new people. However, the *kommune* was not satisfied with the resulting documentation, and responsibility for drafting the LA21 Report was transferred to a planner, who had acted as secretary for each of the implementation groups. A council officer was also available to discuss the strategy with consultees and went out to meetings to explain it. The final LA21 Report covered five strategies: health, social security, quality housing, local identity and public meeting places or facilities. The strategy, however, had no legal status and, due to the lower level of participation in the final editing process, seems to have lost some of its strong sense of legitimacy.

BUILDING UPON LA21 AS PART OF THE PLANNING PROCESS IN TIDAHOLM

The LA21 process was not easily assimilated into the mainstream development planning of the *kommune*. Officials interviewed by Malbert (1998) pointed to lack of knowledge and staff involvement as obstacles. For example, chief officers had not been drawn into the Town and Country Project. The fact that the local politicians 'took over' this work also limited officials' engagement. Staff resources were already stretched without adding further innovative tasks. Overall Malbert argued that the innovative thrust from the LA21 process was not adequately accommodated in the 'ordinary' work of the *kommune*'s administration. The NoordXX1 project also provided evidence of some specific gaps between formal planning practice and the LA21 process. A planner explained that the rural development groups studied the *kommune*'s *oversiktsplan* of 1991, but were very disappointed with it. They saw it as a very generalized document that said little that mattered to them about their area. Malbert also described the problem that mainstream practice had in adapting to the work done with the secondary school pupils. While the official who had led the pupils' work doing urban green area surveys saw it as raising interest in planning, colleagues could not comprehend the connection.

Nevertheless, some officials directly involved in the LA21 work did seek to make connections. The involvement of village-based *byalag* groups through the rural development theme illustrates this. Workbooks were developed as a means of helping the participants to think through their local perspective on problems and options for the countryside aspects of the review of the 1991 *oversiktsplan*. The official managing this exercise saw dialogue with the inhabitants as crucially important. There is also some evidence that the attempt to link LA21 to the *oversiktsplan* had a

two-way effect. The addition of energy, industry and IT to the LA21 themes, and suggestions made to the rural development groups that they should find out more about
the views of the elderly and young people, are examples of the LA21 process being
broadened beyond its environmental foundations and towards the comprehensive
intent of the *oversiktsplan*.

Interviews undertaken in the NoordXXI project a couple of years after Malbert's
research revealed that the previous initiatives had led to general agreement on the
principle of participation and on the role place identity played in this. Those involved in
preparing the new *oversiktsplan* recognized opportunities to include issues that were
previously perceived to be separate from the land use planning process, but that had
been identified through more participatory processes. This enabled those involved to
'knit together' the LA21 and planning processes. As a result, Tidaholm could be
regarded as one of the 'pioneers' in that its LA21 Strategy takes a more comprehensive view compared to other *kommunes*' more environmental LA21 focus. Experience
of LA21 raised new possibilities for extending participation in mainstream planning in
the minds of both elected members and officials. Thus in planning the preparation of
the new *oversiktsplan*, the *kommune* went beyond its minimum statutory requirements
in an effort to transcend the limitations of previous consultative arrangements.

Engendering citizens' ownership of the process was a key aim in Tidaholm
and, in being focused on place identities, the visioning and LA21 processes played
an important role in developing this. Research undertaken as part of the NoordXXI
project thus found that these processes did contribute to a constructive dialogue
focused on problem-solving, and the preparation of the new plan, therefore, would
seem to provide an opportunity to link this cross-sectoral approach more closely to
land use. Issues identified through these earlier processes were fed into the preparation of the new plan with the LA21 strategy being an important source for the
issues report. As such, one key lesson has been that political involvement in and
ownership of the process has raised the possibility of formalizing linkages between
place identity and territorial identity. Another key lesson identified as coming out of
the LA21 process was the value of involving young people, and interviewees were
keen for this aspect to be included in the planning process in future.

The possibility of linking the development of territorial policies more closely to
place is also evident from officers' commitment to enhanced public participation in
the planning process in future. As one planning officer put it, 'to make the municipal
plan more useful you have to include people … and it must be quite specific'.
Officers had also learnt from the previous processes and highlighted the importance
of process rather than end product as a means of securing broad ownership of the
plan, thereby ensuring implementation.

The driving force behind the LA21 process in practice can be seen as the need
to get in touch with those who do not have access to channels of communication that

are open to interest groups such as the business community and non-governmental organizations. Contrary to Newman and Thornley's cases studies of 'negotiation planning', in this area of Sweden where local market forces were relatively weak, the views of business interests were initially not taken into account. However, these were incorporated later as participation gradually broadened. In retrospect, earlier involvement would possibly have engendered greater ownership and responsibility for solutions (as the following case study suggests). This has implications in terms of implementing the final vision, as does the ongoing climate of financial austerity within the council.

Tidaholm's experience shows active participation in the construction of narratives of place identity, but also that this largely occurred outside the formal planning system. It also highlights the importance of key personnel. Indeed, it could be argued that the integration of work begun under LA21 into the planning process is in part dependent upon the commitment of those officers involved, but that transition, the interface of the participatory system with territorial power, is problematic. Thus the LA21 process, and the earlier Town and Country Project, raised a number of important challenges to the *kommune*'s traditional means of operating and engaging with citizens. More specifically, such processes raised issues that had implications for the preparation of the new plan.

In being focused on place identity, such initiatives were successful in mobilizing broad participation and in spreading the sustainable development message and creating new local practices and experiences. However, broad involvement also resulted in a strategy that was difficult to implement as market forces concurrently restructured local production, services and the capacity of the state to 'deal with all the problems'.

FALKÖPING: PARTICIPATION, PLACE IDENTITY AND RURAL DEVELOPMENT

Falköping is a cameo of the pressures on rural areas all across Europe. In the heyday of small dairy farming during the nineteenth century even the poor soils above the town of Falköping were farmed. Now pine and spruce forests claim the marginal land. Small, family-run farms are amalgamating as they struggle for viability. About 700 people are employed in agriculture or closely related jobs and young people are draining away from the land. The rural population is thus fading away. The town of Falköping has some 16,000 inhabitants, and seems to be holding its own, though its image is bad: 'The most boring town in Sweden'.

Falköping Kommune, the local government unit, covers an area roughly 90 kilometres by 60 kilometres. The total population is not much over the 30,000 mark, with about 6,000 living in villages and 9,000 scattered in farmsteads. Twenty-one of the 45 parishes have populations of less than 200. Can this level of settlement, and the lifestyle and landscape that it has reproduced over 200 years, be sustained? The existence of the *kommune* testifies to the tensions between place and territory. It was formed in 1974 by merging eight smaller *kommunes*, which in turn had been established in 1952 through merging 52 parishes. However, the rural communities have a surprisingly strong set of institutions and a culture of civil society that is symbiotic with place identity. Eighty per cent of the 86 political associations or societies in the *kommune* are located in the rural areas, and there are 13 rural development groups, 10 bearing the name of their parish, which was the name of the *kommune* for that locality from 1863. In this way, the past is a key narrative in place identity, and rural development is a discourse through which struggles can be fought for that identity against territory and the exogenous rationality of market-led change.

Similarly to Tidaholm, the *kommune* of Falköping initiated a LA21 process in 1995. However, there was no precursor equivalent to Tidaholm's Town and Country Project. As a first step the *kommune* decided that it was necessary to 'to get its own house in order first' before attempting to engage the public in LA21. It was considered important that the *kommune* demonstrate leadership by addressing its contribution to meeting wider environmental aims. The *kommune* began by applying environmental criteria to its own operations, with a green purchasing project. An LA21 strategy was drawn up and adopted in the winter of 1997–8. The process was led by a special committee of 13 elected members, on which all the political parties were represented, under the umbrella of the planning committee. In addition, an officers' working group and six reference groups were set up, consisting of representatives from organizations and interested individuals. Some groups included local residents while others consisted of business interests only.

As in Tidaholm's Vision 2010 exercise, the reference groups were organized by sector (business, inhabitants, pensioners, youth, shopping, farmers, manufacturing industrialists). These groups sought to address how the *kommune* should proceed on environmental questions. The themes set by the officers' working group were: food and water; energy; transport and communications; business; bio-diversity; rural development; trade; public health; private organizations and clubs; and public education. The *kommune* had invited the reference groups to identify themes but this 'blank sheet' approach proved time-consuming, and it was concluded that elected members were ideally placed to lead discussion. The resulting LA21 Strategy was presented to the public through the hearing process. Four open meetings were organized in local areas. Rural meetings attracted a higher turnout (roughly 25) than the one in Falköping town, where fewer than 10 attended.

Although the strategy listed key goals and proposed action, there was no indication of resources to be allocated to tasks or follow-up action. No connection was made to the *oversiktsplan* or to the *kommune's* economic plan (*virksomhets-plan*), nor was there mention of monitoring to measure progress towards implementation. It was not until responsibility for the implementation of LA21 was transferred from Building and Land Use to the Economic Development Section of the *kommune's* administration that work with business interests led to environmental solutions and the opportunity for concrete results. As a result, some projects did eventually proceed and had wider impacts in changing the way in which the *kommune* consults.

One such project was 'Green Market Sweden', which sought to consult businesses on environmental issues and encourage them to operate in more environmentally sustainable ways. This involved persuading businesses of the economic benefits to be gained by investing and operating in more environmentally sensitive ways, e.g. shared waste and heating systems. Another waste management/recycling company, although not involved in LA21, was involved in a *kommune*-initiated, but informal, follow-up group to discuss a proposed recycling centre – this represented a new way of working adapted from the reference group approach used for LA21. This new way of working is also evidenced in discussions involving retailers in improvements to Falköping town centre. Through their involvement in these schemes, business interests believe that they have established a link with the *kommune*.

Concerning the relationship between these innovations in participation and the planning process, Falköping's *oversiktplan* was about ten years old, a not untypical situation. Some officials felt that the reference group technique could be adopted in the preparation of the new *oversiktplan* and offered a more dynamic, participatory approach than traditional planning methods. However, despite this claim, at the time of the research, the *kommune* had no concrete proposals for varying its traditional process for the preparation of the plan and was considering contracting the work to a planning consultant. Officers interviewed in the NoordXXI research also conceded that sometimes the *kommune*'s ideas are not the same as the people's, and that 'it can be hard trying to connect them'. Crucially, political commitment to the LA21 process was relatively weak. The political party most committed to LA21 held only a narrow majority on the council, and politicians also recognized that participatory approaches would make demands on scarce resources.

Thus in Falköping the discourse associated with LA21 was primarily about the greening of existing *kommune* policies and practices. Despite the significant pressures exerted by agricultural change and the fiscal crisis in local government on existing narratives of place identity, the LA21 process did not produce a clearly articulated place narrative through a broadly participatory process. Mechanisms to connect the LA21 outputs to the *oversiktplan* were weak, and became even more tenuous with the shifting of LA21 implementation to Economic Development and the contracting out of the *oversiktplan* review. As one officer put it, 'people don't know anything about planning … building development is not a big issue and the town plan is a technical plan, therefore land use planning is not an issue'.

The conclusion must be that in the case of Falköping, Newman and Thornley (1996) are right in arguing that the planning process is not particularly participatory, though because of the weak development pressure there is no real evidence of the kind of private sector-led 'negotiation planning' either. Development planning remained a technical and rationalistic discourse, mainly of interest to the professionals themselves. However, that is not the end of the story in Falköping. While the formal planning documents seem to largely ignore the experience of place as to make it incomprehensible, a strong place narrative is being produced and reproduced through other means that more directly confront the problems of restructuring within the countryside. It is a narrative written by 'souls on fire', people who are passionate about place, identity and participation. 'Rural development' is the discourse, and the practice is built through networks linking the Economic Development section of the *kommune*, a key institution of civil society known as the *bygdegards forening*, and market opportunities.

Central to this discourse is the recognition of alternative, ecologically friendly methods of agricultural production. Such approaches recognize the fundamental forces that are at work, the contested nature of place identity and the link to everyday life. This 'small is beautiful' philosophy infuses the *kommune's* approach to rural regeneration. According to this, rural development means working on the ground and with individuals, sustaining and reusing a traditional culture and agricultural practices to create new economic opportunities.

Community associations and other locally initiated self-help organizations have recently begun to organize around rural development issues. They often have agreed common goals and are increasingly seeking to influence the *kommune* on issues such as the quality of local roads and maintaining essential services. This process has been supported by the *kommune* through its participation in the national Rural Development Programme (1994–7). In 1999, the *kommune* organized a series of meetings around a document intended to inspire local people to prepare local rural development plans. These initiatives, therefore, sought to link directly into place identity in developing strategies to address rural development issues.

More recently, the *kommune* initiated a new pilot Rural Development Initiative. One of the first tasks of the development worker appointed to the project was to prepare a Rural Development Plan covering the *kommune* area. As part of this process, the development worker helped organize approximately 40 meetings in various settlements throughout the *kommune*. In doing so, the worker sought to establish contact with 'souls on fire' or committed activists in building local momentum. As

Box 7.3 Examples of rural development projects in and around Falköping

Sorgarden, a dairy farm that supports one family, exemplifies the revitalization of tradi-tional culture and agricultural practice. The family at the Sorgarden farm have ten cows that produce milk which is turned into cheese in their own micro-dairy on the farm. They sell some of their cheese to the big factory down the road, but increasingly they sell direct from the farm, using the views of the landscape and products with high added value to build a customer base.

The remote village of Jala is a dispersed scatter of timber houses several kilo-metres from anywhere else and within a flat, forested landscape. Jala's *bygdegards forening*, a historical institution, is a member organization with residents paying a nominal annual membership fee (about €10). The defining feature of this voluntary body is that they own the community hall in each village, and that hall can be the focus for a range of self-help activities that sustain a community and its rural culture and way of life. As part of its rural economic development strategy, the *kommune* is offer-ing villagers 150,000 kroner (more than €16,000) from a fund for rural initiatives to help fund local initiatives. The 'burning souls' active in these local associations use the money to buy materials but the villagers themselves will do the work. It is a practi-cal demonstration of the value these people attach to their community and place.

Ecology and environment are also part of the rural place narrative that contests the re-making of countryside into agri-business. In 1930, Lake Hornborgasjon was totally drained to create more land on which to grow oats for cattle feed. But plough-ing eroded the level of the land, leading to flooding. In the early 1990s the Swedish Environment Protection Agency responded to lobbying from ornithologists and ecol-ogists and restored the lake and the shoreline environment. Repairing the environmental damage and creating this nature reserve was Sweden's biggest single conservation project. Each spring thousands of cranes arrive, which in Nordic mythol-ogy are bringers of good luck. Bird watchers and tourists flock to the lake, which sees 150,000 visitors each April. As one interviewee put it, 'If you restore a lake and invest in it, you get birds, fish, tourism, but above all, the identity of the area changes. People get pride in the place.'

such, the initiative is seeking to build upon local initiative that draws extensively on place identity. Activities directed at mobilizing broad participation seem to have paid off in securing wide ownership of the resulting Rural Development Plan. Previously, many of the community associations felt that they were too small to have any influ-ence over the *kommune* and relied upon informal, political lobbying to put forward their views. Networking with other associations has resulted in a number of small settlements coming together to discuss common problems and interests. By joining forces, the associations hope to lobby for the establishment of a community board representing rural communities' wider interests.

Rural Falköping's problems begin outside the area, with the rationalizations of farming and the fiscal crisis in local government. Local communities are beginning to

recognize the scale of the challenge that confronts these places but remain optimistic that a passion for place identity can offer a viable alternative future. As one
interviewee put it,

> we face great threats but have a huge opportunity to recreate a living cultural
> landscape. The way forward is through self-help, respect for the environment,
> clean agriculture, and networks of burning souls who can be examples for oth-
> ers to follow. It means local engagement, having pride in your area and its
> culture and environment, and valuing nature and friendship.

CONCLUSION

Both these case studies from rural Sweden demonstrate the potency of local narratives of place identity, and the extent to which such narratives can be
constructed through direct action and participation. However, the relatively high
level of local activity should not blind us to the underlying structures that have pre-
cipitated the need for such actions. Global economic change is reflected in the
increasing size of farms, the jobless growth in Tidaholm's factories, the closure of
village shops, the dwindling willingness and capacity of even Swedish local government to provide the kind of public services that sustained twentieth-century
rural communities. Equally, responses like LA21 are global in their origins, albeit
they beg the need for local action. In greening procurement policies, improving
water management and working for energy efficiency the *kommunes* are making
their contribution to a global environmental agenda. What is perhaps missing is
the higher level visions which would permit these local actions to have a wider
impact.

In 1996 Newman and Thornley saw the impacts of exogenous changes on
Swedish planning as creating a situation where faltering steps towards more participatory planning had been side-stepped by powerful developers. They presented
evidence of this in relation to major development projects in Sweden's big cities.
Our case studies have focused on parts of Sweden where 'building development is
not a big issue'. Nevertheless, the evidence from both Tidaholm and Falköping is
that the production of an *oversiktplan*, notwithstanding the attempts in legislation to
broaden its scope and to encourage wider participation, has remained a largely
technical and exclusionary discourse. The concerns of this plan are territorial and
routine rather than with place identity and innovation, although there is some evidence of the beginnings of a change in attitude on the part of elected members and
officials. To this extent we agree with the diagnosis of Newman and Thornley that
while the planning system seems to provide structural opportunities for a long-term,

comprehensive and integrated approach with plenty of public participation, the realities of decision-making are different.

However, to leave it there would be to miss an important part of the story from Tidaholm and Falköping. The intensely participatory structures and practices linked to narratives of rural place identity, and the traditional civil society institutions based on old parishes, have considerable resonance as a basis for engaging residents collectively in discussions and actions about the future of their place. Practices under headings outside of the formal practices of master planning – such as the above Town and Country Project in Tidaholm, or rural development projects in Falköping – can be very fertile discourse structures for building place identity narratives. Such practices, however, are substantially located outside the mainstream territorial administration system, and depend to some extent on officials who are able to provide support on the edges of 'community' and 'kommune'.

It is the interface of such actors with territorial and economic realities that will decide to what extent these alternative place narratives can become embedded in mainstream institutions and procedures and have a longer term effect on governance structures. The LA21 process is particularly interesting in this respect. Our cases suggest that to a large extent the 'body' of routine rejected the innovatory 'implant', and that LA21 was largely driven from above to meet formal and procedural requirements. However, it would be reductionist to dismiss it so easily. LA21 processes in both case studies did confront representative democracy (and its functionaries) with a different discourse about its relationship to communities, with which they engaged, if but briefly. As such, creating narratives of place identity is a negotiated and contested process which can take time, and needs to be embedded in the realpolitik of the governance and economic systems.

CHAPTER 8

IDENTITY, SUSTAINABILITY AND SETTLEMENT PATTERNS
Cliff Hague

Urban form, spatial concepts and sustainability

This chapter looks at the relationship between urban and rural areas, and particularly the location for new urban growth, which has been a fundamental concern in urban and regional planning. Prevention of urban sprawl has been a key justification for planning. The European Spatial Development Perspective (ESDP) identified 'continuing urban sprawl' as a spatial development issue of European significance (CEC, 1999: 65). 'Control of the physical expansion of towns and cities' is described as being particularly important to sustainable development (CEC, 1999: 22). Uncontrolled growth is equated with increased levels of private transport use, increased energy consumption, more costly infrastructure and services, and negative impacts on the countryside and on the environment (CEC, 1999: 65).

The antidote to suburban spread is the 'compact city', which is the most articulated Euro-narrative of urban place. The Green Paper on the Urban Environment (CEC, 1990) was a conscious attempt to connect a European legacy of urban form with concerns for sustainable development. The contrast is with the low density, car-based North American city; so, as with the whole European integration process, geo-political identity and competition are involved. The ESDP (para. 84) stated that:

> Member States and regional authorities should pursue the concept of the 'compact city' (the city of short distances) in order to have better control over further expansion of the cities. This includes, for example, minimization of expansion within the framework of a careful locational and settlement policy, as in the suburbs and in many coastal regions.

The compact city underpins and supports polycentric development and urban networks as the key ideas on urban form in the ESDP. At the urban-region scale, the form and location of new development, and its relationship to infrastructure, to the landscape and to the existing built environment, are critical factors in redefining urban–rural relationships. However, implementation of the ESDP aspirations about sustainable development, compact cities and new urban–rural relationships through regional scale spatial planning begs major questions. What is the essence of the place narrative and how is it translated from a general concept to a specific reality? Who has the power to construct it and who challenges it? How do institutions and practices such as day-to-day development regulation, the legal system for contesting planning decisions and the structure and operation of the house building industry, influence meanings and implementation between different countries? This chapter looks at some of these issues.

Growth and integration in the regions round the North Sea is required to achieve a better spatial balance at an EU level. These regions need to maximize their potential, both to add to aggregate European competitiveness and to counter the dominance of the 'Pentagon'. However, as noted in Chapter 1, narratives of identity are likely to be both complementary and contradictory between spatial scales. Thus at an intra-regional scale, more growth may threaten the natural and cultural environment, extend commuting, increase car usage and associated emissions, create congestion and change the character and identity of settlements. As the ESDP observed, 'In many urban areas in the EU, development pressure on areas surrounding cities has become a problem' (CEC, 1999: 65).

The NoordXXI InterReg IIC project looked at how partner regions tackled the problem. While the pressures of development were broadly similar across the partner regions, the spatial concepts that have underpinned planning responses show some significant differences. History and culture, legislation, spatial planning institutions and tools, as outlined in Chapter 4, as well as the organization and delivery of new housing, all influence the actual development pattern and discourses about its acceptability. How have these complicated the progress towards competitiveness, cohesion and sustainable development?

The European Green Paper conceived of cities as 'projects for a new style of life and work' (CEC, 1990: 19). Such cities were to offer 'density and variety; the efficient, time- and energy-saving combination of social and economic functions; the chance to restore the rich architecture inherited from the past' (CEC, 1990: 19). This synthesis of tradition and innovation has appeal as a conceptual place narrative, though it is based on conviction rather than evidence (Pratt and Larkham, 1996). However, as the ESDP shows, the notion that a compact, contained and relatively high-density city is a more sustainable urban form than low-density suburban spread, has endured as a fundamental belief in European Commission thinking.

The ESDP explicitly praises the Dutch approach to the 'compact city' (CEC, 1999: 66), which has been strongly rooted in spatial planning policy in the Netherlands. The 1990s spatial policy (Ministry of Housing, Physical Planning and Environment, 1991) contained two important spatial principles: (a) the proximity principle aimed at achieving compact towns; and (b) accessibility profiles, which attempted to 'get the right business in the right place'. These principles were supported by other measures such as a restrictive parking policy, traffic calming and limiting of car access, and the redevelopment of station areas. The compact city model was at the core of this policy. Thus the national government was substantially involved in the selection of locations to take considerable amounts of new housing development, but also in the restriction of urban development in buffer zones and other open spaces. It is interesting to see that the fifth Dutch national spatial planning document (National Spatial Planning Agency, 2001) expressed some reservations about the policy pursued in the 1990s. In particular, 'the growing demand for quality' had not been completely satisfied, and key locations for intense development close to public transport (the 'A locations') 'were often less accessible than was hoped' (National Spatial Planning Agency, 2001: 10). In short, there was something of a gap between the concepts in the strategy and the form of implementation, in terms of 'funding, support and consistent enforcement' (National Spatial Planning Agency, 2001: 10).

The ESDP also noted that the UK had a strong record in brownfield urban development (CEC, 1999: 66). This approach was strengthened in the UK by the report of the Urban Task Force (1999), which advocated the compact city, and made the connection between the essentially aspatial concept of sustainable development and a discourse about place and the location of development: increased density reduces the amount of land needed for roads, open spaces and buildings. The Task Force further stated that a moderate density of 40–60 dwellings per hectare could sustain community facilities within walking distance of homes, while also supporting an efficient bus service, and so providing an alternative to the car.

It is argued that a dispersed urban form results in more and longer car journeys that contribute to pollution levels generally, CO_2 emissions and global warming. Such views shaped UK planning policy guidance from central government (Department of the Environment and Department of Transport, 1994; Scottish Office Development Department, 1999) – brownfield sites had to be prioritized for new housing development, and the location of new housing needed to be integrated with transport. These policy statements drew on the ECOTEC (1993) study, calling for higher urban densities in general and for exceptionally high densities around public transport nodes. Though planning guidance did not expressly refer to the 'compact city', the overall effect of its policies was to promote stronger urban containment (Breheny, 1996).

In the UK, as noted in Chapter 4, local government is viewed primarily as a deliverer of services consistent with policies set by central government. This makes national planning guidance a key influence on local spatial planning practice. As well as the guidance on transport, NPPG3 on Housing (Scottish Office Development Department, 1996) was especially important at the time of our study when considering development around and beyond the edge of the city. It required planning authorities to give priority to the reuse of brownfield land. Where greenfield locations have to be allocated for housing development, NPPG3 says that regard should be given to energy conservation and efficiency. Such greenfield sites should either be adjacent to existing settlements without affecting their environment and amenity adversely, or they should be in new settlements that can be served by pub-lic transport. NPPG3 reasserted some traditional aims of planning policy as contributing to sustainable development. Thus plans should seek to prevent the coalescence of settlements and ribbon development, safeguard green belts and protect prime agriculture land from development.

The technical discourses and planning policies on the compact city as a step towards sustainable development – such as those identified above in the Green Paper on the urban environment, the ESDP, the Netherlands and the UK – have tended to focus on the land use–transport relation as a means to environmental sus-tainability. Spatial organization has been seen as conducive to reduction of the need to travel, and to maximizing public transport's share of overall travel (modal shift). However, Frey (1999: 33) found that many of the claims in support of centralized and decentralized cities are not substantiated, and that there is no unimpaired evi-dence that one or the other city model would have any significantly higher or lower energy consumption.

Hague and Storey (2001a) reviewed a range of literature on settlement pat-terns, settlement size, settlement form and density, concentrating in each case on the relationship to travel and energy efficiency. This revealed, for example, that there is no simple relationship between urban size and travel demand (Owens, 1986; Bozeat, Barret and Jones, 1992). Nor is density the only factor that influences car use – in urban areas access to a car largely reflects levels of incomes and fuel prices. Banister (1992) questioned the validity of the notion of self-containment, and suggested that in a car-based society a series of small free-standing towns in close proximity to each other would probably be the most efficient form. The main argu-ments for and against the compact city can be found in Frey (1999: 24–5). Thomas and Cousins (1996: 56) summarized the benefits that are cited for the compact city, as follows:

> less car dependency, low emissions, reduced energy consumption, better public transportation services, increased overall accessibility, the re-use of infrastruc-ture and previously developed land, the rejuvenation of existing urban areas and urban vitality, a high quality of life, the preservation of green space and a milieu for enhanced business and trading activities.

The conceptual place narrative of the compact city is also contested by the every-day practice of civil society. For example, van der Aa and Huigen (2000b: 10), say of the Netherlands: 'The government has tried numerous measures to get people out of their cars and onto the trains. ... However, the number of cars is still increasing.' Given that much of the evidence is inconclusive, we must infer that the policy pre-scriptions in favour of compact, contained cities are rooted as strongly in values as in science. The compact city is a conceptual place narrative developed by planners, politicians and environmentalists, that counters the narrative of the consumerist, car-based low-density city. It is partial for cohesion, since it looks to shared spaces and facilities. However, the car-based place narrative is strongly embedded in everyday practice in northern Europe, and powerfully promoted through the global motor industry and Hollywood.

This conclusion points to some fundamental questions about the impact of pro-public transport policies on competitiveness. If such policies succeed in freeing road space for commercial vehicles, then presumably competitiveness is increased. However, if the form of the policy is simply 'anti-road', then there is likely to be a negative impact on place competitiveness. This is because the increased use of fast modes of transport as opposed to slower bulk modes (such as rail freight) is linked to current business practice, the 'just-in-time' approach, which relies on quick delivery from production plants rather than on storage. This business approach is increasingly reliant on fast, congestion-free transport.

GREEN BELTS

The green belt has been the strategic planning concept most directly connecting urban form not only with a compact city, but also with maintaining place identity. It is the most important policy for the urban fringe and to define the urban–rural relationship. For example, Scottish national planning guidance (Scottish Office Development Department, 1996) saw green belts as means to:

•   maintain the identity of towns by establishing a clear definition of their physical boundaries;
•   provide countryside for recreation or institutional purposes of various kinds; and
•   maintain the landscape setting of towns.

Elson (1999: 156) called green belts 'an icon of planning culture'. Planners have sought to maintain a clear visual distinction between town and country. Opposition to ribbon development, and a belief that the town should be the antithesis of the countryside, underpinned the foundations of the British planning system from the 1940s onwards. The green belt is often counterposed to urban sprawl, and so equated with the compact city, though a compact city is not necessarily a contained city. The Royal Town Planning Institute (2000) suggested that 'the search for more sustainable patterns of development' required some reconsideration of green belts. In terms of place identity and sustainable development, the questions to be set against the green belt are:

- Does the green belt, through preventing the coalescence of settlements, actually help define and maintain place identity?
- Is this achieved at the expense of other aspects of sustainable development, e.g. increased travel distances or social inequity?
- Is the green belt related to competitiveness, and in particular to structural change in agriculture and in urban development?

While the general literature on identity discussed in Chapter 1 (e.g. Rose, 1995) recognized the important link between boundaries and identity, no research appears to have been done on the extent to which place identity depends on towns being freestanding. How crucial is it to a sense of place identity that the identity is strongly defined at the level of the settlement, as distinct to the neighbourhood or the conurbation/region, for example? The answer is that we do not know, though research within the NoordXXI project found that Scottish house-builders felt that coalescence of settlements did not adversely affect the marketability of houses in them.

Hall et al. (1973) made the important point that unless there was decentralization of employment, a green belt would tend to increase travel to work distance. This study instigated a debate about the social equity aspects of urban containment. Hall and his colleagues argued that the restriction of supply of development land at the edge of the urban area increased land prices and housing densities, thereby benefiting landowners and disadvantaging those at the lower end of the housing market. A substantial literature has developed on the impact of planning controls on house and land prices. This puts particular emphasis on the impact of restrictive planning policies in areas of high demand for housing, e.g. Evans (1987, 1991, 1996), Bramley, Bartlett and Lambert (1995); Bramley and Watkins (1996). There is, however, still some dispute regarding the magnitude of the effects of land supply constraint on new house prices and densities (School of Planning and Housing/Department of Building Engineering and Surveying, Heriot-Watt University, 2001).

There is also a question about the impact of green belt policies on labour markets, competitiveness and hence economic sustainability. Undersupply of land for housing can be relevant both to macro-economic concerns about inflation and to regional economic development efforts. Similarly, there is evidence that the demand for industrial and commercial properties, an essential basis for business competitiveness, has been shifting towards lower density units in prestige landscape settings with good access to a road network and plenty of employee parking (see e.g. Ratcliffe and Stubbs, 1996). These trends seem to be especially marked for new growth industries and those involved in research and innovation, the kind of firms that are seen as drivers of competitive regional economies. Such practices will contest place narratives based on green belts.

Nor should we ignore the restructuring of agriculture. The green belt idea was formulated in an age when a high priority was attached to domestic food production, and when the countryside was equated with agriculture. Farmland adjacent to urban areas is notoriously difficult to farm efficiently, because of issues such as trespass. However, at the start of the twenty-first century there is pressure to remove the protection that agriculture has enjoyed through the EU's common agricultural policy. Thus the agricultural sustainability case for green belt protection is now tenuous, and the application of global competitiveness criteria to agriculture contradicts green belt policy.

In summary, there is a strong policy consensus at European and national level in the UK and in the Netherlands in favour of urban containment and compact cities, as means to achieve sustainable development. The aim is to prevent urban sprawl and settlement coalescence. A green belt is seen as an effective and acceptable way to do this. However, there is less clarity about what should be the structure of settlements and the pattern of new developments in the region around the city, other than to avoid low-density dispersal, and to protect landscape. Research evidence on the virtues of compact settlements is not decisive: density is not the sole influence on travel patterns; location of employment matters. Restrictive planning regimes are also likely to push up land prices, an effect which benefits landowners but can lead to shortages of affordable housing for lower income groups, thus raising issues of social justice. The contained and compact city encircled, as in the past, by its pastoral green belt is a potent image of place identity, but what relation does it bear to reality and to other narratives of place identity? We now turn to our case studies, which we use to show how major place narratives have been constructed through planning practice in different contexts.

ABERDEEN: POLYCENTRIC GROWTH AND NEW URBAN–RURAL RELATIONS

Aberdeen is the third largest city in Scotland, with a population of around 217,000. Since the 1970s, development in and around the city has been dominated by the need to manage growth triggered by the discovery of North Sea oil. Recurrent booms and slumps and balance of payments crises in the 1960s and early 1970s meant that UK governments attached national priority to expeditious exploitation of these offshore reserves. The oil crises of 1973–4 and 1978–9 increased the pressure from oil companies and the UK to reap the benefits of North Sea oil. Aberdeen became the onshore base for the organization of the industry. Because of the international nature of the oil industry, there has been considerable in-migration. In some senses then the situation triggered by oil-led growth in the region around Aberdeen in and after the

1970s anticipated the themes and challenges of European spatial planning a generation later. There was the need to ensure global competitiveness, while securing
economic, social and territorial cohesion. The environment had to be conserved in the
face of the threats posed by oil and its related onshore developments. The city of
Aberdeen became, along with Stavangar in Norway, 'gateway cities' for the oil industry that were of continental significance, locked into global networks that primarily
focused on Houston, Texas. This growth was on Europe's periphery, not in the 'Blue
Banana', and could be read as a precursor for a polycentric development of the
European territory. So how did planning practice respond to the global pressures that
were so dramatically changing the place identity of this traditional Scottish town and
its rural hinterland?

The strategic planning response, led from 1975 until 1996 by Grampian
Regional Council, and continued thereafter by the two unitary councils jointly
charged with producing a structure plan for the area, has been to absorb as much
growth as possible within the city of Aberdeen itself. Policy has sought to be consistent with national guidance from central government, which exercised control
through powers to require alterations to structure plans and through call-in and/or
appeal decisions on planning applications. The spread of the city has been constrained by a green belt. The objectives of the long established green belt policy are:

*   to maintain the identity of Aberdeen and surrounding urban areas by clearly
     defining their boundaries and preventing coalescence;
*   to maintain the landscape setting of the city; and
*   to provide countryside for recreational purposes (Aberdeen City Council and
     Aberdeenshire Council, 2001).

The green belt is seen as successful. It has prevented 'unnecessary sprawl'
(Aberdeen City Council and Aberdeenshire Council, 2001: 50), although the city's
built-up area expanded by 16 per cent between 1975 and 1998 (Aberdeen City
Council, 1998: 3). Limited land availability within the green belt meant that most
new housing was deflected to towns and villages beyond the green belt. The population in the travel to work area (about a 25 km radius from Aberdeen) more than
doubled since 1971. Table 8.1 shows the scale of population and household
change in Aberdeen and in the pre-1996 district council areas of Gordon and
Kincardine and Deeside, which adjoined the city.

The strategy sought to direct housing development to settlements within corridors served by public transport links into Aberdeen, but it would be misleading to call
this a growth corridor approach. Prevention of coalition of settlements has been a key
and consistent aim in Scottish national planning guidance. Similarly there has been a
strong policy seeking to locate new development as a physically contiguous extension of an existing settlement or as infill on available sites within existing settlements.

Table 8.1 Population and household change in and around Aberdeen 1981–94

	Aberdeen City	Gordon District	Kincardine & Deeside District
Population 1981	202,190	63,184	41,891
Population 1994	212,645	79,471	55,958
Average per annum % change	0.4	2.0	2.6
Households 1981	79,486	22,248	15,047
Households 1994	94,965	30,050	21,036
Average per annum % change	1.5	2.7	3.1

Source: Grampian Regional Council, 1995

Ribbon development and sporadic development in the countryside have been seen as the antithesis of good planning.

Although the peak of the oil boom has passed, there will be a continuing need to plan for household growth in Aberdeenshire, the post-1996 authority that includes Gordon and Kincardine and Deeside. The structure plan area forecasts predicted an increase of 23,563 households in the Aberdeen and Aberdeenshire area between 1998 and 2016, with two-thirds of this increase going to Aberdeenshire (Aberdeen City Council and Aberdeenshire Council, 1999: 79). There are signs that concepts of sustainable development and compact cities are having an effect, with a renewed emphasis on development within the city, particularly on brownfield sites. The role of the green belt has been reasserted to this end. It is a component of the strategy of 'focusing development into settlements and encouraging the redevelopment of brownfield sites and thus ... particularly ... protecting ... the natural environment and reducing the need to travel' (Aberdeen City Council and Aberdeenshire Council, 2001: 50). To a large extent the mechanism to deliver the reuse of brownfield sites and a compact city has been what is termed 'windfall', that is sites not actually identified in the statutory development plan for housing use. In effect, planning policy has squeezed the market and allowed differential land values to trigger changes of use.

The 1997 Grampian Structure Plan and the 1998 Aberdeen Local Plan both identified sustainable development as a key principle. In both cases sustainable development was interpreted primarily as 'that which maintains or improves the quality of life whilst conserving the environment for future generations' (Grampian Regional Council, 1997: 12). The 1998 Local Plan also quoted the understanding of sustainable development in the City Council's Corporate Development Strategy. This was less narrowly environmental in its emphasis, and included 'to seek to ensure economic prosperity ... tackle inequalities and widen opportunity and be based on a partnership involving all sectors of the community ...' (Aberdeen City Council, 1998: 2). The written report of the latest structure plan, *North East Scotland Together*, is also 'firmly based on the concept of sustainability' (Aberdeen City Council and Aberdeenshire Council, 2001: 7).

In summary, spatial planning has responded to pressure for global competitiveness, in the form of major oil-related housing growth, through a policy of absorbing some development within the city confined by its green belt, but mainly directing growth to smaller free-standing settlements in or beyond the green belt. The place narrative has been couched increasingly in terms of sustainable development and a compact city, though the basis of the policy is rooted in a traditional set of planning ideas equating place identity with the landscape setting of Aberdeen and non-coalescence of settlements. How have others reacted to the way that the 'space of flows' superseded the 'space of places' (Castells, 1989) and to the place narrative of spatial planning?

Implementation of this strategy changed the identity of the towns receiving major increments of new housing. It could scarcely have been otherwise given the scale of the changes. House-builders and the everyday practice of home-seeking in-migrants fashioned dormitory towns, whose visual character became that of modern suburbia. Most of the jobs are in Aberdeen while most of the new housing has been built some distance away across the green belt. The spatial strategy has necessitated commuting. Portlethen, about 10 km out of Aberdeen on the main road south, is a good example. This suburban settlement expanded rapidly during the 1980s and 1990s. Between 1991 and 1998 there was an 18 per cent increase in units of housing stock in the town. It is a dormitory town, with over 64 per cent of residents commuting to Aberdeen at the time of the 1991 census. Notwithstanding the railway connection, there is a lot of car-based commuting from here into Aberdeen. Portlethen is protected by green belt to the north and south, and has developed between the main arterial routes of the railway line and the A90 dual carriageway road from Aberdeen to the South. A further 400 houses were planned in the latest structure plan. A major out-of-town retailing development adjacent to the A90 improved shopping facilities in Portlethen and for other places in the southern corridor. However, the visual effect created a sense that Aberdeen, and its urban character, now began some 10–15 km to the south.

Some are critical of the extent to which the quantity and quality of new housing developed in settlements outside Aberdeen has undermined traditional place identity. For example, a member of the Mearns Community Council said that the town of Laurencekirk had been 'polluted' with too much new housing. He argued for more scattered, small-scale development within or joined to existing villages/towns. Similarly a community councillor in Ellon said that new housing was 'By far the biggest issue which has been consistently on the agenda over the past

20 years. There's always been pressure for new housing and Ellon Community Council has fought to maintain the character of Ellon throughout.' However, the community councillor noted that there was not unanimity within the 'community': 'There are basically two camps – "local" locals who resist any changes, and others who accept that housing has to go somewhere.' In both these examples there is some equation of identity with authenticity, both of the town (before 'pollution') and of long-term inhabitants ('local' locals). The distinction between indigenous residents and newcomers suggests that the dispersal of housing to small towns has not been entirely successful in terms of social cohesion.

An official in the economic development agency, Grampian Enterprise, observed that 'Housing is dominated by middle market "boxes"'. However, house-builders argued that house types reflect what people want and are prepared to buy, and that the market itself regulates the scale of new developments: 'We can't build huge developments in small towns anyway, because you can't sell them unless it's over a number of years.' In effect the builders argue that place identity reflects market demand and structures, and the everyday choices of households. They equate brownfield housing sites in Aberdeen with flats, so that the shortage of greenfield sites in the city means that families seeking conventional houses are excluded and forced to commute from the towns in and beyond the green belt.

The house-builders were essentially pragmatic about the spatial aspects of land allocation; their main concern was that the planning system releases insufficient land in aggregate. However, they were unhappy with the green belt, and felt that a better planning policy would be to allocate a large area for new development, then reserve part of it for a park, since 'People use parks; they don't use green belt'. Another housing developer said, 'The countryside is *not* for urbanites' recreation. It's where people make a living. I don't believe that the green belt is successful in maintaining the city's landscape setting either, because land has been released from it anyway'. Pressure builds until green belt land is eventually released at a planning appeal. 'Aberdeenshire and Aberdeen City Council simply don't allocate enough land for housing. I would say that no major housing development has been granted over the past number of years apart from by appeal.' Negotiation on applications, appeals, objections to the 'effectiveness' of sites in the annual housing land audit, and speculative purchase of options on sites with latent development potential are key means used by house-builders to translate their place narrative into reality.

Grampian Enterprise has a place narrative that is primarily about the competitive region. From this perspective the green belt unnecessarily constrains the supply of industrial land. 'It really functions more as a green "collar" than as a green belt. Green "rope" or "wedges" would perhaps be better', said one of the house-builders. The rationale for the green belt was felt to be primarily cosmetic, whereas a spatial policy concerned with reducing commuting distances would be prepared to countenance more development in the green belt. One of the key objectives of the new structure plan was to provide the opportunity for people to live close to their work. Objective 4 sought 'To locate homes, jobs, and services in scale with each other and with the role and function of each settlement' (Aberdeen City Council and Aberdeenshire Council, 2001: 10). A Grampian Enterprise official noted some of the political tensions and practicalities involved: 'There's an ongoing conflicting debate between City and Shire. The Shire wants small-town development, but the structure plan has not set up enough brownfield sites for development. There are small pockets of industrial land, but not enough sites of suitable size and quality.'

Thus a new urban–rural relationship has developed around Aberdeen over the last 30 years. It is polycentric in residential terms but still relatively mono-centric in employment terms and in respect of the shopping hierarchy. However, only 36,000 people work in Aberdeen city centre (Aberdeen City Council, 1998: 110) out of a total workforce of just over 150,000 (Aberdeen City Council 1998: 91). Car-based commuting and traffic congestion have been unintended outcomes that the latest plans are trying to address. Table 8.2 summarizes the place narratives involved.

EAST LOTHIAN: PROTECTING EDINBURGH'S PLACE IDENTITY

East Lothian has also been an area under pressure for new housing and has additionally seen relatively little dispersal of employment or retailing. There are important similarities with our first case study – in particular the national planning context, and a general growth context on Europe's periphery – but there are also some significant differences, mainly concerned with the relationships between local authorities. Whereas Aberdeenshire is the only council sharing a border with the City of Aberdeen, East Lothian is one of three councils that surround the City of Edinburgh on its landward side. East Lothian covers a much smaller area than Aberdeenshire, and virtually the whole of that area is within commuting distance of Edinburgh. Between 1975 and 1996 Lothian Regional Council was responsible for structure planning. Edinburgh dominated that council to a much greater extent than did Aberdeen in the Grampian Regional Council. Edinburgh's influence was exercised through its relative size and consequent numerical representation, but in less tangible ways as well. These derived from its capital city status and social, economic and political dominance in the region. The mental maps of Edinburgh as a place apart have been means to reproduce this status through spatial planning.

In 1995–6 East Lothian experienced the largest percentage increase in population from in-migration of all the Scottish local authorities. This reflected the general economic strength of Edinburgh, a city whose economic base is in services, and

Table 8.2 Place narratives about development in and around Aberdeen

What?	Who?	Where/how?
Maintain the identity of Aberdeen (and other settlements) by protecting its landscape setting through a green belt, defining a clear urban/rural boundary, and avoiding sprawl and settlement coalescence. Aberdeen can be a compact city. Free-standing towns in transport corridors in Aberdeenshire can be sustained by new housing, creating a polycentric growth pattern and a new urban–rural relationship that constitutes sustainable development.	Spatial planners in central government, former regional council and post-1996 unitary councils, and their politicians (though there may be shire/city and political tensions on some aspects).	National planning guidance, structure plans, implemented through local plans and development control. Restriction of supply of land in Aberdeen encourages developers to reuse brownfield sites.
Aberdeen and Aberdeenshire should be places where people can live in the houses and locations of their choice. For many this would mean a family house on greenfield land near the edge of the city.	House-builders and their customers. Builders are also competing with each other.	Challenge planning policies through applications, appeals, objections; contest amount, effectiveness and marketability of sites. Market properties to customers. Acquire options to buy land if planning permission can be secured.
Aberdeen and Aberdeenshire should be a competitive region offering good opportunities for business.	Grampian Enterprise, but support also from councils.	Site identification and marketing to business. Promotional materials. Consultation with planners.
The character and identity of the towns should be protected and enhanced.	Community councils with support from planners, politicians and Grampian Enterprise.	Response to consultations on plans and planning applications. Local initiatives.

especially financial services, economic sectors that have prospered with globaliza-tion and European integration. 'East Lothian's continuing growth reflects its contribution to the Edinburgh housing market, the impact of changing household structures and the area's considerable attractiveness as a place to live' (The City of Edinburgh Council, East Lothian Council, Midlothian Council and West Lothian Council, 2000, para. 42). East Lothian's population rose from nearly 79,000 in 1981 to approximately 88,000 in 1996, an 11 per cent increase. Estimates are that it will rise to 91,500 by the year 2006 (East Lothian Council, 1998). East Lothian has plenty to offer house-buyers: 'Quality of life, value for money in housing, schools, the coastline, and it's on the main road south', as a member of the local enterprise company observed. 'East Lothian has a housing market all of its own – the English love it', said the marketing manager of a major house-builder. Other characteriza-tions by house-builders in our focus group were 'commutable', 'accessible', 'cheaper than Edinburgh', while one gave it the epithet of 'a dormitory, and a geriatric rest home in certain parts'.

Sub-regional differences within East Lothian have significantly affected its planning and identity. The western area comprises urbanized, former mining settle-ments. This area is closest to Edinburgh, though green belt policy has sought to avoid coalescence. It is accessible by road, and there are stations for commuter trains. In the Lothian Structure Plan that was approved in 1997 (East Lothian Council, City of Edinburgh Council, Midlothian Council and West Lothian Council, 1997: 79–80), these places are 'the west sector of East Lothian', 'a marketable area (that) will relieve pressures on more environmentally sensitive areas'.

In contrast, the eastern part remains a landscape of prosperous estates hid-den behind high stone walls, of farm 'steadings' (outbuildings – often now converted for housing), pantiled cottages and mature shelter belts. Haddington is the traditional market town of this neat county. 'Many of these towns and villages are renowned for their historic and architectural interest, and this makes them attractive places to live in and to visit' (East Lothian Council, 1998: 4). This description covers not just the inland settlements but also the string of villages along the coast, where there are also important nature conservation constraints. A resident of one of the vil-lages, interviewed in this research, confidently defined the identity of her village as 'rural', and argued that to protect that identity any new development needed to be small scale and incremental. The structure plan saw the eastern part of East Lothian as one of three 'main areas of restraint' (East Lothian Council, City of Edinburgh Council, Midlothian Council and West Lothian Council, 1997: 89). Thus spatial planning has sought to conserve a place identity defined by history and architecture, whereas the historic identity of the former mining settlements has given way to the pragmatic sobriquet of 'a marketable area'. These place narratives of practice have even been characterized in a recent top-selling detective novel:

He drove out of Edinburgh along the A1. Traffic was light, the sun low and
bright. East Lothian to him meant golf links and rocky beaches, flat farming land
and commuter towns, fiercely protective of their own identities. The area had its
share of secrets – caravan parks where Glasgow criminals came to hide – but it
was essentially a calm place, a destination for day-trippers, or somewhere you
might detour through on the route south to England. Towns such as Haddington,
Gullane and North Berwick always seemed to him reserved, prosperous
enclaves, their small shops supported by local communities which looked
askance at the retail-park culture of the nearby capital. Yet Edinburgh was
exerting its influence: house prices in the city were forcing more people further
out, while the green belt found itself eroded by housing and the main arteries
into town from the south and east, and over the past ten years or so he'd
noticed the increase of rush-hour traffic, the slow, pitiless convoy of commuters
(Rankin, 2001: 52–3).

A continuous green belt around Edinburgh was established in 1957 (see Figure
8.1). It has been a principal part of planning policy ever since, and has significantly
structured planning practice in East Lothian. It has three purposes:

- to maintain the identity of the city and its neighbouring towns by clearly establishing their physical boundaries and preventing coalescence;
- to protect the countryside for recreation and institutional purposes;
- to maintain the landscape setting of the city and neighbouring towns.

The consistent priority has been to protect the landscape setting of Edinburgh, and
through that, its identity as a distinctive, self-contained city. The implications of such
separation for social and territorial cohesion between the capital and its landward
neighbours have not been addressed. New housing has been developed in East
Lothian while jobs and retail development have stayed in Edinburgh. The potential
for development alongside the dual carriageway main A1 road which links East
Lothian and points south to the Edinburgh by-pass is negated by the green belt and
other restrictive national planning policies. A senior East Lothian planner noted that
local politicians 'feel that the green belt policy is to the benefit of Edinburgh but to
the dis-benefit of East Lothian.'

Green belt policy has also restricted residential development opportunities on
some of the more attractive sites adjacent to, and on the Edinburgh side of, the former mining towns. If steering new housing to such towns is a means of creating a
new identity and attracting new investment, then it seems logical that more land
release there, allowing more housing closer to Edinburgh, would enhance regeneration. Such releases would also make it easier to defend a very restrictive policy in
the east of East Lothian. An appraisal of the existing green belt against the aims of

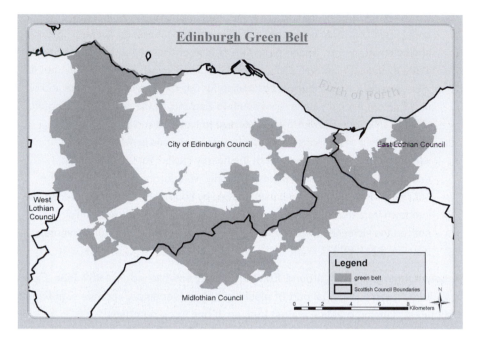

Figure 8.1   Map of the Edinburgh Green Belt

sustainable transport and social justice would yield different results than an approach that primarily concentrates on visual aspects of identity. That said, not all the Edinburgh green belt is of outstanding visual quality. It has been cut through by major roads and is home to some uses such as used-car yards that pre-date the planning system.

The place narratives of the spatial planners have been coherent – free-standing compact capital city; green belt; marketable areas for housing in East Lothian's western sector; conservation of villages and landscapes in the east – but they have been contested. Development plans have proved effective, albeit technical and rationalistic, discourses for this narrative of place identity. House-builders have argued for more substantial land releases and have fought long public inquiries in pursuit of planning permissions. In the 1990s the situation was particularly fraught because the structure plan had become seriously outdated. Preparation to replace the 1986 plan began in 1991, but approval only happened in 1997.

Once the Consultative Draft Lothian Structure Plan was produced in 1993, East Lothian District Council prepared an authority-wide local plan that was consistent with the draft structure plan. However, central government delayed amending and approving the structure plan. This left the draft local plan in limbo, so that it could not be finalized and placed on deposit until 1998, when it immediately attracted a flood of objections over issues of housing land. A local plan inquiry, which also took in nine conjoined planning appeals, ran from November 1998 until June 1999, picking through the detailed disagreements about the meaning of policies in the structure plan, and about windfall and effective sites. The Reporter's recommendations appeared in February 2000. The structure plan saw provision of land for housing as only one of its objectives, and not an overriding concern. It sought to achieve a more sustainable development pattern, and to protect and enhance the environment, including the green belt and the amenity of towns and villages. Such ambiguity about priorities amongst different policies is likely to lead to conflicts fought out at planning inquiries, especially as house-builders are more single-minded in their concerns.

The Lothian Structure Plan implicitly had seen rising land and house prices as a cost worth paying in return for protecting most of the green belt, and the general environmental quality of areas such as the villages of East Lothian. In the ten years to July 1997, prices for greenfield land in Edinburgh increased by 247 per cent to over £430,000 per acre. In East Lothian the rate of increase was even higher – 453 per cent from 1987 to 1995, to £212,000 per acre (Walker Group evidence to the local plan inquiry). As a number of our interviewees recognized, high and escalating prices create particular problems for households with young children, for whom extra housing space may only be attainable if there is inheritance or two wages coming in.

Central government's decisive support for the green belt was reflected in its decisions on structure plans, planning applications and appeals. A house-builder at the focus group said: 'The problem in respect of the green belt may be more with the Scottish Executive than with East Lothian Council planners.' Another house-builder added:

> Edinburgh is famed for its landscape setting – nobody rational would deny that
> there should be some control; but green*field* must be distinguished from green
> *belt*. For example, there are ample opportunities for development around
> Musselburgh, which would not compromise the setting of the city at all. Few of
> the original green belt principles are still valid.

In the NoordXXI project a workshop was held in which one exercise asked the professional planners from the partner regions present to allocate a set amount of new housing development in East Lothian against defined criteria. Those looking to stress sustainable development favoured sites close to Edinburgh even though such sites lay in the green belt. This suggests that there are grounds for questioning the equation of green belt with sustainable development. Similarly, a house-builder at the focus group said, 'The green belt is in fact the most sustainable location for new housing. This is because it's the most accessible location in terms of access to work. The only good reason for now preserving the green belt is to maintain the landscape setting of the city.'

Thus structure planning has prioritized the reproduction of Edinburgh as a free-standing capital city set in a landscape demarcated by a green belt. This has commanded popular support from civil society in Edinburgh, and in particular from an active and vocal grouping of amenity organizations. Similarly there has been a political consensus in the city on retention of this imagery, though that has not prevented substantial edge of city development of business and retail parks in the 1990s, often on land owned by the city council. One result was political tensions between the Edinburgh authority and those adjoining authorities – East Lothian, West Lothian and Midlothian – over development around the city's fringes. Non-coalescence and the green belt have defined these places as 'others' in terms of Edinburgh's identity, and this was one reason why Lothian Regional Council proved to be a fragile territorial unit, whose demise in 1996 was not mourned outside of Edinburgh.

In respect of East Lothian itself, planning practice has reproduced the 'rural/village' place narrative of the pre-1975 county council with respect to the east of the area. However, in the west, the previous narrative of place identity as a set of mining communities has been significantly changed, by a combination of the closure of the mining industry (other than some open-cast activity) and the growth in its stead of house-building and commuting. The loss of the identity that mining once provided is likely to be sensed by some residents in these towns, and some institutions from that earlier era are still visible in the townscapes – e.g. the social clubs and the co-operative stores. However, faced with major economic restructuring of traditional forms of production, planning has been more able to reproduce the place identity of agriculture and the countryside than that of urban mining communities. Table 8.3 summarizes the place identities in East Lothian.

THE GRONINGEN-WEST BORDER ZONE: DESIGNING AN AUTHENTIC PLACE IDENTITY

What have been the spatial planning place narratives about urban–rural relations in the Netherlands and how have they been constructed and contested? As is often the case in international projects, it was not possible in NoordXXI to make a direct and systematic comparison. Groningen is in one of the less economically successful regions of the Netherlands. Growth pressures have not been as strong as those around Edinburgh and Aberdeen. This relative absence of international development pressures must have given more prominence to local planners and designers to create their own place narratives. Equally important are the institutional differences and the comparison in the spatial planning concepts and methods that shape decisions about where to locate new development and what form the development should take.

Table 8.3 Place narratives about development in East Lothian

What?	Who?	Where/how?
Maintain the identity of Edinburgh (and other settlements) by protecting its landscape setting through a green belt, defining a clear urban/rural boundary, and avoiding sprawl and settlement coalescence. Reuse brownfield land within Edinburgh.	Spatial planners in central government, former regional council and successive Edinburgh councils, and their politicians. Strong Edinburgh amenity lobby.	National planning guidance, structure plans, implemented through local plans and development control. Restriction of supply of land in Edinburgh encourages developers to reuse brownfield sites.
Regeneration of former mining settlements in west of East Lothian, while avoiding their coalescence or strip development along the A1.	East Lothian Council (officers and members), supported by structure plan authorities, house-builders and their customers. However, some East Lothian councillors would want more economic development sites.	Structure plan, local plan and development control, backed by national planning guidance.
Conservation of the rural landscape and settlement identity in eastern sector.	East Lothian Council (officers and members), supported by structure plan authorities, and community councils.	Structure plan, local plan and development control, supported by central government guidance and advice notes.
East Lothian should be a place where people can live in the houses and locations of their choice. For many this would mean a family house on greenfield land near the edge of the city or in one of the villages.	House-builders and their customers.	Challenge planning policies through applications, appeals, objections; contest amount, effectiveness and marketability of sites. Market properties to customers. Acquire options to buy land if planning permission can be secured.

The population of Groningen province only increased by 0.7 per cent between 1980 and 1999. However, issues about the expansion of the city of Groningen emerged in the extensive public consultation that the province undertook in the preparation of the Provincial Plan for the Environs (POP plan), described in Chapter 6. The process of preparing the plan led to a focus on a number of key concerns about the urban–rural relationship. These centred on the balance to be struck between economic growth and preservation of the quality of the physical environment. The landscape and environment should be protected as characteristic of the area's identity. New house-building should be regulated to maintain open spaces and respect the style and character of villages. Organic farming was favoured, as well as some diversification into targeted, high-quality tourism, along with opportunities for small-scale business in the rural areas. Thus Groningen should not try to be like the Randstad. It should compete using its own strengths – space, tranquillity, clean air, and job opportunities. There was also support for aspects of the compact city idea, including restrictions on car use within the city and concentration of development.

The fifth national spatial planning report (National Spatial Planning Agency, 2001) was produced through an intensive consultation process with the Dutch regions, and endorses the ideas in 'Compass for the North' about the North of the Netherlands as a mainly rural area of tranquillity, space and nature. It argues that in this area there will be no significant change in the relationship between the city and the countryside: 'It is important to combine living and working in the urban areas and to keep the rural areas between cities open. That means that a demand for primarily inner city and green urban living/working environments will have to be met' (National Spatial Planning Agency, 2001: 38). The identity of the area is very much defined in terms of its landscape conservation areas.

In summary, the responses of local people and of central government showed a strong commitment to the environmental quality of the province, while also recognizing the need for change and new development. As in Scotland, landscape protection and place identity were seen as important. However, there was nothing like the same adversarial relationship with house-builders – in fact dispersed communities competed for new housing allocations to underpin strengthening of local services in direct contrast to the local antagonism to in-migration and resulting dormitory status expressed in Scotland. Following the consultation, a draft POP plan was produced in June 2000, which defined the main spatial policy aims for the province as the development of strong towns and a healthy countryside, and the conservation and further restoration of the regional identity of the Groningen landscape.

In the light of the POP and the NoordXXI project, a project was contracted to planning consultants in May 2000 by the province of Groningen regional authority. The brief was to produce proposals for the development of the town, the countryside and the aquatic system for a zone running some 10–15 km from the western fringe of the city of Groningen. The area included four small towns, while the remainder was sparsely populated with a few villages. Dairy farming was the main land-use. The consultants immediately made it clear that the key priorities were seen to be to 'protect and strengthen ecological, landscape and recreational qualities' (Kuiper Compagnons, 2000: 2).

The consultants' report gave considerable emphasis to the cultural landscape and history of the area, beginning with the formation of the landscape 7,000 years ago. The report stressed and described village identity, before discussing soils and hydrology, and then landscape and ecology. Description, analysis and design of these 'authentic' qualities of the area were the means to construct the place narrative. It was argued that until the 1950s, development to the west of Groningen was gradual, and its cultural heritage was clearly visible in the countryside (dikes, canals, railways, roads, reclaimed land). The countryside is now changing dramatically as a result of economic growth and related spatial claims. This relatively empty area was depicted as threatened by change in the form of the advancing western fringe of the town, the growth of businesses, expansion of the road network, other infrastructural activities, and the need for land for all sorts of activities on the edge of town.

The consultants then developed their analysis into a first draft strategy. The theme they took to conceptualize the design was 'embracing the emptiness': 'the characteristic emptiness will be cherished' (Kuiper Compagnons, 2000: 14). The aims included: a clear transition between the town and the countryside; a network of recreational routes extending to the centre of the town; farming should continue to set the spatial image of the landscape; the open nature of the countryside should be maintained. There was also a series of aims relating to the water systems. The declared intention was to enhance the sense of the cultural landscape and place identity.

By October 2000 a policy decision had been taken by the Municipality of Groningen to expand to the east and not to the west. Thus substantial elements of the detail in 'embracing the emptiness' had to be reconsidered. However, the underlying ideas were retained – a design approach that respects and enhances features of the historic landscape, water systems and natural ecology, while recognizing the need to diversify the agricultural base, make it more ecologically sensitive and create new opportunities for recreation. 'Embracing the emptiness' was a more pure, less compromised or negotiated place identity narrative than anything seen in the Scottish examples. It is not a coincidence that it was constructed in Groningen, where the ideas for 'quality by identity' that underpinned the whole NoordXXI project were also fashioned. Kuiper Compagnons were developing a narrative already mobilized among politicians, planners, academics and local civil society that was able to connect landscape, ecology and history to a place narrative in which Randstad-style globalized urbanization was 'the other'. The institutional context of consultants and the mental maps of designers also facilitate an approach that drives to a solution rather than gets enmeshed in negotiation, implementation and compromise, the everyday practice of public service professionals. As noted previously in this book, the traditions of negotiated consensus are strong in the Dutch polity and, as in the POP itself, there are institutional mechanisms that work towards agreement and co-ordination of inter-agency action within what remains (by UK standards at least) a robust public sector. The narrative of place identity developed through the planning system is as such less contested than in the Scottish examples, and is summarized in Table 8.4.

AN ASIDE ON THE NORWEGIANS

The Swedish and Norwegian regions who were partners in NoordXXI decided not to get involved in the project called 'border zones' on which this chapter has been based. That itself said a lot about mental maps and contrasting institutional struc-tures in the different countries. Planners in the two Scottish regions confronted a situation where strategic planning of land for new housing was, if not *the* key issue, then one high up on the list. East Lothian's professionals had endured a massive, adversarial local plan inquiry where the pent-up frustrations of house-builders with the planning of housing land allocations in the whole of Lothian were released. The vocabulary and everyday currency of such procedures on this issue – housing mar-ket areas, effective sites, windfall sites, etc. – could be translated into Norwegian, but the concepts meant nothing to planners in the counties of Østfold or Buskerud. The idea of major national/international house-building companies speculatively looking for land for extensive estate development was literally foreign to the Scandinavians. Tenure structures in Norway retain land ownership and succession in families and so promote a more incremental approach, with most new private

Table 8.4 Place narratives about development on the edge of Groningen

What?	Who?	Where/how?
'Embracing the emptiness' – retaining and enhancing authentic place identity based on landscape, water, and villages. Sustainable development.	POP respondents, Groningen municipal council, planning consultants and national spatial planning agency.	Landscape design-led approach through non-statutory advisory report/innovative planning exercise.

house-building being single developments of detached, family properties that conform with the zoning in the detailed local plan.

National law in Norway prevents development on arable land. There is a strong
cultural element to this stance – historically Norway has been a rural society, yet one
in which arable land was scarce due to basic physical geography. While the policy
can have an urban containment effect it does not constitute a specific spatial concept: it only says where a town should not develop, and does not create any
diagram or image of what pattern of urban development is desirable or sustainable.
The disposition of arable land around any settlement will be unique if not random,
and therefore there is not the prescription of a preferred development solution, such
as the green belt concept provides. The town of Askim in Østfold, for example, has
areas of arable land quite close to the centre of the town, probably less than 2 km
from the railway station. This land has not been developed, whereas there has been
considerable development of non-arable land further from the centre. The effect is
that the town is elongated in an east–west direction, but relatively narrow in a
north–south direction. Other things being equal, this is likely to extend some travel
distances and to encourage car-based travel rather than walking. However, it does
save arable land, which some would see as an important contribution to sustainable
development.

In short, the construction of place narratives for settlements in Norway seems
to have been more linked to everyday practices in civil society, rather than through
strategic spatial planning interventions. However, it could be that development pressures have simply not been strong enough to prompt more conscious spatial
planning narratives of place. It is interesting to note that the Buskerud County Plan
has been keen to constrain the physical spread of Oslo suburbia. To do this a green
zone has been declared in parts of the E18 transport corridor, with the aim of preventing coalescence of settlements, and to emphasize a distinct identity. There are
obvious links to the idea of a green belt.

CONCLUSION

The case studies reveal the extent to which spatial planners take a leading role in
the creation and implementation of place narratives. This is not surprising – our
argument is that the construction, manipulation, negotiation and implementation of
such narratives is an integral part of the role of planners. It also appears that the
narratives in Scotland and the Netherlands are substantially the same, certainly in
respect of green belts and containment and pursuit of the compact city, though
this is not so in Norway. It also appears that the narratives of the local authority
planners are more contested in Scotland than in the Netherlands. While this finding

may to some extent be a consequence of the way that research was undertaken within the project, or a reflection of differentials in development pressures in the regions we studied, we believe the finding to be robust and explicable. It partly reflects institutional differences, mental maps and training of planners, with more local 'ownership' of plans and designs in the more decentralized Dutch system, and a more consultative process from central government to listen to local authorities in the formulation of national strategy. However, we should never overlook the wider structures – Aberdeenshire in particular reflects the attempts of spatial planning to accommodate global development pressure on a scale that had no equivalent in Groningen.

We believe that the processes by which planners' place narratives are implemented and contested are integral to the narrative itself. They shape its integrity and comprehension. In this respect the nature of Scottish development plans as statements of policies primarily demonstrating conformity with national guidance has the effect of confusing and fragmenting the place narrative, which becomes contingent on interpretation and cross-reference. Thus, while statutory planning has constructed a place narrative based on a green belt, and this notion of place perhaps more than any other associated with planning commands popular support, in reality the green belt concept is embedded in a technicized, rationalistic and discretionary process that is most fully expressed in adversarial public inquiries. In these circumstances it is no surprise to find that the Royal Town Planning Institute believes that the public does not really understand the nature of a green belt, and that people mistakenly presume a common sense interpretation ('it's green and can't be built upon') to be robust. Adversarial inquiries in the plan-led UK system tend to lead to the atomization of the coherence of these place narratives. In addition, a structure plan is a relatively weak co-ordination mechanism. In aspiring to deliver sustainable patterns of urbanization through locating development so as to minimize dependency on the car, the planning system in the UK has no real control over public transport provision or over the provision of water and sewerage to make sites developable.

Finally, we should question whether the dedication to maintaining place identity through preventing coalescence and protecting the landscape setting of settlements really enhanced the European aims of competitiveness, cohesion and sustainable development. This chapter has shown that both in theory and in practice, traditional containment and dispersal policies are likely to extend travel distances, are exclusionary in nature, and work against territorial cohesion. They are at best indirect supports to competitiveness, and at worst undermine it. It is thus time to reconceptualize the urban containment narratives of place identity, and also how such place identity narratives are created.

CHAPTER 9

DESIGN AND PLACE IDENTITY
MARILYN HIGGINS

This chapter follows through concerns with quality and place identity down to the level of townscape and the design of areas of a town. It uses ideas developed in the early part of the book, and in particular in Chapter 1, to analyse the new interest in urban design. It then draws on one of the most exciting elements in the NoordXXI project, the collaborative design work done by students from Heriot-Watt and the NLH in the towns of Ellon in Aberdeenshire and Askim in Norway. This was a very rich learning experience for the students and staff involved in the project. Not only did they come to appreciate differences in design cultures, but also to experience at first hand some of the differences in the ways that planning and the institutions of planning operate in practice. Practising planners and local politicians were also involved in the projects in Ellon and Askim, so not only was it an international exercise in student collaboration, but it also straddled the academic/practitioner boundary. We now push the project a stage further by applying a critical social science perspective to the narratives of design that dominated this part of the NoordXXI project.

THE RECONSTRUCTION OF THE DESIGN NARRATIVE WITHIN PLANNING

Design is one discourse of place identity, but the other discourses about identity influence the design process. Across the globe, communities cherish the local vernacular as a countervailing reference (that is simultaneously both real and symbolic) in opposition to 'modern' design. Such communities look to planning systems to defend the quality of their place, but issues of design carry surprisingly little weight in many of Europe's statutory planning systems, where the prime concerns are with quantitative aspects of the use of land. In contrast to this popular misconception of planners as guardians of the physical qualities of space and place, a complex web of cultural, social, economic, political, historic and environmental factors underpin the design of our everyday environment, influenced by a wide range of players. The aim of this chapter is to explore the relationship between design and place identity, its evolving role in national and local planning processes, and how different narratives about place identity might be reconciled in the design process. The subplot is the story of a NoordXXI design project involving Scottish and Norwegian students, which illustrates how international comparison can be a creative and critical force.

The pluralistic nature of narratives about place identity lies at the heart of this book. The design of our environment constitutes a physical and three-dimensional manifestation of place identity. This applies to any site, space or building and the whole is more than the sum of its parts: it is the *relationship* between all these individual elements that gives places their character and identity. Design components within the environment are obviously physical and often local; building form is highly influenced by the part of the world in which it is located, including the nature of the topography, climate, local materials and construction methods. But globalization during the twentieth century challenged these traditional images.

As long ago as the 1920s the aesthetic in modern architecture – its fundamental discourse – became explicitly and unashamedly an 'international style'. In the name of democracy and functionalism, the same aesthetic was to be found in Dessau, New Haven, Barcelona and Bexhill-on-Sea as new technology in concrete and glass rode roughshod over any notion of the local vernacular. Franck and Lepori (2000: 138) observed that through modernism 'architects sought to transcend the particularities of specific locations ... substantial differences in climate, culture and program were often largely ignored'. Despite the often democratic intent, this was an exclusive discourse, conducted amongst design professionals, and legitimated by claims to expertise and taste.

However, everyday practice of developers (both private and public agency) and consumers has subverted this exclusion. In the insular UK, modernism was often on the fringes, rather than at the heart of, planning practice. In other countries also, planning controls, and the skills of those taking planning decisions, only embraced the design discourse to a limited extent: plans are two-dimensional, often policy-led documents; in many European countries control of development is largely an administrative process requiring checks for conformity with the plan, and design is often seen as a matter of taste rather than rational choice.

The really interesting facets underpinning design decisions are the less obvious ones: the cultural, social, political and economic factors. Each individual space and building carries with it a number of possible readings in relation to these. It is very definitely a three-dimensional product of its age and all that this entails, whether global brand or medieval theology, but the meanings and identities of places, as shown in previous chapters, are likely to be contested and open to different interpretations. Consciousness of difference, tolerance of diversity, and sensitivity to the power relations woven in and through design need to be embedded into design discourses that have a history of elite control and of uncoupling the visual and functional aspects of place from other bases. An added layer of interest incorporates the fourth dimension, time, as few buildings or spaces remain the same for very long. Planners need to recognize all these diverse factors and competing interests while both responding to and influencing the changing dynamics. If this were an easy task, design would not be such a fraught issue.

It is ironic that a set of dichotomies has typically underpinned thinking about design in planning, as these dichotomies have often obscured the real issues to do with quality and place identity. The following outlines seven dichotomies:

visual	–	functional
product	–	process
professional	–	public/users
strategic	–	site specific
traditional	–	modern
plans/principles	–	implementation
urban	–	rural

All of the above are important in the planning process and in influencing the design of our environment. We need to get away from the dangerous 'either/or' mindset and move toward an understanding of the paradox underlying these dualities. 'The model of isolation and separation among parts permeates so many aspects of modern life. Too often we conceive and design buildings as objects, separated from context and use' (Franck and Lepori, 2000: 132). 'Good design', can emerge from such integration.

The importance of 'good quality design' is being increasingly acknowledged by the public, national and local government agencies, and planners. This reflects the wider dynamics of post-Fordism in which 'design' has been one of the key means of replacing economies of scale through standardization with individual choice within branding. The differentiation between 'town planning' and 'urban design' is the reconstruction of professional practice and identity around this same, fundamental transition. John Gummer, as Secretary of State for the Environment in the later stages of Margaret Thatcher's Conservative regime, initiated the 'quality agenda' (Department of the Environment, 1994). Design was recognized as a 'material consideration' in the planning process, in contrast to the 1980s view that design could be left to the market. The establishment of the Commission for Architecture and the Built Environment (CABE) in England signalled a more proactive approach to design within planning. Lord Rogers' Urban Task Force report even went so far as to put the importance of design at the centre of regeneration efforts (Urban Task Force, 1999). The establishment of the Urban Design Alliance (UDAL) in 1999 has brought together a range of professions and organizations with an interest in improving the quality of our surroundings. The government produced *By Design – Urban Design in the Planning System: Towards Better Practice* (Commission for Architecture and the Built Environment, 2000) which sets out in a very clear and practical way the various tools that can be used within the planning system to encourage good design. It includes a section with tips and techniques for public involvement and gives an example where this has worked in practice (Commission for Architecture and the Built Environment, 2000: 73–6). Around the same time, another hands-on document was produced by English Partnerships and the Housing Corporation (2000): *Urban Design Compendium*. This is a well-illustrated guide to urban design principles, including how to determine the character of a particular area – 'everywhere is somewhere' (English Partnerships *et al.*, 2000: 22–4). Planning schools have generally incorporated more design into the curricula since the early 1990s.

'Good design' thus becomes an economic and cultural imperative in cities, small towns, villages and the countryside. In this sense design encompasses all the different elements within our surroundings and how they relate to people: buildings and the spaces between them, movement patterns, activities, structures and landscape all contribute to the overall picture. Whereas in the past, design of the environment emphasized purely physical and visual elements, the new consumerism requires a wider, more inclusive and participatory discourse encompassing context, activities, movement, public spaces and the human aspects of development.

This is not to argue that visual aspects and aesthetics should be underplayed; rather that they need to be seen in relation to the wider picture. Thus the Urban Design Alliance is sponsoring the Placecheck scheme, which is a tool to help local communities 'assess the qualities of a place, showing what improvements are needed and focusing people working together to achieve them' (Cowan, 2001: 4). There is even a National Placecheck Day and this bottom-up approach is freely available on the World Wide Web (www.placecheck.co.uk). A very successful community-led initiative, Village Design Statements, was started by the Countryside Commission in the 1990s and has taken off so rapidly that already several hundred of these have been carried out around the English countryside. These statements give guidance for all development based on the character of the area, so at their very heart is place identity and the uniqueness of the settlement (see Countryside Commission, 1996).

Design is as much about process as it is about product, and the interaction between the two is a powerful determinant of outcomes. 'Listening transforms the relationship between designer and place, between designer and client. Designers thus become facilitators as well as directors of an orchestra' (Franck and Lepori, 2000: 22). However, for a long period the dialogues of planners and designers were closed to the voices of women, ethnic minorities, children and teenagers, the elderly and the disabled. Indeed, many planners themselves have not felt equipped with the necessary skills, knowledge and vocabulary to positively contribute to design debates. This lack of confidence has discouraged confronting design issues and many poor quality development proposals have passed through the planning system.

A lack of design skills has also led planners, especially in Britain, to sometimes take the easy option of encouraging pastiche solutions as opposed to good quality new design, whereas Tibbalds (1992) emphasized the importance of learning from the past but not copying. Other European countries have been more successful in embracing the modern aesthetic but infusing it with qualities appreciated by the public (see Figure 9.1). Quality will result from a genuine dialogue between designers, planners and groups within the community; no one of these interests has a monopoly on design judgement.

THE DESIGN DISCOURSE

If we are to explore relations between design, place identity and participation, then the design discourse within planning has to be the starting point. What kind of language and concepts have been used by those with the power to define the nature and product of deliberate place design? We have already noted that the discourse was not very permeable to voices from outside the design professions. In an extreme statement of this exclusionary stance, Thomas Sharp, a leading British architect–planner in the 1940s and 1950s, argued that 'Planning is design: design is one man's responsibility (with, of course, the subordinate help of assistants)' (Schuster Report, 1950, para. 119). This dogma depicting design as a private

Figure 9.1   Modern design in Amsterdam: Eastern Docklands

process sat uneasily in a real world where planning practice was infused with negotiation and compromise and depended on a range of public agencies and the market for implementation. However, the pedagogy of planning education remained a powerful means to reproduce this exclusive viewpoint through design projects. Presentation, aesthetics and functionalism typically defined the parameters by which the projects were conducted and assessed. Even when planning education from the 1970s onwards began to become less rooted in design, design projects within programmes typically remained immune to insights from statistical probability or social science. Thus a key part of the design discourse was a view that planners had a responsibility to (re-)create places to conform to a set of professional understandings about quality. What have been the building blocks of those understandings?

Cullen (1961) is recognized as a seminal text that popularized the word 'townscape', and elaborated the idea that places were more than 'architecture' or collections of individual buildings. This was one of the first approaches to concentrate on the 'art of relationship' in the environment, and to explain the importance of 'serial vision' (the human experience of moving through spaces), details and qualities of spaces and interesting juxtapositions that contribute to place identity. Though Cullen emphasized the importance of optics and the human view, his concern was very much with the visual and physical aspects of the environment. People rarely figured in his scenes of interesting and pretty townscapes. Thus this important text provided a vocabulary and set of visual motifs that both opened and closed professional understandings of the nature of place.

Christian Norberg-Schulz's *Genius Loci* (1980) is another landmark text amongst urban design professionals. Again written by an architect, it explored determinants of the spirit of a place, including 'psychic implications', with a metaphysical and visual orientation. His illustrations from all over the world convey powerful images of the influence of geography, climate, local materials and vernacular building traditions. The 'genius loci' idea is precisely the kind of essentialist narrative of place identity that was criticized in Chapter 1. Both Cullen and Norberg-Schulz made little distinction between people on the basis of age, gender, class or physical ability. People tended to be lumped into one category with one visual aesthetic.

It is perhaps significant that one of the most influential critiques of orthodox planning and design came from Jane Jacobs, a layperson and woman. Jacobs (1961) highlighted the importance of social space on the 'sidewalks' and human activities on the street, seeing cities as a setting for interaction. Jan Gehl furthered the debate about public life on the streets and put many of his ideas into practice in the city of Copenhagen (Gehl, 1987; Gehl and Gemzoe, 2000). His emphasis is on the quality of design in the public realm to encourage human interaction and active use of outdoor spaces to enhance the quality of life. However, again, these authors tend to treat people equally without really acknowledging the needs and perspectives of different groups. They also highlight problems and solutions while largely ignoring the processes that underpin good design.

Kevin Lynch, another major contributor to urban design as a narrative, first studied the strategic importance of urban design in terms of place identity and the effect it had on people's personal orientation within their environment (Lynch, 1960). He coined the phrases 'legibility' and 'imageability' and his central thesis, following extensive interviews with members of the public, was that the interaction between self and place was important to emotional stability. He therefore recommended that new development accentuate the features that people inherently use to navigate their way through their surroundings, including paths, nodes, landmarks, districts and edges. This concept was expanded and supplemented by the seminal book *Responsive Environments*, which developed practical design principles aimed at meeting the needs of users of space, including legibility (ease of finding one's way around), permeability (connections between places), variety and interest, robustness, richness, personalization and visual appropriateness (Bentley *et al.*, 1985). This 'responsiveness' acknowledges that solutions should be tailored to different contexts, while recognizing general principles.

The literature summarized above which has underpinned the urban design discourse is divorced from social science traditions, though these traditions have much in common with a branch of architecture that emphasizes cultural identity. Canter (1977: 123) acknowledged the complexity underlying people's experience of place, summarized by symbols: 'A particular physical location can have its psychological power.' He summarized the nature of places as the intersection of physical attributes, activities and conceptions (1977: 158), an understanding of which should directly influence planners and decision-makers (1977: 125). Place was seen as temporal, an inter-related continuum of space, time and meaning, a collective consciousness where meaning has both perceptual and associational aspects (Motloch, 1989: 231). Design education should therefore promote an understanding of the nature of places visually, ecologically and culturally, including the processes of place-making and the cultural and individual character of perception (Motloch, 1989: 237).

Such insights have come to the fore within urban design: 'Increasingly, architects and planners recognize that there is no single, universal answer; contextualism, regionalism, historic preservation and sustainable architecture all reflect the acceptance of multiplicity and the rediscovery of the connections between geographical and cultural location and design' (Franck and Lepori, 2000: 138). Punter and Carmona (1997) conclude that planners and designers are too often ignorant of the large body of social science literature that promotes an understanding of people's sense of place, including environmental psychology and the role of culture. Madanipour (1996) also recognizes that different people experience surroundings in different ways. This pluralistic view challenges traditional assumptions of the more physically oriented theories and emphasizes the experiential dimension of varying place identities.

This brief overview has shown that the design discourse has developed from an extremely narrow and elitist base to a recognition of the need to engage with the voices of others. The concepts and language through which the discourse is constructed now include a number of elements seen as contributing to 'good design' that are open to interpretation by businesses and civil society, and form a potential basis from which to build narratives of place identity. Examples would include: strengthening a sense of place through contextual analysis, mixed uses, lively and interesting street frontages, high quality materials, security and safety issues, high-standard open space and public circulation, good visual and pedestrian connections, clarity between public and private space, attention to climate and natural features, sustainability factors, and public and user involvement. However, very sweeping and anodyne statements remain embedded in the design discourse, which is littered with contested words like 'character', 'appropriate', 'in keeping' and 'sympathetic', that are presented as if they were uncontroversial.

NATIONAL PLANNING POLICY INFLUENCES ON DESIGN IN NORWAY AND SCOTLAND

We have argued that there has been a reconstruction of the design discourse within planning, making it potentially more accessible to a wider range of participants, while also constituting a set of concepts that can be manipulated to construct narratives of place identity. We now explore how these possibilities have been translated into practice. International comparison is particularly appropriate to this purpose, since it allows us to explore how far territory and the restructuring of space set parameters within which a design-led narrative of place identity is produced and reproduced. To this end we begin by looking at the extent and ways in which national planning policy has developed the themes of design and place identity. Our study looks at Norway and Scotland, as these were the countries where the NoordXXI project took on an innovative exercise to apply the ideas of 'quality by identity' through urban design.

Ever since 1965, the Norwegian Planning and Building Act included what has been called both a 'beauty paragraph' and a 'sleeping paragraph' (Ploeger, 1999: 48). This paragraph required reasonable judgement to be made about the beauty of surroundings and buildings when considering new development proposals, but the provision has not often been used in practice. This contradiction is indicative of the extent to which the local level of planning in Norway was an administrative routine, based on ensuring that new development met largely functional and land use criteria. Implicitly the 'sleeping' status of these powers also recognized the extent to which the small towns and villages that so characterize the Norwegian settlement system have been incremental products of small scale, even individual, developers and quasi-state agencies such as housing co-operatives.

However, the role of design was strengthened in the Planning and Building Act 1995 by several last-minute amendments (Bettum, 2000: 26). Securing aesthetic considerations was made a central consideration of the planning system and a circular was produced emphasizing the importance of aesthetic issues (visual qualities in buildings and their surroundings) at all spatial planning scales (county plans, municipal development plans and building development plans), relevant for both the private and public sector (Rundskriv/ H-7/97, circular letter, 1997).

Norway thus made strides in the late 1990s to institutionalize design control and emphasize it as an aesthetic matter incorporating issues such as architectural design and built form, but also cultural landscapes and place identity (Ploeger, 1999: 47). Municipalities were strongly encouraged to produce aesthetic guidelines to influence local politicians, professional planners and architects. The circular was accompanied by a substantial handbook aimed at local authorities and developers, giving guidance and well-illustrated examples of how quality can be promoted, including appropriate legal tools (Miljoeverndepartementet/Ministry of Environment, 1997). We would argue that this new emphasis on design could reflect a number of concerns – perceived threats to place identity, and the links between design, competitiveness and sustainable development are certainly amongst these.

Throughout this guidance, there is a strong encouragement of new development that sits well within its unique setting in terms of building form, plot size and land use but that also is in tune with the present age and contemporary approaches to design and aesthetics. Perhaps the greatest contrast between Norwegian and Scottish national guidance is that the Norwegian contains more unashamedly modern design compared to the Scottish pastiche. The Norwegians go for bold, simple designs that don't seek to replicate the romance of a past age; they look more to the future, while relating well to landform and landscape. This is true in illustrations for housing, offices, bridges, ski jumps and street furniture alike.

Thus the substance of the new design narrative is tuned both to place identity and to competitiveness (see Figure 9.2). The design of physical surroundings is explicitly seen as important for national cultural identity as well as for local socio-cultural identity (Ploeger, 1999: 49). Norway is a predominantly rural country with a valued and dramatic landscape, and the guidance is particularly strong on integrating the built with the natural environment. These aims dovetail with the emphasis on

Figure 9.2   Modern design in the centre of Oslo

sustainability issues being promoted nationally, for example through the Environmental Cities programme, where improving five cities includes aesthetic regeneration (Miljoeverndepartementet/Ministry of Environment, 1995).

In practice, towns have differed considerably in terms of how the national policy intentions have been implemented at local level. Baerum, west of Oslo, is an example of an authority that has produced aesthetic guidelines requiring an analysis of, among other things, context, views, cultural heritage and topography (Baerum Kommune 1997 and 1999). Successful implementation of national policy is dependent on local awareness and skills, and these are patchy. Ploeger concludes his analysis of design in the Norwegian planning system by pointing to essential ingredients that are still lacking: planners' design skills, effective public discourse and an understanding of people's everyday aesthetic concerns (Ploeger, 1999: 53).

As noted already, central government in the UK put a new emphasis on urban design in the 1990s. Though this was more marked initially in England than in Scotland, there are now some seminal publications from the Scottish Executive, notably *A Policy on Architecture for Scotland* (Scottish Executive, 2001a) and *Designing Places: A Policy Statement for Scotland* (Scottish Executive, 2001b). The national architecture policy explicitly recognizes the role that the built environment plays in the promotion of national culture, social inclusion and economic competitiveness and the importance of meaningful dialogue between designers, clients, users and communities (Scottish Executive, 2001a: 2–3).

The fact that the document is exclusively about 'architecture' and not more inclusively about urban or environmental design is indicative of the resilience of the orthodox discourse on design, and of the extent to which planning remains marginalized by its exclusion from that discourse. Similarly, while the role of communities is very generally promoted, there is no recognition in the 'architecture' policy of the multiplicity of interests that this includes, or practical steps toward implementation. Good design is not explicitly defined, but on the whole is considered to be a result of partnership in the building process (including the general community dimension), a reflection of Scottish culture (without defining it), value for money and sustainability in the long term.

Designing Places helps to flesh out the national architecture policy and lists six qualities which define good design, the first of which is distinct place identity, followed by safe and pleasant spaces, ease of movement, a sense of welcome, adaptability and good use of resources (Scottish Executive, 2001b: 10–11). The establishment and maintenance of a distinct identity is seen as benefiting both users and investors (Scottish Executive, 2001b: 18) and therefore establishes an explicit link between place identity and economic concerns. Particular opportunities for creating a sense of identity are listed as: landscapes, natural features, buildings, streets, street patterns, spaces, skylines, building forms, practices and materials that should inspire patterns of new building (Scottish Executive, 2001b: 30). This list is somewhat vague and the dichotomy between what already exists and appropriate new patterns is far from clear.

Like the Norwegian guidance, the new policy integrates the importance of both urban and rural design, emphasizing the crucial role that setting plays. This contrasts with previous documents produced in Scotland, where the norm at national level has been to separate urban and rural design, with particular reports aimed at design in the countryside (see Scottish Office Development Department, 1998; and Scottish Office Environment Department, 1991, 1994). While Scotland, like Norway, has a substantial rural land area, the lack of engagement of design policy with urban areas reflected and further increased the extent to which central government discourse about planning has presented planning as being about the control of development rather than social inclusion. In tune with some of the conclusions in this book, the new policy also recognizes that good design can be a contested issue between different members of the community, advocating an open and democratic process for setting priorities, shaped by public priorities, presumably referring to the democratic process carried out by elected representatives (Scottish Executive, 2001b: 33).

The two national design policies for Scotland were produced too late for the student project discussed in the next section, so the major piece of government guidance that was used in that project was *Planning in Small Towns* (Scottish Office Development Department, 1997). The major aim of this Planning Advice Note prepared by central government to foster 'good practice' is to 'provide the context within which opportunities for positive change can be identified and promoted to help reinforce the character and identity of small towns' (Scottish Office Development Department, 1997: 2). The importance of a sense of place is promoted through a townscape audit which includes cursory mention of public involvement, but is described in an annex very much as a desk and site study with a comprehensive list of issues to be considered (Scottish Office Development Department, 1997: 40–61).

The Planning Advice Note is a particularly interesting text, since almost by definition it is an attempt to create a dominant narrative of the place identity of small Scottish towns (defined as the 400 places with a population between 1,000 and 20,000). It begins by an assertion that development that is unsympathetic to 'the character' of such towns has eroded their identity. Thus the idea of identity is fundamentally linked to a historical narrative as expressed through the built form. The word 'legacy' figures prominently, and these small towns contain more than half of Scotland's conservation areas.

Through this Planning Advice Note we see that the planning system at national scale is intimately creating and disseminating meaning and modes of perception to mould collective identities for small town Scotland. The 'feel' of such places is defined by their physical features, with a strong emphasis on architecture and the historical geometry of the streets. Such continuity contrasts with restructuring of the towns' economies, which had been based on fishing, agriculture, mining, textiles, etc. Similarly the changing service economy is also undermining the historical functions of many small towns. Thus the Planning Advice Note expresses a place narrative that is critical of the banal practices of everyday life, in so far as these are expressed in traffic growth, 'insensitive development', etc. However, the counternarrative expressed in the Planning Advice Note is essentially backward-looking, and sidesteps any critical analysis of the political economy that is creating the changes to the form and fabric of these small towns.

The use of coloured photographs and sketches is fundamental to the place narrative that the Advice Note sets out. Through these a fable is written. Steeples and trim cobbled streets, elevations that are generally plain but proportionate to one to another and cast in vernacular stone, shop fronts with warm clutter and family pride ('Don Philpott and Daughter', 'Gardner and Son', 'Scott Brothers'), chimney pots and once gas-lamps, old red post boxes and clocks with Roman numerals, a mill wheel, a spade, the juxtaposition of land and sea – all these elements intricately laced around a lattice of streets, speak of a sturdy independence, of a people living honestly within their means, of respect for tradition and learning and traditional institutions, of a hard life lived close to the elements. The people in the photos appear to be exclusively white, well fed, disproportionately middle aged or elderly, clean children with caring mums: implicitly dads are at work and don't shop or push buggies.

This is a narrative that has been extensively exposed and criticized within Scottish culture, known as *kailyard*. It is a tradition that celebrates the parochial virtues of an idealized past community.

The threats to this narrative are also expressed through the visuals in the Advice Note. The villains of the piece are there in the boarded-up shop fronts and the garish insignia of downmarket supermarkets, the tarmac, railings and signage of the highway engineers, the mundane metal of jostled cars and delivery vans. These are 'the other' in this narrative, the signifiers of outsiders, a visual expression of an urban world of assembly lines and anonymous, even amoral functional relations, of institutions beyond local control. However, there is an alternative to this path, and it is about harmonizing identity with modern economic imperatives. Heritage can be used to create economic development (a lighthouse museum, a woollen mill, a mining museum, a maritime heritage centre, etc.), tasteful new, clear factories can be slotted in so that they do not break the skyline, buildings can be restored, vistas created, pedestrians given priority over cars, and large supermarket buildings can be fitted modestly into the roofscape. In summary, design is central to the contestation of place identity that is an ongoing process in the small towns of Scotland (see Figure 9.3).

Figure 9.3 Pastiche housing design in Elgin, Scotland

STUDENT CASE STUDY: ELLON, ABERDEENSHIRE, SCOTLAND AND ASKIM, ØSTFOLD, NORWAY

The NoordXXI project sought to address issues of design and place identity through a collaborative student project that was undertaken in a working partnership between local authorities (Aberdeenshire Council in Scotland and Askim Kommune in Østfold County, Norway) and universities (Heriot-Watt University, Edinburgh and the National Agricultural University of Norway in Aas). Thirty town planning, land-scape architecture and land management students participated in cross-disciplinary, trans-national teams analysing the two medium-sized towns of Ellon (population 9,000), Aberdeenshire and Askim (population 13,500), southeast of Oslo. These towns were chosen to illustrate the NoordXXI theme analysing place identity dilemmas brought about by development pressures experienced in towns in the commuting catchments of larger cities. The students spent roughly a week in each town, working up their designs in mixed-nationality teams of four or five, so that their expectations of place identity and design approaches might be challenged through exposure to those from another culture, and hence other narratives of place identity.

Ellon experienced phenomenal housing growth as a result of the discovery of oil in the North Sea, increasing population five-fold between 1965 and 2000. Askim became industrialized with the opening of the Viking rubber factory in the 1920s. At its peak in the late 1960s the factory employed 2,600, and about 70 per cent of the town's jobs were in manufacturing, but its closure in 1991 has left a very dominant building in the town centre, and today only about 15 per cent of jobs are industrial. Askim is linked to Oslo by rail; recent growth pressure in the wider conurbation has increasingly brought incoming commuters, who now stand at half the workforce. The population grew from 3,544 in 1991 to over 13,500 in 1999, with about 30 per cent of workers commuting to Oslo.

The brief for each student group was to do a character analysis of the town and then produce an urban design strategy springing from it. Each group focused on a different aspect of the strategy: conservation and enhancement, movement, development opportunities, and landscape. A key text was *Planning in Small Towns* (Scottish Office Development Department, 1997), including its emphasis on place identity.

Consistent with the NoordXXI emphasis on participation and youth involve-ment in particular, one important ingredient of the project was to obtain ideas from local people about their own sense of place identity and not just look at the physical aspects, a particular danger when time is limited. Given constraints of time and the fact that it was a student project, it was decided that young people should be the target group. This saved time by allowing us to interview school pupils in their lunch break, for example, rather than trying to collect a representative cross-section of the population. Similarly, by concentrating on youths the exercise was able to link with the NoordXXI theme that recognized the importance of young people's perceptions in shaping the future of places (see the foreword by Øivind Holt). This worked especially well in Askim, where the visit started with a tour in small groups led by local young people.

A talk was given by Professor Arne Bugge Amundsen of the Cultural Studies Department of the University of Oslo, who had undertaken a study of the meaning and relevance of local identity in Askim, concentrating on young people, as part of NoordXXI (Amundsen, 2001). He challenged the prevailing ethos amongst planners, politicians and other professionals who look too often at the physical aspects (in the Norberg-Schulz tradition mentioned above) to the exclusion of the human/cultural/historical dimensions. To understand the 'cultural construction' of place identities it is necessary to have a discourse with local people as individuals, politicians, officials, and organizations. Thus the students were exposed to the idea that there will probably be conflicting narratives of identity within the same place.

To explore local identity in Askim, Amundsen analysed school essays on the subject written by teenagers, conducted interviews with local officials, took part in discussion groups with young people and studied local printed material. From these he articulated three major themes of identity, based around losses, deficiencies and possibilities (Amundsen, 2001: 22–32). For some inhabitants the decline and loss of the farming and rubber industries was the dominant narrative – Askim was a place that had lost its defining economic bases and their associated social relations and cultural artifacts. In contrast, the young people in their school essays emphasized the deficiencies in Askim, characterizing it as particularly lacking activities for young people. While they appreciated the sporting facilities and cinema, they were critical of lack of green in the centre, litter, badly kept houses and the eternal teenage lament of 'lack of things to do'.

The third strand had to do with development potential and was promoted by the local planners and politicians, whose emphasis is on 'urbanity, modern culture and competence' (Amundsen, 2001: 33). The municipal plan defines Askim in relation to possible future alternatives for development; the administration tries to articulate a future vision by connecting the fragments left by changes over the years to make it a strong regional centre. The head of the municipal culture department also talked to the students and emphasized the importance of recent incomers, both young suburban families and ethnic minorities, continuing the industrial transformation to an 'open, tolerant and liberal local society' (Amundsen, 2001: 32). There has been an influx over the last ten years of Turkish people, some of whom have opened restaurants in a part of town by the railway tracks, nicknamed 'kebab land' by the students. This interpretation challenges the traditional narrative of Askim's historical identity. Similarly, the narrative of deficiencies has no real equivalent in the Scottish Planning Advice Note's narratives about small town life.

Amundsen's empirical work in Askim thus confirmed that there are many identities, depending on whom you ask, depending on age, gender, social status and ethnicity (Amundsen, 2001: 38). An understanding of identity as a reflection of how local people think and talk about their community also helps us understand that planners and politicians also have their own view, one of many. Theirs, however, is a powerful and influential voice. The big contribution that Amundsen's study makes is not to pose a solution, but to open up questions and dialogue to promote future understanding. It stresses the importance of asking the right questions in finding the right answers.

In contrast to the Askim cultural analysis, in Ellon, planned surveys of young people were not possible in advance of the student visit, given time and resource constraints. A small survey of young people (aged 12 to 30) on the street was undertaken, asking people to describe Ellon to a friend who had never visited the town and then asking what were the three best and worst characteristics. While statistically insignificant, the results were an important starting place for design strategies and gave the students added valuable experience of devising and analysing questionnaire surveys. Ninety-four young people were interviewed and the results produced an image of a small, quiet, boring town; the shops, restaurants, pubs and sporting facilities were valued but also seen as lacking in number and/or quality. A good sense of community was also valued, as was the open space and attractive countryside setting. Young people wanted more entertainment, shops and facilities. Just over half said they were proud to come from Ellon. One group asked whether interviewees would be prepared to see Ellon double in size if that was the only way to add facilities and the answer was generally 'yes'. Similarly to in the Askim survey, young people tended to view the small town in terms of deficiencies, seeing the town in terms of facilities it lacked (Ellon Student Project, 2000: 37–9).

The themes set by the tutors for the students to build their designs around approximated to different narratives of place identity: movement through space – clean and easy (Ellon/Askim); development opportunities – big and bright; a place to see and be – 'touch/feely'; and building the future with the past – memory and imagination.

The 'building the future with the past: conserving and enhancing Askim – memory and imagination' group engaged with the historical narrative of loss that Amundsen's analysis had identified. Their work also had resonance with the Scottish Planning Advice Note. They devised a strategy for raising the profile of historic and symbolic areas in Askim (e.g. the Viking graveyard and the park by the railway station in the town centre), enhancing the aesthetic image while providing opportunities to move forward from the industrial period. In this way, a deliberate blend of old and new proposed conservation, not just for the sake of it but also to reinforce the sense of places that have meaning for the local community. The group made an interesting comparison of local traditional and more modern building styles and found interest in the diversity. One conclusion was that building style mattered less than building form, morphology, orientation, use and size.

The 'place to see and be' in Askim group responded in a particularly innovative and creative way, suggesting that a Millennium Monument be erected in the town centre marking the loss of the rubber factory. People would be able to sign the tall slender column and it would gradually slip into the ground. This monument would signify the past and the 'loss', which would be buried in a positive way while allowing the memory, the signatures, to remain visible below ground through clear glass. In this way, memory and pride could be acknowledged in a way that allows the town to grow and move forward in a constructive fashion.

The thrust of much of the student work in both towns was to strengthen areas that were especially significant to narratives of identity. In Askim, this focused on the area in the centre around the former rubber factory, which, interestingly, no one proposed to demolish (see Figure 9.4). Instead, students proposed that the factory be kept and used for a mixture of residential, commercial, retail and recreational uses. They also proposed the upgrading and linking of major open areas in the centre that have been filled up with cars. In line with sustainability aims, a reduction in car parking was proposed because the unreflective everyday practice of this fairly typical small Norwegian town meant that there were 2,000 spaces in the town centre for a

Figure 9.4 The disused rubber factory looms over Askim

town with a population of 13,500. The upgrading of the public realm was linked to adjacent public uses: a shopping centre, a proposal to reinstate an art deco cinema into a cultural complex and a new swimming pool (the narratives of deficiency and potential).

In Ellon, proposals revolved around strengthening the role and accessibility of a riverside park in the centre, near the old bridge across the river that created Ellon ('island') in the first place (see Figure 9.5). Students also proposed additions and improvements to the shopping facilities in the centre. While it may seem simple to propose improvements to the key places that give each town a strong sense of unique identity, it is true that too often in practice these are precisely the areas that can be taken for granted and not accorded enough attention. Sites were never seen in isolation. In line with the Planning Advice Note, improvements to movement patterns emphasized pedestrian connections and parking control while respecting historic street patterns, restricting traffic in the heart of the towns. A key element was giving young people new indoor and outdoor spaces where they could come together both formally and informally. In this way, responding to Amundsen's interpretation, they were able to address losses and deficiencies and help set agendas for the future, building on the past while seizing new opportunities.

The project, like design itself, was about process as well as product. It was obvious in Askim that a greater number of local politicians were more involved in the

Figure 9.5 Ellon: the islands and bridge that first gave the town its identity, now spoiled by twentieth-century insertions

detail of planning issues given the smaller scale nature of local authority boundaries. Some 35 elected members are based in Askim and are responsible for the town and environs, whereas Ellon is represented by two who sit on a council of 66, meeting in Aberdeen and representing over 220,000 people across a vast area in comparison. The Mayor and Deputy Mayor of Askim took a keen interest in the student work and were involved in the project. The final student presentation was filmed for the local television station and was the subject of a two-page spread in the local newspaper. Also in Askim, students met a much greater range of non-planners who were involved in the planning process: the Head of Culture of the local authority, a local artist, the Head of Community Affairs and the manager of the renovated art deco cinema. Thus the design process was notably more democratic and inclusive in this Norwegian town than in its Scottish equivalent.

Norwegian planning and design appeared to be bottom-up, whereas in Scotland the system is centralized and top-down. The Chief Planner of Askim said that Britain is regarded as a 'planner's paradise' because of the status of the profession and the relative lack of political interference. Students also noted other key differences in the way that culture was expressed through planning policies to contribute to place identity. In Norway, agricultural land is scarce and heavily protected, arable fields can be found in the midst of settlements and are sacrosanct. In Britain, where old forests have disappeared over the last centuries, woodland is held dear and generally protected from development. Norwegians tend to build in their more plentiful woodland and the British on their farmland.

The house-building industry in Britain is mainly made up of large national volume house-builders who tend to build the same houses up and down the country. House construction in Norway is much smaller scale, generally carried out by local builders in small numbers who are keyed in to local building traditions. Despite the more prescriptive local building plans, new houses there tend to be more dissimilar to each other because of the way the building industry is structured. It was therefore fascinating to observe the way in which the Norwegian students warmed to Ellon's ranks of suburban houses! They admired in particular the sharp break between the edge of the estates and the open fields, and the relatively compact urban form, in contrast to the ribbon development back home. The green belt has been one of the strongest planning tools in Britain driving urban containment policies but in Norway, settlement patterns, taking off from their agrarian roots, have been more dispersed and scattered; there is no green belt aesthetic there.

The project also highlighted interesting differences between the skills and outlook of the British and Norwegian students, which may be a reflection of their education or their culture, or both. The Norwegians were especially good at thinking about the detail of design for individual sites, whereas the British were better at taking a strategic look across an area. The British students were infused with a sustainability aesthetic and abhorred the seas of parking lots in Askim. The Norwegians tended not to get so upset at this, saying that people were used to parking right outside the shops; these views were perhaps conditioned by the small town background of most of the students, from a country where a large proportion of the population lives outside big cities and the car is seemingly a universal part of the household.

Now that some time has passed since the student project, it is interesting to revisit the towns to see what difference the proposals and the process might have made. In Ellon, there was an exhibition of the student work in the local library. In 2003, a programme for town centre environmental improvements is ongoing, the designs for which have been driven by outside consultants. The local plan in force when the students made their visit did not contain many design policies, but the consultation draft of the current Aberdeenshire Local Plan (Aberdeenshire Council, 2002) is much stronger on this. A key general policy concerns the layout, siting and design of new development, the thrust of which is couched in general terms about respecting the character of the surroundings, but criteria are given for good design and new innovative design is specifically encouraged. There is also an eleven-page appendix on design that goes into much more detail about design criteria.

In Askim, the project was successful in raising awareness of urban design and quality issues in the town centre with both politicians and the public. A significant debate was sparked; the chief planner afterwards appeared often in the press and not everyone agreed with his views. Following the student project, consultants were appointed to produce a town centre master plan, including design issues, to feed into a new plan at the level between the development plan and the local building plan. The design guidelines produced about issues such as building height and styles could not be agreed by the politicians and therefore have not been implemented. Property owners and neighbours are being consulted about appropriate next stages. Amundsen's ideas about losses, deficiencies and development have made a deep impression on the chief planner, who is actively trying to use these concepts in the future planning of the area, along with some of the students' ideas.

CONCLUSION

It is clear that design issues in the environment are rising up the agendas of national and local government, the planning profession and local communities. In small towns such as those discussed in this chapter this reflects a combination of the restructuring of traditional local economies and a sense that the continuity of the 'character' of the settlement is under threat. Thus the strengthening of a historically rooted place identity is seen as a key aim of such design interventions. This does not

mean copying architectural styles, but undertaking a careful analysis of the buildings, materials, views, and street patterns of places and designing something
appropriate for the future. This is the dominant narrative in small town design in
Scotland and was also evident in the articulation of the narrative of 'loss' in Askim.
It is essentially an exclusionary narrative that in planning terms emphasizes control,
though it also embraces the need for actions to achieve enhancements. The outsider in this narrative is the homogenization that globalization can bring, though
ironically there is a homogenization of the counter strategy – a risk of standard 'historical' street furniture, 'traditional' shop fronts and signs, 'heritage' museums, etc.
The tensions created by the diversity of narratives that are likely to exist in any place,
the sense that all places are intertextual sites (i.e. sites where different 'texts', experiences and understandings, cross, and meanings are contested or negotiated, not
unambiguous), the sense of local engagement of a range of stakeholders who feel
that they can influence outcomes – all these are likely to infuse the design process
with the imagination and creativity it needs to overcome the confines of the more
narrow professional discourse.

More community involvement in the design and planning processes, including
usually excluded groups, can guide professionals and politicians in their decisions.
Community narratives must be listened to and planners need to think not of place
identity but of place identities, just as it is more helpful to think of design qualities as
opposed to quality in the absolute. Plurals reflect the pluralism inherent in the concepts. This inevitably brings conflicts which cannot be avoided; it is impossible to
keep everyone happy, but the need to work with diversity should be the starting
point of the design process, not a painful afterthought. Conflicts should be acknowledged and dealt with, not brushed aside. Planners need to be aware of the cultural
and social underpinnings of their own favoured place narratives.

The NoordXXI student project was one very small example where the issues discussed in this chapter were made explicit to the students through action learning, in
the hope that it would influence their future professional practice. There are no easy
recipes or absolute solutions in design and the process is crucial in informing the outcome. Places and sites are where memories and meanings and investments collide:
awareness of this may help practising planners to negotiate new connections.

PART THREE

CONCLUSIONS

CHAPTER 10

RECONCEPTUALIZING THE NARRATIVES OF PLACE IDENTITY IN PLANNING
PAUL JENKINS AND CLIFF HAGUE

INTRODUCTION

When we were asked to undertake the research projects which underpin this book, as part of the NoordXXI project, we were attracted to the themes of place identity and participation in planning in the widening European context. However, as noted in the preface, we initially did not plan to produce a book exploring these concepts, rather we were immersed in the logistics of organizing data collection from six partners in four countries, so that we could meet the tight timetables set within the project. However, the process of undertaking international research, working with academics from other countries and participating in workshops with practitioners from different planning systems was – as ever – an experience that began to prompt new ideas. Why were some practitioners much more certain about the identity of their region than others in different partners? Why was the concept of 'housing market areas' so familiar to Scots but so strange to Scandinavians? Why were the local politicians so engaged in Askim, but less visible in some other places? Why did Scandinavian towns look different from Dutch ones, and why were both so different in urban form from their Scottish equivalents? The findings of the various linked research projects provided some answers but raised other questions.

So, with the encouragement of the NoordXXI project managers, we set about re-interpreting the research material by reflecting on the project results and connecting this to critical analysis and relevant social science literature. The contributors to the book came together to discuss the issues and re-work our drafts as new perspectives were increasingly developed and shared. At the same time, while the demands of other research contracts reduced the time we had planned to devote to the book, they also extended and deepened our understanding of the subject material. A contract to be the UK's European Spatial Planning Observatory Network (ESPON) Contact Point, and another from the UK Office of the Deputy Prime Minister (Hague and Kirk, 2003) for work on polycentric development, bolstered our grasp of the European context. In parallel we undertook work for the Scottish Executive on participation in planning (Jenkins, Kirk and Smith, 2002) and then an international review of mediation and engagement in plan-making for the Office of the Deputy Prime Minister (School of the Built Environment, Heriot-Watt University *et al.*, 2003).

The book thus benefits from, and reflects, the ongoing nature of our research into very practical questions within planning. However, this means that the research

method we are adopting here is more one of analytical induction, and *post hoc* interpretation, rather than hypothesis testing. The specific research which has produced
this book (i.e. the re-interpretation of the NoordXXI contract research) is in effect
being used to refine hypotheses that we have been developing through our wider
work. The veracity or not of these hypotheses would require wider 'testing' than we
were able to do with the time and resources available to us. In building on our work
in NoordXXI we wanted to be able to address issues of relevance to other European
researchers, and – importantly – planning practitioners. This is part of the interest in
producing a book in the Royal Town Planning Institute Library Series. We hope that
we have produced a text that is of interest to a wide readership who can reflect on the
issues, the research questions raised and the partial responses we have put forward,
and eventually add to, amend or critique these.

All the authors of this book are currently within the School of the Built
Environment at Heriot-Watt University,[1] but each has had a quite distinctive professional career path which reinforces our different research (and teaching)
specialisms. Our collective experience in planning worldwide underpins our interests in place identity and participation in planning. We feel strongly that modern
planning is at an important juncture in its evolution. Whereas it was dominated by
architect–planners with their associated modernist social engineering in the immediate post-war welfare states in Europe, it has transmuted through various
paradigms, as discussed in Chapters 2 and 3. These paradigms are still all evident
in planning practice across Europe and further afield, and we have, as authors, all
practised within these paradigms in one way or another.

The book argues that increasingly multicultural societies make socio-cultural
values more important than ever in planning. Together with the environmental, economic and political impacts of globalization, it is the 'cultural turn' that now makes
place identity so important and so contested. Similarly in Europe the territorial context
for planning has started to change rapidly. As Jenkins points out in Chapter 2, these
changes have in fact been ongoing worldwide, but arguably the hegemony of the profession in the European welfare states has protected it from this to a relatively high
degree, unlike in most of the so-called 'less developed world', where the challenges
of global economic and social forces for land use management, including planning,
are immediate and often devastating, and where planning as an integral part of wel-
fare-statism never achieved any real hegemony. We have thus come to interpret the
research material from different backgrounds and different dominant interests, but
agree on the changing role of planning in Europe, and the opportunity this provides
for re-emphasizing the role of place identity in new territorial identities, as a basis to
widen participation in planning as a form of governance. However, we are equally
aware of the dangers of much political and economic change which drives many of
the processes underway in governance – and hence also in planning – in Europe.

This summarizes the core thesis of the book: in a context of change in European territorial identities, there is an opportunity (even necessity) to emphasize the importance of socio-cultural identities linked to place, in relation to the typically more dominant legalistic and technical discourses in planning. The often informal nature of ongoing changes in territorial identities carries the possibility that powerful political and economic actors will manipulate this opportunity to dismantle aspects of the post-war rationale for planning as a tool for social–democratic redistribution without any clear public mandate for this. Ironically, therefore, even where wider participation in planning is promoted, this is in carefully controlled contexts with specific aims that are often subsumed. Thus while grounding of strategic and local planning, environmentally responsible action, rural service provision and urban design in place identities has been promoted in the early twenty-first century, we perceive that 'glass ceilings' to participation exist that need to be challenged if action is to move beyond rhetoric and tokenism.

Our concern for the role of planning as essentially a form of redistribution does not mean that we hanker after a return to the 'northern hegemony' that this so often entailed. Rather, globalization has not only challenged this role, but also potentially permits new forms and attitudes to redistribution, and this needs to be reflected in new forms of planning. Thus, although this research focuses on Europe, much of our other work is international, and we are seeking forms of planning which are relevant not just in the changing context of Europe, but worldwide. We believe that the fuller recognition of socio-cultural values embedded in place identity and the proactive furtherance of wider participation in planning are essential in all circumstances for planning to continue to evolve.

A SUMMARY OF THE ARGUMENT

Returning to the experience of the research, and through this to the experience of the planners and politicians in the local authorities investigated, we suggest that the four key queries raised initially by Amundsen (2001) can help us summarize our argument: what, who, how and why?

What is the substance of place identity in the examples from European spatial planning that form the core of the book? We saw in Chapter 1 that identity often involves counter-position with 'the other', establishing a relation of difference with other places and other social groups. We have seen narratives of identity being written for a new Europe and for trans-national Euro-regions, for intra-national regions and for sub-regions and for towns. In each case a sense of 'the other' is fundamental to the identity. Thus the new Europe is precisely *not* the old Europe of nation-states warring with each other over territory. Neither can the old divisions of class be spoken, nor is Europe the USA. The USA is another 'other' and its pre-eminent place narrative of contemporary competitive and consumerist urbanism is one that the EU seeks to challenge.

So what is the narrative of Europe as a place that underpins the EU as a territory? Above all Europe wants to be seen to be a cohesive place – after two world wars and the divisions of the Iron Curtain, could it be otherwise? However, cohesion does not equate with uniformity, and there are aspects of 'old Europe' that give the new territorial unit richness in diversity. These include landscapes and cultures, regional identities and a proud legacy of city-states and trans-national trading associations. Thus Europe envisages itself in this discourse as a place where sustainable development ensures care of the natural environment and of the cultural heritage. It is a continent of compact cities, not sprawling US-style suburbia. Andersen (2002: 41) also notes that 'Europe distinguishes itself precisely from North America, both through political tradition and the public regulation of basic welfare benefits…efficiency cannot be achieved only through cuts in people's welfare and rights in the labour market'.

Forging a place identity for trans-national regions within Europe has proved problematic, as the discussion of the North Sea Region showed. There are limits to what can be administratively willed from above. Community councillors whom we interviewed felt no affinity at all with a North Sea Region, while the basic geography of the region also puts it at variance with the development trajectory styled on Europe's 'pentagon' that is favoured by the European Commission. Similarly, at sub-national level, administrative creations of new regional territorial units such as Västra Götaland appear to lack a substantive place identity. In part this reflects the power of landscapes in defining sub-regional identities, and the traditional strengths of these in cultural understandings of place (an example of path-dependency). However, the creation of such units to pursue global competitiveness risks constructing place narratives in anodyne terms that ape the presumed place-less priorities of global companies (e.g. 'viable business', 'opportunities and creativity', and even 'sustainable growth').

It is in the rural areas undergoing restructuring and in the de-industrialized towns where the problems of place identity are most acute, and the content of new place narratives is most interesting and contested. In Askim the memories of rural work and of the rubber factory linger but are not shared by the youth, who define the place by the desiderata of metropolitan consumerism, which it lacks. Drammen wants to be the Venice of Norway but is 'Harry-town'. In Aberdeenshire and East Lothian the scale and form of recent house-building has been the focus for the contestation of place identity. The most powerful evocations of place identity have been those that assert 'quality by identity' – the Compass for the North and the POP plan that see Groningen province as a tranquil area based on traditional landscapes and green production, a green alternative to the Randstad; the green town of Tidaholm as discerned through the Town and Country Project; the sense of community and sustainable farming methods that fires the souls in Falköping. In Aberdeenshire the Structure Plan used the language of the novelist Grassic Gibbon to express the narrative that links all these endeavours, 'Nothing endures, nothing but the land'.

Yet in all the examples there is the persistent sense of everyday practice writing a different narrative. People buy the standard suburban houses on new estates appended to vernacular villages. They drive to the city to work and shop or go to the cinema, returning to sleep. They leave the remote rural areas to seek higher education and the norms of consumerism, and don't return, except as tourists. Thus in every situation there is no single, still less unambiguous, place identity, no clear authenticity. Identities are cross-cutting, contingent and contested from above and from below, and from different social positions such as age or migrant status (e.g. 'incomers' versus 'long-term residents').

Planning, which more than any other profession or form of state action has place identity as its reason for being, has struggled to come to terms with these challenges. Planning's modernist place identity project was clear, comprehensible and credible for a generation or more – new towns, efficient roads, separation of living and industrial areas, modern houses replacing slums. If each place would look the same that was an expression of egalitarianism that was to be welcomed; progress for all was the aspiration. The collapse of this vision and of the welfarism behind it has left a vacuum in which planning too often becomes a place narrative that looks backwards, cherishing the urban elements of an age that has disappeared, a cosy ramble for the middle aged and middle class. It is perhaps in the small towns and rural areas where this tendency is most pronounced. In the cities, the pulse of multiculturalism is unstoppable and planners have increasingly to learn how to dance to its different tunes. This is not a call for planners to reimpose some design orthodoxy, to reinvent some elitist vision of place that will be good for the populace. Rather the narratives of place that planners should write are those that are learned from the people of the place itself, but planners should no longer be ignorant about what these narratives signify, or whose narratives they are. There is real scope for a new, radical critique of the assumptions that underpin conventional policies such as green belts, compact cities and the knee-jerk protection of old buildings, and a restructuring of place narratives around equity in diversity.

Who is engaged in defining new place and territorial identities? Our argument is that place identity is being changed by globalization and by everyday life, but that the conscious construction and advocacy of new place narratives is, perhaps inevitably, a process dominated by officials and politicians. Planners are key actors in this process; most of the key participants in the substantive work on place identity in NoordXXI were planners, though they came from a variety of backgrounds. While it may sound obvious, we feel it is worth stating that planners have a particular professional concern with place and the qualities of place. This is not to say they monopolize such concerns but it does mean that interpretations of planning that disregard place in favour of some generic process are missing an important objective reality.

Other professionals also have a stake in the narratives of place identity. Indeed we have seen examples of them playing the leading role, and being frustrated by the barriers presented by the discourses of statutory planning practice. The active engagement of teachers and environmental professionals underpinned Tidaholm's Town and Country Project; economic development was critical in Falköping, while in Aberdeenshire the local enterprise agency, Grampian Enterprise, had its own narratives of place identity that partly overlapped with those of the planners. Tourist development is another key driver of place identity construction. Nor should we overlook the part played by professional planners working for house-builders, certainly in the UK, in fashioning narratives of place identity through the use of concepts such as 'marketability' when debating sites, house numbers and house types through the planning process.

We have also seen the part played by politicians, and particularly those in ruling groups, in the promotion of place identity as the basis for underpinning territorial identity. This seems to have been more evident in Scandinavia and the Netherlands than in Scotland. This might reflect the more local base of politics in the smaller administrative units in these countries, compared with Scotland, though the key politicians in the POP case were those from the provincial council. It may be that our samples were small, and further distorted by our research focus. We believe that elected members are under-researched in planning generally, and that the growing importance of planning for place identity and the contestation of territorial power makes a strong case for further research on what kind of politicians exert what power and how over planning outcomes. Representative democracy is both an important part of democratic planning and under great pressure: the way it develops in different institutional contexts deserves critical scrutiny and calls for new interpretations.

Notwithstanding the dominance of officials and politicians, we have argued that participation of civil society is now a necessary part of the planning process. In Chapter 3 we suggested that the structural context for participation had been changed by the fiscal and political crises of social democratic welfare states, but also by the failure of the individualist model of the New Right to totally replace such institutions. Thus the Third Way is seen as a viable political programme, but also as one requiring mechanisms to proactively reach out to civil society, to listen, include and involve. Our examples in later chapters show citizens playing active parts, notably in Falköping and Tidaholm, but also in Scotland's community councils and in the POP plan. A notable feature of the NoordXXI project was the attempts made to involve young people in constructions of place identity.

However, participation is not inevitable, and when it takes place may be very narrow in scope. There are important questions, raised in Chapters 6 and 7 in particular, about the extent to which orthodox planning discourses are exclusionary. Again more research is needed, and more action-research such as that supported through NoordXXI to exchange experiences and apply innovative methods in different institutional contexts. Our feeling is that the more planning can be construed and understood as a credible and comprehensible means for collaborative negotiation around discourses of place identity, the more participatory and relevant it is likely to become. We feel that in fact the term 'participation' may be indelibly tarred with its narrow image, especially in the UK, where it constitutes a discourse that is routine and restricted, rather than innovative and inclusive. A new language is needed to release the full potential that is latent in planning for place identity under conditions of diversity (Hague *et al.*, 2003).

How are place narratives written, and what methods of participation are involved? We have noted the existence of multiple narratives and mechanisms for their construction. Examples would include the elegiac booklet on the old villages of East Lothian (Anderson, 2000), or the various tourist brochures or publications seeking to entice inward investment. We have also stressed the practices of everyday life, within the overall parameters set by globalization and consumerism, as significant means of constructing place identity. For instance, we took photos of several McDonald's stores in the different NoordXXI regions and asked participants in the project which came from where. They found it hard to tell.

At a pan-European scale, the ESDP has been a crucial document to elaborate definitive concepts of the new place identity, most notably polycentric development, new urban–rural relations, parity of access to infrastructure and knowledge, sustainable development of the natural environment and cultural heritage, gateway cities and compact cities as an antidote to 'urban sprawl'. How did the ESDP do it? Above all by avoiding definitive political commitment to one place over another. European language elides politically contentious choices. Competitiveness, cohesion and sustainable development merge into each other, symbolic diagrams express the key concepts, but maps in a master plan style, showing what development is likely to go where, were avoided. Similarly, the spatial vision documents produced for the North Western Metropolitan Area and for the North Sea Region were new types of planning document, seeking to set a tone and establish a territorial identity and highlight the need for integration of sectoral investments rather than resolve development controversies. This reflects both astute politics and the reality of the lack of executive authority. The regional strategy for Västra Götaland (Västra Götaland Region, 1999) is similarly a vision rather than a spatial plan.

In more formal 'planning' terms, we have noted a number of different approaches to constructing narratives of place identity. The Compass for the North (of the Netherlands) in a sense underpinned the whole NoordXXI project and was an important innovation. The POP plan that followed in Groningen was an innovative attempt to integrate four different types of plan. The *North East Scotland Together* structure plan was also a new form of collaborative strategic planning in a new unitary structure of local government. New ideas and techniques from POP were applied in the Buskerud County Plan, though as Chapter 6 shows, with less impact. However, there were also important continuities in the way planning policies tackled issues of identity. This is shown particularly in Chapter 8 by the example of green belt policies in Aberdeen and Edinburgh, where prevention of the coalescence of settlements and the protection of the landscape setting of the city – i.e. visual identity of place – is the key rationale. There were also attempts to use design to emphasize or redefine place identity at a local level, as Chapter 9 showed.

Overall, we see throughout the book how planners have to negotiate place identity through the discourse structures of statutory planning and as a form of mediation both with the market and between different territorial scales. The long drawn-out local plan inquiry in East Lothian is perhaps the outstanding example. There planners were committed to policies seeking to preserve the rural identity of the east of the county, just as their predecessors had done. Yet they had to accommodate allocations of land for housing prescribed by the then regional council; meanwhile the house-builders had been denied a proper opportunity to challenge those same allocations in the structure plan. At the same time community councils were hostile to the loss of traditional place identity, and for them the planning system represented the main bulwark against further incursion. Neither the plan nor the legalistic procedures of the public inquiry provided a basis for the debates about place identity that should have taken place.

The evidence so far from this admittedly limited number of cases is that the Dutch system of statutory planning was probably better equipped to handle narratives of place identity than the others. Again some caution is needed, since development pressures were less intense there than in some of the other examples. The statutory plans in Norway and in Sweden seem to have had particular difficulty in accommodating new narratives of place identity. The more strategic plans in these countries had been largely geared to integrating the space requirements generated by strong welfare state development programmes, while the detailed plans are precise and localized documents to control building, to the point of being myopic about overall place identity.

Thus there are institutional differences and contingencies that can make a difference; however, we would hypothesize overall that statutory systems by their nature are restrictive and exclusionary discourses ill-equipped to promulgate or negotiate place identities in situations of diversity. If this is the case, and if there is a higher political priority attached to place identity (as we have argued), then the implication is that other non-statutory means will need to be created to allow the construction of place identities as a basis for development policy. In this scenario, planning as only a regulatory activity, constrained by the rule of law, is likely to be marginalized and reduced to an administrative routine. In Tidaholm we saw the Town and Country Project, and then the Local Agenda 21, being used to build narratives of place identity. Youth parliaments also offered possibilities in some of the NoordXXI partners. In Falköping it was the rural development process that set 'souls on fire'. These and other institutional forms have more flexibility than statutory planning, and would seem to have more capacity to involve marginalized groups, and to begin to negotiate a shift of resources in their favour.

This latter point is important. We noted in Chapter 3 the risk that participation becomes a fetish defining how you do planning without careful reflection on the power structures created by such approaches within centralized statutory systems. As the redistributory capacity of planning as part of a welfare state apparatus has dwindled, so it becomes more crucial to scrutinize how the emergent structures of planning privilege some interests over others. How aware are the planners and the political elites of the diversity of the society for which they are planning? We would advocate that all stages of plan preparation need to work around the recognition that there are different identities of place that need to be negotiated, rather than proceeding from the assumption that the values of the elite are those that express 'the public interest'. This does not prevent a plan from being partial, even didactic, e.g. for its interpretation of sustainable development, but it does mean that plan-making becomes a critical, self-aware and reflective process.

Why has planning become more involved in, and open to, issues of place identity and participation? Our view, argued throughout the book, is that these trends sit within a structural context. Globalization creates new economic spaces and undermines traditional place identities. In this process of change there are various territorial changes and opportunities, particularly exerting pressures on nation-states from above (the supra-national level) and from below (regions and city networks). As class has been deconstructed by economic and political change, so identity has become a crucial basis for political action. Achieving broad legitimacy for action – as opposed to uncontested leadership status – has led to the need for outreach in new forms of governance. The socializing experience of consumerism as the basis for everyday life itself redefines the relation between voters and their elected representatives, just as the privatization of welfare redefines the role and capacity of states vis-à-vis their civil societies. Successful planning thus becomes the effective delivery of innovatory programmes and measures that voters and key stakeholders can identify with. Participatory negotiation of place identity is central to this process.

Having reasserted the importance of structure, within the traditions of political economy approaches to planning, we hasten to add that we do not underestimate the importance of agency, contingency, path dependency and difference. While all the partners in NoordXXI were experiencing similar pressures (ex-urban and suburban residential spread, increased commuting, loss of shops and other rural services, decline of traditional industries, and awareness to address the challenges of sustainable development and to conserve natural environments and the built environment heritage), they went about their work in different ways that largely reflected their institutional contexts and histories. We firmly believe that agencies, policies, plans and actions matter and can make a difference to outcomes and that planners need to play proactive roles in this context.

MAIN HYPOTHESES EMERGING FROM THE RESEARCH

The following summarizes the key themes – and within these, the main hypotheses – emerging from this research.

1. PLACE IDENTITY IN RELATIONAL SPACE

This book has tried to address two main issues in relation to place identity and planning: 1) How do we perceive place identity and how is this changing? 2) What is the relevance of this for planning?

In relation to the first issue, we have argued that place identity has always been a factor inherent in planning, as underpinning the core set of values which planning sets out to uphold is the concept of public interest as opposed to private interests. This concept, however, has to relate to a 'public' and here our research shows that the concept of what is a 'public' is affected by both place identity and territorial identity. In other words we can only perceive of a collective 'public interest' in any real way where this 'public' so identifies itself and where institutional structures permit (or encourage) this identification, and its expression. These two attributes – of the mental models underpinning our cultural perception, and of organizational forms which permit this to be expressed – are key elements of institutionalist analysis (Jenkins and Smith, 2001).

We have argued in Chapter 1 that one major issue here is the changing collective sense(s) of identity. When modern planning was established in Europe there was a much more hegemonic structuring of public identity, although even then already 'tiered' through the concepts of locality and nation-state. There were very different forms of territorial identity associated with this as modern forms of government in the post-war welfare states developed in the northern European countries this research has focused on. In the UK the nation-state dominated, whereas in Sweden and Norway the local authority had much more significance, and perhaps regions had more importance in the Netherlands, although parts of the UK – such as Scotland – retained strong cultural identities.

Thus, although even at this time there were multiple identities, place identity as the basis for territorial identity was relatively uncontested, albeit with exceptions (such as Northern Ireland or the Basque country). This was reflected in the structure of governance; while based on geographical areas (e.g. wards and electoral boundaries) and representative democracy, the dominant welfare nation-states also operated with fairly high degrees of corporate interests – business and organized labour for instance. Hence in a predominantly working-class industrial European city a household would expect its interests to be defined and supported through its local MP, city councillor and trade union. The sense of place identity was reinforced by various aspects of socio-cultural life – football teams or neighbourhood organizations, for example.

Two major changes in our more recent social structure have multiplied the basis for cultural identities, and with this the basis for place identity: much more mixing of social groups (across previous class divisions as well as ethnic and regional groups), and a vast widening of cultural diversity and related interest groups such as age, gender, sexual orientation, etc. This demonstrates the relational aspects of place, i.e. where we live in will not have moved spatially, but our perception of it will have changed – quite often radically. This has both stimulated and been supported by increasing mass media activity. The result is for all of us a plethora of cultural identities which we carry and alternately display depending on the circumstances. This means the system of representative governance based on fairly simple forms of place identity – in tandem with that based on work interests – has been eroded. The effect is a tendency to voter apathy, narrow majorities, interest group lobbying, etc. in politics, with it becoming ever more difficult to determine what is the 'public interest'.

As such, the fundamental role of planning in determining what might be in the public as opposed to private interest has also become ever more difficult. The planning process has become much more complex and, at the same time, tends to be dominated by those 'in the know': the planners themselves of course, but also the lobbyists such as specific private sector, or non-governmental, interests. These groups may have more understanding and influence on the system even than elected representatives, who often have limited understanding before taking up public responsibility, especially at local authority level. Thus, as with governance in general, planning is seeking ways to become more legitimate and deliberately targeting different groups other than the place-based public, e.g. young people. This is needed of course, but the issue of who has a right to influence decisions on the public interest in relation to specific places – which is the role of planning – does not become any simpler because of this. Added to this, as argued in the book, we have changing territorial identities, and hence even the structured forms of representation are changing.

2. PARTICIPATION, REPRESENTATION, TERRITORIALITY AND GOVERNANCE

Another major theme running through the book has been the relation – usually tension – between participatory and representative forms of governance. As noted above, modern planning was born in the era of developing welfare-oriented nation-states, and the role of the general public was to express through their representatives whether they disagreed with what was being assessed as in the public interests by these representatives and their specialist advisors (i.e. planners). As Chapter 3 has shown, the form of planning that resulted then has changed, now in its third paradigm. This largely reflects the cultural and economic changes which the nation-states and societies of the West have gone through in the past half-century or so. We are facing much more complicated governance issues today. On top of this – in Europe, but also elsewhere (see below) – we are facing changing territorial identities and hence the political space within which governance works is changing, and this directly affects the issue of representation.

The difficulty for the modern politician – at local, regional or national level – is to know how successful she/he is in representing her/his constituents. However, the predominant political party-based decision-making also undermines this representativity. Thus even if a representative knows what his/her constituents want, she/he may not want – or be allowed – to represent this as it goes against a party line. With increasing cultural and economic fragmentation within the boundaries of the electoral representative territories (i.e. wards, constituencies), the vast variety of differing views means it is also much more difficult to ascertain what is in fact the position of the majority in order to represent this anyway. This is a particular problem for 'first-past-the-post' electoral systems.

One of the reactions to this has been to accept that some forms of participatory democracy need to co-exist alongside the representative forms, and also that representative forms need refining. This refinement includes redefinition of territorial boundaries, but predominantly the changing of electoral systems, moving to proportional representation. In tandem, however, a wide variety of mechanisms of participatory democracy are being used – some to try to understand 'public opinion' better (such as polls and focus groups), some to permit direct public expression of interest (referenda), some to encourage more political engagement (working with young people in particular) and some to actually permit different forms of participation in decision-making. Local Agenda 21, for instance, included a wide variety of these mechanisms.

The problem of how to balance these different forms – and how to integrate participatory forms of democracy with representative forms – has not been solved by any means. As we can see from various chapters in this book, while there have been many 'experiments', there has been limited integration of decision-making. Perhaps the most successful example has been in the Netherlands, where widespread acceptance of negotiation has been embedded for a longer period in political life and public attitudes. On the other hand, the need to build forms of public legitimacy for political decision-making – especially vis-à-vis other political/government actors – is increasingly seen as important. Hence we see a variety of new territorial identities being formed through alliances and the widespread use of participatory techniques to underpin their legitimacy.

This would seem to bode well for democracy, as the quite structured and closed forms of governance instituted after the Second World War are opening up and seeking different forms of public engagement in the face of multiplying socio-cultural identities and changing territorial contexts. It does raise the problem of how these different territorial identities are expressed in spatial terms – and particularly so for planning, as it deals with spatial issues. Hence while a range of innovative participatory democratic mechanisms are being used to underpin new territorial identities, it is also the case that the contexts for these are very carefully controlled and indeed largely manipulated to specific goals, which may not even be open for discussion. This reflects the – probably dominant – reason why new territorial identities are being forged: changing patterns of economic distribution.

3. PLANNING AND REDISTRIBUTION IN AN ERA OF GROWING 'GLOBALIZATION'

Modern technology permits new forms of distribution of economic action and results, and, although this has taken some time to be implemented, there is an increasing disassociation of economic activity from spatial bases. This is not to say that work is not undertaken in places, but these places are increasingly impermanent. This has many effects on the places we have studied – often in economic decline, or partially so (with other places in economic ascendancy). It is not clear if this process will continue relatively unchecked, or if new forms of political control over resources will arise and effectively constrain the process normally called 'globalization'. This recent manifestation of changing global economic distribution is of course not the first – just a new wave spurred on by the cycles of capital and the opportunities of technology (Robertson, 2003). As in the past, there will most likely be new forms of authoritative controls established, which will probably – as before – tend to benefit the politically and economically more powerful. The period of flux which we are currently experiencing will also, no doubt, permit some shifting of relative economic and political power worldwide in new configurations.

Thus the new wave of economic distribution termed 'globalization' is creating new economic structures, and also having social and cultural effects. What concerns us here is the role of economic *re*-distribution, which is even more under threat in this period. Each wave of changing economic structure – the agricultural revolution, the industrial revolution, and the current 'de-spatialization' of economies – has led to periods when relatively small groups benefit disproportionately, often with disastrous consequences for those at the bottom of the socio-economic structure. Subsequently there has been a political backlash leading to new forms of control and redistribution – at least within the dominant polities. It is not clear how this will evolve in the current situation, but the need for some form of supra-national controls which benefit more than a minority of strong nation-states and companies is ever more apparent.

One of the trends in the current phase of globalization, given the effective weakness of any current supra-national controls, is the creation of larger economic blocks which can both protect themselves against the bigger economic players (such as the USA), and create internal advantages. The EU is, of course, a major example of this macro-regionalism. Within these major economic regions there is also the possibility, and demand, for redistribution; and the fact that the European Commission has this function is the single most important feature in a 'knock-on effect' in terms of the subordinate levels. In other words, the authority of nation-states is challenged by strong meso-regions within these (usually city-regions) through accessing this redistribution. This has led, as we have argued in the book, to new forms of territorial identity forming. As these are as yet not well defined (or their rights are not well defined or challenged), this has led to various attempts to legitimize their proposals through forms of participatory democracy, as noted above.

Our concern here is with the need for regulation or clarity in the forms of redistribution sought – or possible – through these new governance partnerships involving different tiers of government and different actors. How truly representative are these, and to what extent have issues of economic restructuring been clearly enunciated in their attempts to develop legitimacy? It seems to us that much of the participatory democratic innovation we encountered in the case studies was often manipulated to keep public opinion on board, but did not fundamentally affect issues of redistribution. The case of LA21 in Sweden comes to mind particularly, producing sound environmental and social 'visions', but having limited effect on any real political and economic action.

Planning, as stated in Chapter 1, is essentially a political function. Its main objective is to redress potential imbalances between public and private benefit in relation to space – whether for economic, social or cultural use/value. As we know it in Europe, it is essentially a part of post-war social democracy, whatever the politics of the planner. The nature of the redistributive role of planning has of course varied in the past half century, with its low point (when planning almost disappeared altogether) in the neo-liberal 1980s – at least in the UK. However, in the new global restructuring, with the strengthening of macro-regional economic blocks and rearguard actions by nation-states, the role of planning in redistribution through space can potentially be strengthened. The tendency is to promote larger meso-level strategic planning, although the need for legitimacy has led to increasing interest in locality planning.

Our concern here is that while the opportunity perhaps exists for a better balance between participatory democracy and representative democracy in planning, which needs to be an integral and explicit part of each planner's role, at the same time planners need to be clear what their redistributive role can be and attempt to clarify the potential effects of their planning, opening this up for participatory engagement as well as the social and cultural objectives. Planners can never be neutral, in that their action always has political, economic and social consequences. Of course many actions by planners do not have major consequences, but the sum of these do, particularly the issue of whether planning is seen as essentially top-down and dominated by the city-regions and nation-states, or whether it is bottom-up and focused on people in places.

We argue that it has to be both, and here Scandinavia, with its strong local governments, is a useful model, albeit being eroded through the processes described above. The Netherlands, with its long tradition of public negotiation, also has much to offer vis-à-vis negotiation in planning. The UK itself is reviewing the nature of its planning system, at the same time as reviewing its systems of governance, and as such may develop new and clear roles for planning in this regard. Planners thus need to be aware of the opportunities and constraints the changing situation in each context provides. Part of this awareness is a keener understanding of the global context for economic, social and cultural development, and the role planning can play in wider contexts. Planning grew from a local to a strategic concern through the first half of the twentieth century, and needs to more fully comprehend trans-national and supra-national issues in the twenty-first century. This includes issues related to its inherent role in redistribution.

CONCLUSION

In conclusion, as teachers/researchers in planning with a firm basis in practice, we see the obvious need for strategic planning as well as local planning. However, we would argue that these do not have to be mutually exclusive activities, or ones which operate in different parts of the bureaucratic psyche. Rather, we would argue that in the present context of territorial change in Europe, with its relatively strong traditions of planning and still important links between planning and broader governance issues, there is an opportunity for a new form of planning to evolve. The planning 'system' needs to be more varied and adaptable and needs to permit the counter-balance of multiple-defined place identities with micro- and macro-level economic strategies and widening and more flexible forms of governance.

Our vision for this would be planning which is based on place identities, and which through this raises strategic issues for negotiation – a term we prefer to participation. In other words, bottom-up planning will lead to strategic issues and these do not necessarily have to be imposed, or sealed off above the 'glass ceiling'. This form of planning would be akin to that promoted by 'collaborative planning', although we would stress that, as noted in Chapter 3 and shown in some of the research reported here, the arenas and agenda-setting for negotiation in planning are always open to manipulation and can never be 'level playing fields'. Thus, to assume that these will be established by goodwill would be naive and it is clear that a new generation of politically aware and active planners, as well as a planning-aware and active public, needs to develop, to impress on political and economic actors the necessity of such an approach.

This then leads us to the role of the planner. The modern planner has often been seen as striving to provide objective technical advice and promote rationally negotiated development. In fact the parameters of action of the profession have been dominated by the governance situations within which planners work, and these, we have argued, have tended to reflect political and economic values more than social and cultural values. This has been played out in various different ways in the countries we have researched in this book, but generally speaking the planner as specialized, rational negotiator has been the norm. Some planners, of course, have played – and continue to play – different roles: the private sector planner, or in-house planner within a private sector organization for instance has a specific economic objective, while the 'community planner' working as an agent for civil society groups and organizations (Friedmann, 1998) has more political objectives. Both have social implications, whether implicit or explicit. However, the arena and agenda-setting for planning is largely determined by planners within the governance system, and local authority planners in each of the countries studied evidenced similar stresses on their role between strategic regional and national objectives (often coming top-down from central level and seen as politically motivated) and private sector-led economically motivated demands and forces, with social and cultural issues seen usually as a weaker 'outsider', referred to for example in relation to conservation/design and environmental issues.

We suggest that to achieve a new form of planning that values place identity, uses this as a basis for land use planning, environmental protection, rural development and/or urban design, and factors this in equally in its planning role in relation to the real political and economic context, requires an analysis that will permit the planner to step outside their traditional expert role to see the constraints created by the governance and planning systems that they operate within, and to apply themselves to overcoming these constraints. This will require a professional mind-shift from that which celebrates a form of 'objectivity' to one which recognizes the essential social–democratic ideals which underpin the function of 'planning' as a form of governance and proactively promote this. It will also mean specifically developing skills in analysis of the dominant tendencies in any situation of negotiation (generally political and economic) and an ability to be aware of the limitations this can create for different socio-cultural groups' engagement. All in all, planning education will thus need to have a more political economic approach and focus on participation, negotiation and/or mediation as key tools of the planner, and will also need to include training for the public and politicians as well as for planners. We hope the experience of 'reflection in practice' of the research for NoordXXI, as related in this book, can assist, and even inspire, this process.

CHAPTER 2

1   As well as attempts to define regions in geographical/environmental forms – i.e. bio-regionalism. These, however, have had less impact on changing territorial definitions than economic factors such as the definition of labour pools, transport networks, etc.

2   We understand governance as the sphere of relations between government and other actors in civil society or non-governmental sectors – including the private sector. It also refers to the processes of interaction between these in defining roles and relationships. The idea of governance is that government does not work in isolation but in the above sphere and through these types of relations and thus government has to be seen in this context.

3   Healey (1997) and Vigar et al. (2000) have recognized that successful implementation of a collaborative approach necessitates wider institutional, legal and political restructuring, and they refer to the need to design an appropriate 'hard infrastructure' or formal structure. However, they do little to investigate how this can develop.

CHAPTER 3

1   That is within each of the constituent parts of the UK, as planning is a devolved matter. Healey's (2001) and Vigar et al.'s (2000) research on planning refers specifically to England.

2   The teams commissioned to undertake both research projects were composed of members of staff from the former School of Planning and Housing in Edinburgh, which provided technical support to the NoordXXI project, and now forms part of the School of the Built Environment, Heriot-Watt University.

CHAPTER 4

1   Newman and Thornley consider the Eastern European system as a separate form, which is not included here.

2   In the Netherlands the main strategic planning instrument is the *streekplan*, prepared for the 12 provinces, with *structuurplans* being prepared for seven city regions. In Sweden the main strategic planning instrument is the *lans stragey*, prepared for the 24 county councils, whereas in Norway it is the *fylkesplan*, prepared for the 19 county councils. In Scotland this level of strategic planning is the

structure plan prepared by unitary local councils or, more usually, groups of these (previously these were prepared also at regional level).

3   In the Netherlands the framework plan is the *structuurplan* (whole local authority or city regions) and the detailed plan is the *bestemmingsplan* (whole or part of the local authority area). This latter can include *stadsvernieuningsplans* for urban renewal. In Norway each *kommune* prepares a *kommuneplan* (master plan) covering the whole municipality, and a more specific *reguleringsplan* for areas where new development will take place. The *kommune* may also prepare *kommunedelplan* (sub-master plans) and *bebyggelsesplan* (building development plans). In Sweden the framework plan covering the whole municipal area is the *översiktsplan*, and *detaljplan* are prepared for small areas where more complicated development is foreseen. For areas not covered by a *detaljplan*, special area regulations or *omradesbestammelser* can be adopted. In Scotland, below the strategic level the only statutory instrument is local plans (covering the whole or part of the local authority area), though other instruments such as master plans may be used for specific areas (Jenkins, Kirk and Smith, 2001).

4   There has, however, been an increase in the number of 'forums' which include both politicians and other interest groups, as well as attempts to include young people more directly in the political process (e.g. youth parliaments).

CHAPTER 6

1   However, one of the overall outcomes was a commitment to feedback and to evolution of the consultative process. Towards the end, the planners indicated they were considering how to continue to use the momentum generated to continue to monitor and engage over implementation of the plan in practice.

2   Indeed the neighbouring Friesland province adopted a very different top-down and closed approach to the development of its regional physical plan in 1995 (Needham, 1997).

3   The fact that 28 new council members were elected (out of the 55 total), three of the six provincial executive were new, the Queen's commissioner was also relatively new in post, and there was a 'personal chemistry' between some of these key individuals, both enabled the province to adopt this new way of working and led them to want to consolidate their political position through the process.

4   Such as the promotion of decision-making based on 'black and white' choices related to scenarios.

5   The regional commissioner was responsible for establishing this group with staff from his own departments and other state agencies. Participating members included Environment, Municipal Department, (Military) Preparedness, Agriculture, The County Physicians Department, the Road Agency and the Labour Agency.

CHAPTER 7

1   Eckerberg (2001:15) suggests that Sweden 'could be labelled the leading country in Europe concerning the implementation of LA21'.

CHAPTER 10

1   Previously the School of Planning and Housing at Edinburgh College of Art – an Associated College of Heriot-Watt University up to 1 August 2002.

BIBLIOGRAPHY

Aberdeen City Council (1998) *Aberdeen City Local Plan Consultative Draft,* Aberdeen: Aberdeen City Council.

Aberdeen City Council and Aberdeenshire Council (1999) *Structure Plan Area Forecasts. Technical Report,* Aberdeen: Aberdeen City Council and Aberdeenshire Council.

Aberdeen City Council and Aberdeenshire Council (2001) *North East Scotland Together: Finalised Aberdeen & Aberdeenshire Structure Plan 2001–2016,* Aberdeen: Aberdeen City Council and Aberdeenshire Council.

Aberdeenshire Council (2002) *Aberdeenshire Local Plan: Consultation Draft,* Aberdeen: Aberdeenshire Council.

Alma, R. (1999) *Rond en om Deventer: Stad en platteland in Zuidwest-Salland,* Groningen: REGIO-PRojekt Uitgevers.

Ambrose, P.J. and Colenutt, B. (1975) *The Property Machine,* Harmondsworth: Penguin.

Amdam, R. (2001) 'Empowering New Regional Political Institutions: A Norwegian Case', *Planning Theory and Practice,* 2(2), 119–85.

Amin, A. and Thrift, N. (1995) 'Globalisation, Institutional "Thickness" and the Local Economy', in P. Healey, C. Cameron, S. Davoudi, S. Graham and A. Madanipour (eds) *Managing Cities: The New Urban Context,* Chichester: Wiley.

Amundsen, A.B. (2001) *Articulations of Identity: A Methodological Essay and a Report on Askim and Tidaholm,* NoordXXI Report no. 19. Available online at <http://www.noordxxi.nl>.

Andersen, H.T. (2002) 'Globalisation is affected by local factors: shifts in the relationship between state, region and city', in Miljøministeriet/Ministry of the Environment (ed.) *European Cities in a Global Era: Urban Identities and Regional Development,* Copenhagen: Ministry of the Environment.

Anderson, B. (1983) *Imagined Communities: Reflections on the Origin and Spread of Nationalism,* London: Verso.

Anderson, D. (2000) *Old East Lothian Villages,* Ochiltree, Ayrshire: Stenlake Publishing.

Arnstein, S. (1969) 'A ladder of citizen participation', *Journal of the American Institute of Planners,* 35(4), 216–44.

Askim Student Project: Edinburgh College of Art/Heriot-Watt University and Agricultural University of Norway (2000) *The Askim Reports,* Aas, Norway: NLH.

Baerum Kommune (1997) *Veiledning til Etiske Retningslinjer,* Sandvika: Baerum Kommune.

Baerum Kommune (1999) *Kommuneplan 1998–2015 m/arealdel,* Sandvika: Baerum Kommune.

Bailey, N. and Turok, I. (2001) 'Central Scotland as a Polycentric Urban Region: Useful Planning Concept or Chimera?', *Urban Studies,* 38(4), 697–715.

Baker, M. (2001) 'Some reflections on strategic planning processes in three urban regions', *Planning Theory and Practice,* 2(2), 230–4.

Banister, D. (1992) 'Energy Use, Transport and Settlement Patterns', in M.J. Breheny (ed.) *Sustainable Development and Urban Form,* London: Pion Limited.

Barke, M. and Harrop, K. (1994) 'Selling the Industrial town: identity, image and illusion', in J.R. Gold and S.V. Ward (eds) *Place Promotion: The Use of Publicity and Marketing to Sell Towns and Regions,* Chichester: Wiley.

Beauregard, R. (1989) 'Between modernity and post-modernity: the ambiguous position of U.S. planning', *Environment and Planning D: Society and Space* 7(4), 381–95, reprinted in S. Campbell and S. Fainstein (eds) (2003, 2nd edition) *Readings in Planning Theory,* Oxford: Blackwell.

Bentley, I., Alcock, A., McGlynn, S., Murrain, P. and Smith, G. (1985) *Responsive Environments: A Manual for Designers,* London: Architectural Press.

Bettum, L.C. (2000) 'Nodes in Suburbia: A Sustainable New Era for Suburbia at the Dawn of a New Century?' unpublished dissertation for Diploma in Town and Country Planning, Edinburgh College of Art/Heriot-Watt University.

Blakeney, J. (1997) 'Citizen's Bane', *Plan Canada,* 37(3), 12–17.

Bozeat, N., Barret, G. and Jones, G. (1992) 'The potential contributions of planning to reducing travel demand', in *PTRC 20th Summer Annual Meeting, Environmental Issues: Proceedings of Seminar B,* London: PTRC.

Bramley, G., Bartlett, W. and Lambert, C. (1995) *Planning, the Market and Private Housebuilding,* London: UCL Press.

Bramley, G. and Watkins, C. (1996) *Steering the Housing Market: New Building and the Changing Planning System,* Bristol: Policy Press.

Breheny, M (1996) 'Centrists, Decentrists and Compromisers: Views on the Future of Urban Form', in M. Jenks, E. Burton and K. Williams (eds) *The Compact City: A Sustainable Urban Form?,* Oxford: Oxford Brookes University.

Brennan, G.H. and Buchanan, J.M. (1985) *The Reason of Rules: Constitutional Political Economy,* Cambridge: Cambridge University Press.

Brundtland Report (1987) *Our Common Future, World Commission on Environment and Development,* Oxford: Oxford University Press.

Buchanan, J.M. (1975) *The Limits of Liberty,* Chicago: University of Chicago Press.

Buchanan, J.M. (1977) *Freedom in Constitutional Contract,* College Station, Texas: Texas A&M University Press.

Buchanan, J.M. (1986) *Liberty, Market and State: Political Economy in the 1980s,* Brighton: Wheatsheaf.

Buchanan, J.M. and Tullock, G. (1962) *The Calculus of Consent: Logical Foundations of Constitutional Democracy*, Ann Arbor: University of Michigan Press.

Bukve, O. (2000) 'Towards the end of a Norwegian regional policy model?', in M. Danson, H. Halkier and G. Cameron (eds) *Governance, Institutional Change and Regional Development*, Aldershot: Ashgate.

CABE – Commission for Architecture and the Built Environment (2000) *By Design – Urban Design in the Planning System: Towards Better Practice*, London: Thomas Telford.

CABE/DETR – Commission for Architecture and the Built Environment/Department for the Environment, Transport and the Regions (2001) *The Value of Urban Design*, London: Thomas Telford.

Campbell, H. *et al.* (2001) 'Regions, territories and strategies: trends in contemporary practice and thinking', *Planning Theory and Practice*, 2(2), 205–34.

Canter, D. (1977) *The Psychology of Place*, New York: St. Martin's Press.

Carlsson, Y. (2001) 'Somewhere between Venice and Harry-Town', NoordXXI Report no. 18. Available online at: http://www.noordxxi.nl.

Cars, G., Healey, P., Madanipour, A. and de Magalhães, C. (2002) *Urban Governance, Institutional Capacity and Social Milieux*, Aldershot: Ashgate.

Castells, M. (1989) *The Informational City*, Oxford: Basil Blackwell.

Castles, F. (1978) *The Social Democratic Image of Society*, London: Routledge and Kegan Paul.

CEC – Commission of the European Communities (1990) 'Green Paper on the Urban Environment', EUR 12902 EN, Brussels: Commission of the European Communities.

CEC (1991) *Europe 2000: Outlook for the Development of the Community's Territory*, Luxembourg: Office for the Official Publications of the European Communities.

CEC (1994) *Europe 2000+: Cooperation for European Territorial Development*, Luxembourg: Office for the Official Publications of the European Communities.

CEC (1997) *The EU Compendium of Spatial Planning Systems and Policies*, Luxembourg: Office for the Official Publications of the European Communities.

CEC (1999) *European Spatial Development Perspective: Towards Balanced and Sustainable Development of the Territory of the EU*, Luxembourg: Office for the Official Publications of the European Communities.

CEC (2001) *Community Initiative Programme 13-12-2001, Interreg IIIB North Sea Region. Community Initiative Concerning Trans-European Co-operation Intended to Encourage Harmonious and Balanced Sustainable Development of the European Territory*, Viborg: Interreg North Sea Region.

City of Edinburgh Council, East Lothian Council, Midlothian Council and West Lothian Council (2000) *Edinburgh and The Lothians Structure Plan: Major Issues Report*.

Cloke, P. (1992) 'The countryside: development, conservation and an increasingly marketable commodity', in P. Cloke (ed.) *Policy and Change in Thatcher's Britain*, Oxford: Pergamon Press.

Cloke, P. Goodwin, M. and Milbourne, P. (1998) 'Cultural change and conflict in rural Wales: Competing constructs of identity', *Environment and Planning A*, 30, 463–80.

Coombes, M.G. and Wymer, C. (2001) 'A new approach to identifying localities: Representing 'places' in Britain', in A. Madanipour, A. Hull, and P. Healey, (eds) *The Governance of Place: Space and Planning Processes*, Aldershot: Ashgate.

Countryside Commission (1996) *Village Design: Making Local Character Count in New Development Parts 1 and 2*, Chelmsford: Countryside Commission.

Cowan, R. (2001) *Arm Yourself with a Placecheck: A Users' Guide,* London: Urban Design Alliance.

Crilley, D. (1993) 'Architecture as Advertising: Constructing the Image of Redevelopment', in G. Kearns and C. Philo (eds) *Selling Places: The City as Cultural Capital, Past and Present*, Oxford: Pergamon Press.

Cullen, G. (1961) *Townscape*, London: Architectural Press.

Danson, M., Halkier, H. and Cameron, G. (2000) *Governance, Institutional Change and Regional Development*, Aldershot: Ashgate.

Davidoff, P. (1965) 'Advocacy and pluralism in planning', *Journal of the American Institute of Planners*, 31, 331–8.

Davies, J.G. (1972) *The Evangelistic Bureaucrat*, London: Tavistock.

de Certeau, M. (1984) *The Practice of Everyday Life*, Berkeley: University of California Press.

de Jong, M.W. (1991) 'Revitalizing the Urban Core: Waterfront Development in Baltimore, Maryland', in J. Fox-Przeworski, J. Goddard and M.W. de Jong (eds) *Urban Regeneration in a Changing Economy: An International Perspective,* Oxford: Clarendon Press.

Dennis, N. (1970) *People and Planning*, London: Faber and Faber.

Dennis, N. (1972) *Public Participation and Planners' Blight*, London: Faber and Faber.

Department of the Environment (1994) *Quality in Town and Country*, London: Department of the Environment.

Department of the Environment and Department of Transport (1994) *Planning Policy Guidance 13: Transport*, London: HMSO.

Duncan, J.S. and Barnes, T.J. (eds) (1992) *Writing Worlds: Discourse, Text and Metaphor in the Representation of Landscape*, London: Routledge.

East Lothian Council (1998) *East Lothian Local Plan 1998: Finalised Written Statement and Plan*, Haddington: East Lothian Council.

East Lothian Council, City of Edinburgh Council, Midlothian Council and West Lothian Council (1997) *Lothian Structure Plan 1994*.

Eckerberg, K. (2000) 'Sweden: Progression despite recession', in M.W. Lafferty and J. Meadowcroft (eds) *Bringing Rio Home*, Oxford: Oxford University Press.

Eckerberg, K. (2001) 'Sweden: Problems and prospects at the leading edge of LA21 inplementation' in M.W. Lafferty (ed.) *Sustainable Communities in Europe*, London: Earthscan.

Eckerberg, K. and Forsberg, B. (1998) 'Implementing Agenda 21 in Local Government: the Swedish experience', *Local Environment*, 3(3) 333–47.

ECOTEC (1993) *Reducing Transport Emissions Through Planning*, London: HMSO.

Ellon Student Project: Edinburgh College of Art/Heriot-Watt University and The Agricultural University of Norway (2000) 'Ellon Student Groups' Contributions to the Local Planning Process: Character Appraisal and Urban Design Strategies', unpublished student project, Edinburgh College of Art/Heriot-Watt University.

Elson, M.J. (1999) 'Green Belts – The need for re-appraisal', *Town & Country Planning*, 68(5), 156–8.

English Partnerships and the Housing Corporation (2000) *Urban Design Compendium*, London: English Partnerships and the Housing Corporation.

Evans, A. (1987) *House Prices and Land Prices in the South East – A Review*, London: The House Builders Federation.

Evans, A.W. (1991) 'Rabbit hutches on postage stamps – planning, development and political-economy', *Urban Studies*, 28(6), 853–70.

Evans, A.W. (1996) 'The impact of land use planning and tax subsidies on the supply and price of housing in Britain: A comment', *Urban Studies*, 33(3), 581–5.

Fainstein, S. (1995) 'Politics, economics and planning: why urban regimes matter', *Planning Theory*, 14, 34–41.

Fainstein, S. (2000) 'New directions in planning theory', *Urban Affairs Review*, 35(4), 451–78.

Faludi, A. and Waterhout, B. (2002) *The Making of the European Spatial Development Perspective: No Masterplan*, RTPI Library Series, London: Routledge.

Faludi, A. and Zonnveld, W. (eds) (1997) 'Shaping Europe: The European Spatial Development Perspective', *Built Environment*, 23(4).

Fitzsimmons, D.S. (1995) 'Planning and Promotion: City reimaging in the 1980s and 1990s', in W.J.V. Neill, D.S. Fitzsimmons and B. Murtagh (eds) *Reimaging the Pariah City: Urban Development in Belfast and Detroit*, Aldershot: Avebury.

Forester, J. (1987) 'Planning in the face of conflict: negotiation and mediation strategies in local land use regulation', *Journal of the American Planning Association*, 53(3), 303–14.

Forester, J. (1989) *Planning in the Face of Power*, Berkeley: University of California Press.

Forester, J. (1993) *Critical Theory, Public Policy and Planning Practice*, Albany, NY: State of New York University Press.

Forester, J. (1999) *The Deliberative Practitioner: Encouraging Participatory Planning Processes*, Cambridge, Massachusetts and London: The MIT Press.

Fothergill, S. and Gudgin, G. (1982) *Unequal Growth: Urban and Regional Employment in the UK*, London: Heinemann.

Franck, K. and Lepori, B. (2000) *Architecture Inside Out*, Chichester: Wiley Academy.

Frey, H. (1999) *Designing the City: Towards a More Sustainable Urban Form*, London: E & FN Spon.

Friedmann, J. (1998) 'The New Political Economy of Planning: The Rise of Civil Society', in M. Douglass and J. Friedmann (eds) *Cities for Citizens: Planning and the Rise of Civil Society in a Global Age*, Chichester: Wiley.

Frouws, J. (1998) 'The contested redefinition of the countryside. An analysis of rural discourse in the Netherlands', *Sociologica Ruralis*, 38(1), 54–68.

Gehl, J. (1987) *Life Between Buildings: Using Public Space*, New York: van Nostrand Reinhold.

Gehl, J. and Gemzoe, L. (2000) *New City Spaces*, Copenhagen: Danish Architectural Press.

Giannakourou, G. (1996) 'Towards a European spatial planning policy: theoretical dilemmas and institutional implications', *European Planning Studies*, 4(5), 595–613.

Gold, J.R. and Ward, S.V. (1995) *Place Promotion: The Use of Publicity and Marketing to Sell Towns and Regions*, Chichester: Wiley.

Goodstadt, V. (2001) 'The need for effective strategic planning: the experience of Glasgow and Clyde Valley', *Planning Theory and Practice*, 2(2), 215–21.

Grampian Regional Council (1995) 'Technical Report, Housing, 1995 Update', Aberdeen: Grampian Regional Council.

Grampian Regional Council (1997) *Grampian Structure Plan*, Aberdeen: Grampian Regional Council.

Griffiths, R. (1998) 'Making Sameness: Place Marketing and the New Urban Entrepreneurialism', in N. Oatley (ed.) *Cities, Economic Competition and Urban Policy*, London: Paul Chapman.

Groote, P., Huigen, P.P.P. and Haartsen, T. (2000) 'Claiming rural identities', in T. Haartsen, P. Groote, and P.P.P. Huigen (eds) *Claiming Rural Identities: Dynamics, Contexts, Policies*, Assen, the Netherlands: Van Gorcum.

Groth, N.B. (2002) 'Urban and regional identity challenged by globalisation', in Miljøministeriet/Ministry of the Environment, Spatial Planning Department (ed.) *European Cities in a Global Era: Urban identities and regional development*, Denmark: Ministry of the Environment, Spatial Planning Department.

Group of Focal Points (1994) *Visions and Strategies around the Baltic Sea 2010: Towards a Framework for Spatial Development in the Baltic Sea Region*, Karlskrona: The Baltic Sea Institute.

GVA Grimley (1998) 'Aberdeenshire Towns, Shopping Study, Final Report', prepared for Aberdeenshire Council and Grampian Enterprise Ltd, GVA Grimley, International Property Advisors.

Haartsen, T., Groote, P. and Huigen, P.P.P. (eds) (2000) *Claiming Rural Identities: Dynamics, Contexts, Policies*, Assen, the Netherlands: Van Gorcum.

Habermas, J. (1979) *Communication and the Evolution of Society*, trans. T. McCarthy, London: Heinemann Educational.

Hague, C. (2001) 'Planning and planning education in a consumer society', *AESOP News*, Summer 2001, 13–16.

Hague, C. and Kirk, K. (2003) *Polycentricity Scoping Study*, London: ODPM.

Hague, C. and Storey, C. (2001a) *Border Zones*, Noord XXI Report no. 4, Edinburgh: Edinburgh College of Art/Heriot-Watt University. Available online at <http://www.noordxxi.nl>.

Hague, C. and Storey, C. (2001b) *Regional Analysis – East Lothian. Quality by Identity*, Noord XXI Report no. 7, Edinburgh: Edinburgh College of Art/Heriot-Watt University. Available online at <http://www.noordxxi.nl>.

Hall, P.A. and Taylor, R.C.R. (1996) 'Political Science and the Three New Institutionalisms', *Political Studies*, 44, 936–57.

Hall, P., Thomas, R., Gracey, H. and Drewett, R. (1973) *The Containment of Urban England*, London: Heinemann.

Harvey, D. (1989) 'From managerialism to entrepreneurialism: formation of urban governance in late capitalism', *Geografisker Annaler*, 71B, 3–17.

Harvey, D. (1996) *Justice, Nature and the Geography of Difference*, Oxford: Blackwell.

Healey, P. (1992) 'Planning through debate: the communicative turn in planning theory', *Town Planning Review*, 63(2), 143–62.

Healey, P. (1993) 'The communicative work of development plans', *Environment and Planning B: Planning and Design*, 20, 83–104.

Healey, P. (1996) 'The communicative turn in spatial planning theory and its implications for spatial strategy formulation', *Environment and Planning B: Planning and Design*, 23, 217–34.

Healey, P. (1997) *Collaborative Planning: Shaping Places in Fragmented Societies*, London: Macmillan.

Healey P. (1999) 'Institutionalist analysis, communicative planning and shaping places', *Journal of Planning Education and Research*, 19: 111–12.

Healey, P. (2001) 'Towards a more place-focused planning system in Britain', in A. Madanipour, A. Hull and P. Healey (eds) *The Governance of Place: Space and Planning Processes*, Aldershot: Ashgate.

Healey, P., Khakee, A., Motte, A. and Needham, B. (1997) *Making Strategic Spatial Plans: Innovation in Europe*, London: UCL Press.

Heclo, H. and Madsen, H. (1987) *Policy and Politics in Sweden: Principled Pragmatism*, Philadelphia: Temple University Press.

Herrschel, T. and Newman, P. (2002) *Governance of Europe's City Regions: Planning, Policy and Politics*, London: Routledge.

HMSO (1997) *Belfast City Region*, Belfast: Public Voices.

Holcomb, B. (1994) 'City make-overs: marketing the post-industrial city', in J.R. Gold and S.V. Ward (eds) *Place Promotion: The Use of Publicity and Marketing to Sell Towns and Regions*, Chichester: Wiley.

Holt, Ø. and Collins, P. (2001) *Final Report: Activities and Results*, NoordXXI Report no. 1. Available online at <http://www.noordxxi.nl>.

Innes, J.E. (1995) 'Planning theory's emerging paradigm: communicative action and interactive practice', *Journal of Planning Education and Research*, 14(3), 183–90.

Innes, J.E. and Booher, D.E. (1999a) 'Consensus building and complex adaptive systems: a framework for evaluating collaborative planning', *Journal of the American Planning Association*, 65(4), 412–23.

Innes, J.E. and Booher, D.E. (1999b) 'Consensus building as role playing and bricolage', *Journal of the American Planning Association*, 65(1), 9–26.

Jacobs, J. (1961) *The Death and Life of Great American Cities*, Harmondsworth: Random House.

Jamieson, A. and Gray, A. (2001) 'Pay bonanza as cities cash in on success', *Scotsman*, 9 March 2001, 6.

Jenkins, P., Kirk, K. and Smith, H. (2001) A Comparative Study of Participation in Planning in the Netherlands, Norway, Scotland and Sweden, Noord XXI Report no. 5, Edinburgh: Edinburgh College of Art / Heriot-Watt University. Available online at <http://www.noordxxi.nl>.

Jenkins, P., Kirk, K. and Smith, H. (2002) *Getting Involved in Planning: Perceptions of the Wider Public*, Edinburgh: Scottish Executive.

Jenkins, P. and Smith, H. (2001) 'The state, the market and community: an analytical framework for community self-development', in M. Carley, P. Jenkins and H. Smith (eds) *Urban Development & Civil Society: The Role of Communities in Sustainable Cities*, London: Earthscan.

Jouve, B. (2001) 'Sectors and territories in territorial planning in Lyons', *Planning Theory and Practice*, 2(2), 222–30.

Kearns, G. and Philo, C. (eds) (1993) *Selling Places: The City as Cultural Capital, Past and Present,* Oxford: Pergamon Press.

Keeble, L. (1964) *Principles and Practice of Town and Country Planning,* London: Estates Gazette (third edition).

Kresl, P.K. (1995) 'The determinants of urban competitiveness', in P.K. Kresl and G. Gappert (eds) 'North American Cities and the Global Economy: Challenges and Opportunities', *Urban Affairs Annual Review*, Sage Publications, 45–68.

Krugman, P. (1991) *Geography and trade*, Cambridge, MA: MIT Press.

Kuiper Compagnons (2000) *Project Border Zone Groningen – West: Functional Analysis and Concept Development Strategy,* Province of Groningen, Groningen.

Kunzmann, K. (1996) 'Euro-megalopolis or Theme-park Europe? Scenarios for European Spatial Development', *International Planning Studies,* 1(2), 143–63.

Kunzmann, K. and Wegener, M. (1991) *The Pattern of Urbanisation in Western Europe 1960–1990,* Berichte aus dem Institut fur Raumplaning 28: Institut fur Raumplaning, Dortmund: Universitat Dortmund.

Landstad (1999) *Inventarisatie van ontwikkelingen en beleid,* Deventer: Province of Overijssel and the municipalities of Bathmen, Deventer and Olst.

Le Gales, P. (1998) 'Regulations and governance in European cities', *International Journal of Urban and Regional Research,* 22, 482–506.

Le Gales, P. (2002) *European Cities, Social Conflict and Governance,* Oxford: Oxford University Press.

Llewellyn Davies & Partners (1977) *Unequal City,* London: HMSO.

Lynch, K. (1960) *The Image of the City,* Boston: MIT Press.

Madanipour, A. (1996) *Design of Urban Space,* London: John Wiley and Sons.

Madanipour, A. (2001) 'Concepts of space', in A. Madanipour, A. Hull and P. Healey (eds) *The Governance of Place: Space and Planning Processes,* Aldershot: Ashgate.

Malbert, B. (1998) 'Urban Planning Participation – Linking Practice and Theory', unpublished dissertation, Chalmers University of Technology, Gothenburg.

Maskell, P., Eskelinen, H., Hannibalsson, I., Malmberg, A. and Vatne, E. (1998) *Competitiveness, Localised Learning and Regional Development: Specialisation and Prosperity in Small Open Economies,* London and New York: Routledge.

McCann, E. (2001) 'State Devolution, Governance, and the Politics of Rapid Urban Development: Lessons from Austin, Texas' Smart Growth and Neighborhood Planning Initiative', paper presented at the Annual Meeting of the Association of American Geographers, New York, NY.

McLay, F. (ed.) (1988) *Workers' City: The Real Glasgow Stands Up,* Glasgow: Clydeside Press.

Metz, T. (2000) 'Planologische proeftuin in Overijssel', in H. Akse, W. Foorthuis, M. Klompe, M. de Lange, B. Neefjes, K. de Ruijter, M. Smit and J. van Starkenburg, *Landstad Deeventer,* pp. 3–8, Supplement bij Stedebouw en Ruimtelijke Ordening, 81(4), 1–32.

Miljoeverndepartementet/Ministry of Environment (1995) *Nasjonalt Program for Utvikling av Fem Miljoebyer (National Programme on Developing Five Environmental Cities),* (T-115), Oslo: Ministry of Environment.

Miljoeverndepartementet/Ministry of Environment (1997) *Estetikk I planog byggesaker. Veileder (Aesthetic in Planning and Building Matters. Guidelines* (T-1179), Oslo: Ministry of Environment.

Ministry of Housing, Physical Planning and Environment (1991) *Fourth Report (EXTRA) on Physical Planning in the Netherlands (comprehensive summary)*, The Hague: Ministry of Housing, Physical Planning and Environment.

Ministry of Housing, Spatial Planning and the Environment (2000) *Spatial Perspectives in Europe*, The Hague: Ministry of Housing, Spatial Planning and the Environment.

Miljøministeriet/Ministry of the Environment, Spatial Planning Department (2002) *European Cities in a Global Era: Urban identities and regional development*, Denmark: Ministry of the Environment, Spatial Planning Department.

Motloch, J.L. (1989) 'Placemaking. Order and Spontaneity', in G. Hardie, R. Moore, H. Sanoff (eds) *Changing Paradigms: Proceedings of Annual Conference Environmental Design Research Association 20*, Oklahoma City: Environmental Design Research Association.

Muchnick, D. (1970) 'Urban Renewal in Liverpool', *Occasional Papers in Social Administration*, 33, G. Bell.

National Spatial Planning Agency (2001) *Summary: Making Space, Sharing Space*, The Hague: Ministry of Housing, Spatial Planning and the Environment.

Needham, B. (1997) 'A plan with a purpose: the regional plan for the province of Friesland, 1994', in P. Healey, A. Khakee, A. Motte and B. Needham (eds) *Making Strategic Spatial Plans: Innovation in Europe*, London: UCL Press.

Neill, W.J.V. (1999) 'Whose City? Can a place vision for Belfast avoid the issue of identity?', *European Planning Studies*, 7(3), 269–81.

Newman, P. and Thornley, A. (1996) *Urban Planning in Europe: International Competition, National Systems and Planning Projects*, London: Routledge.

Nijkamp, P. (1998) 'Infrastructuur en regionale ontwikkeling; Kansen op een welvarende periferie', in J.N.H. Elerie and P.H. Pellenbarg (eds) *De welvarende periferie; Beschouwingen over infrastructuur, economie en het mozaïek van functies in Noord- en Oost-Nederland*, Groningen: REGIO-Projekt.

Norberg-Schulz, C. (1980) *Genius Loci: Towards a Phenomenology of Architecture*, London: Academy Editions.

Office of the Deputy Prime Minister (2001) *Planning: Delivering a Fundamental Change*, Green Paper, London: ODPM.

Office of the Deputy Prime Minister (2002) *Sustainable Communities: Delivering Through Planning*, London: ODPM.

Østrem, E.W. and Edvardsen, M. (2000a) *Regional Analysis – Buskerud*, NoordXXI Report no. 9, Ås: Norges Landbrukshøgskole. Available online at <http://www.noordxxi.nl>.

Østrem, E.W. and Edvardsen, M. (2000b) *Regional Analysis – Västra Götaland*, NoordXXI Report no. 11, Ås: Norges Landbrukshøgskole. Available online at <http://www.noordxxi.nl>.

Owens, S. (1986) *Energy, Planning and Urban Form*, London: Pion Limited.

Paasi, A. (1986) 'The institutionalization of regions: a theoretical framework for the understanding of the emergence of regions and the constitution of regional identity' *Fennia*, 164, 105–46.

Ploeger, J. (1999) 'Aesthetic Planning and Design Control in Norway', *Urban Design International*, 4 (1&2): 47–54.

Porter, M.E. (1990) *The Competitive Advantage of Nations*, New York: Free Press.

Poulton, M. and Begg, H.M. (1988) 'Public choice and a positive theory of planning', *The Planner*, 74(7), 15–17.

Pratt, R. and Larkham, P. (1996) 'Who Will Care for Compact Cities?', in M. Jenks, E. Burton and K. Williams (eds) *The Compact City: A Sustainable Urban Form?*, Oxford: Oxford Brookes University.

Provincie Drenthe (1998) *Provinciaal omgevingsplan*, Assen: Provincie Drenthe.

Provincie Groningen (1999) *Groningers over Groningen*, Groningen: Provincie Groningen.

Provincie Groningen (2000) *Koersen op karater: Ontwerp provinciaal omgevingsplan*, Groningen: Provincie Groningen.

Punter, J. and Carmona, M. (1997) *The Design Dimension of Planning*, London: E & FN SPON.

Raagmaa, G. (2002) 'Regional identity in regional development and planning' *European Planning Studies*, 10 (1), 55–76.

Rankin, I. (2001) *The Falls*, London: Orion.

Ratcliffe, J. and Stubbs, M. (1996) *Urban Planning and Real Estate Development*, London: UCL Press.

Ravetz, A. (1986) *The Government of Space: Town Planning in Modern Society*, London and Boston: Faber and Faber.

Relph, E. (1992) 'Modernity and the reclamation of place', in D. Seamon (ed.) *Dwelling, Seeing and Designing: Towards a phenomenological ecology*, New York: State University of New York Press.

Richardson, T. and Jensen, O. (2000) 'Discourses of Mobility and Polycentric Development: A Contested View of European Spatial Planning', *European Planning Studies*, 8(4), 503–20.

Robertson, R. (2003) *The Three Waves of Globalization: A History of a Developing Global Consciousness*, London: Zed Press.

Robins, K. (1991) 'Prisoners of the city, whatever could a post-modern city be?', *New Formations*, 15, Winter, 1–22.

Rose, G. (1995) 'Place and identity: a sense of place', in D. Massey and P. Jess (eds) *A Place in the World? Places, Cultures and Globalisation*, Oxford: Oxford University Press/Open University Press.

RTPI – Royal Town Planning Institute (2000) 'Green Belt Policy: A Discussion Paper'.

RTPI (2002) *A New Vision for Planning: Delivering Sustainable Communities, Settlements and Places*, London: RTPI.

RTPI (2003) RTPI *Education Commission: Final Report*, London: RTPI.

Rundskriv H-7/97 *om endringer av estetikkbestemmelser I plan-og bygningsloven* (Circular Letter) (1997), Oslo: Kommunalog Arbeidsdepartementet/ Miljoevern-departementat.

Rutherford, J. (1990) 'A place called home: identity and the cultural politics of difference', in J. Rutherford (ed.) *Identity: Community, Culture, Difference*, London: Lawrence and Wishart.

Sandercock, L. (1998) 'The Death of Modernist Planning: Radical Praxis for a Postmodern Age', in M. Douglass and J. Friedmann (eds) *Cities for Citizens: Planning and the Rise of Civil Society in a Global Age,* Chichester: John Wiley & Sons.

Sandercock, L. (2000) 'When strangers become neighbours: managing cities for difference', *Planning Theory and Practice*, 1(1), 13–30.

School of Planning and Housing/Department of Building Engineering and Surveying, Heriot-Watt University (2001) *The Role of the Planning System in the Provision of Housing*, Edinburgh: Scottish Executive Central Research Unit.

School of the Built Environment, Heriot-Watt University with Department of Geography, DePaul University, Chicago, Studio Cascade, Spokane and Christine Platt, Durban (2003) *Participatory Planning for Sustainable Communities: International Experience in Mediation, Negotiation and Engagement in Making Plans*, London: OPM.

Scottish Executive (2001a) *A Policy on Architecture for Scotland*, Edinburgh: Scottish Executive.

Scottish Executive (2001b) *Designing Places: A Policy Statement for Scotland*, Edinburgh: Scottish Executive.

Scottish Executive Development Department (2002a) *Review of Strategic Planning*, Edinburgh: Scottish Executive.

Scottish Executive Development Department (2002b) *Your Place Your Plan: A White Paper on Public Involvement in Planning*, Edinburgh: Scottish Executive.

Scottish Office Development Department (1996) *Land for Housing, National Planning Policy Guideline 3 (Revised 1996)*, Edinburgh: Scottish Office.

Scottish Office Development Department (1997) *Planning Advice Note 52: Planning in Small Towns*, Edinburgh: Scottish Office.

Scottish Office Development Department (1998) *Investing in Quality: Improving the Design of New Housing in the Scottish Countryside: A Consultation Paper*, Edinburgh: Scottish Office.

Scottish Office Development Department (1999) *Transport and Planning, National Planning Policy Guideline 17*, Edinburgh: Scottish Office.

Scottish Office Environment Department (1991) *Planning Advice Note 36: Siting and Design of New Housing in the Countryside*, Edinburgh: Scottish Office.

Scottish Office Environment Department (1994) *Planning Advice Note 44: Fitting New Housing Development into the Landscape: a Design Manual*, Edinburgh: Scottish Office.

Shaw, D. and Nadin, V. (2000) 'Towards coherence in European spatial planning?', in D. Shaw, P. Roberts and J. Walsh (eds) *Regional Planning and Development in Europe*, Aldershot: Ashgate.

Spatial Vision Group and consultant team (2000) *A Spatial Vision for North-West Europe: Building Co-operation*, The Hague: Ministry of Housing, Spatial Planning and the Environment.

Stoker, G. (1995) 'Regime theory and urban politics', in D. Judge, G. Stoker and H. Wolman (eds) *Theories of Urban Politics*, London: Sage.

Stones, A. (1972) 'Stop slum clearance – now', *Built Environment*, 35(2).

Taylor, N. (1998) *Urban Planning Theory Since 1945*, London: Sage.

Taylor, N. (1999) 'Anglo-American Town Planning Theory Since 1945: Three significant Developments But No Paradigm Shifts', *Planning Perspectives*, 13(4), 327–45.

Tewdwr-Jones, M. and Allmendinger, P. (1998) 'Deconstructing communicative rationality: a critique of Habermasian collaborative planning', *Environment and Planning A*, 30, 1975–89.

Thomas, M. (2001) 'Comment on Oxford Planning Theory Conference "New Issues; New Theory"', *AESOP News*, Summer 2001, p. 7.

Thomas, L. and Cousins, W. (1996) 'The Compact City: Successful, Desirable and Achievable?', in M. Jenks, E. Burton and K. Williams (eds) *The Compact City: A Sustainable Urban Form?*, Oxford: Oxford Brookes University.

Thornley, A. (1991) *Urban Planning Under Thatcherism: The Challenge of the Market*, London: Routledge.

Tibbalds, F. (1992) *Making People Friendly Towns: Improving the Public Environment in Towns and Cities*, Harlow: Longman.

Tindall, F. (1998) *Memoirs and Confessions of a County Planning Officer*, Ford, Midlothian: The Pantile Press.

UNCED – United Nations Conference on Environment and Development (1992) *Agenda 21*, New York: United Nations General Assembly.

United Nations Centre for Human Settlements (2001) *Cities in a Globalizing World: Global Report on Human Settlements*, London: Earthscan.

Urban Task Force (1999) *Towards an Urban Renaissance*, London: DETR.

Urry, J. (1995) *Consuming Places*, London and New York: Routledge.

van der Aa, B.J.M. and Huigen, P.P.P. (2000a) *Regional Analysis – Northern Part of the Netherlands. A Study of the Dutch Provinces of Groningen, Frisia and Drenthe*, NoordXXI Report no. 12, Groningen: University of Groningen. Available online at <http://www.noordxxi.nl>.

van der Aa, B.J.M. and Huigen, P.P.P. (2000b) *Regional Analysis – Deventer sub-regionen. A Study of the Landstad*, NoordXXI Report no. 13, Groningen: University of Groningen. Available online at HTTP: <http://www.noordxxi.nl>.

Västra Götaland Region (1999) *Västra Götaland: Regional Development Strategy*, Secretariat to the Regional Executive Board and the Regional Development Secretariat, Västra Götaland Region, Gothenburg.

Västra Götaland Regional Executive Board (1999) 'Basic Data for a Regional Development Plan for Västra Götaland (abstract). Part 3 – Strategies and measures', paper presented in the Interreg IIC project 'NoordXXI'.

Vigar, G., Healey, P., Hull, A. and Davoudi, S. (2000) *Planning, Governance and Spatial Strategy in Britain: An Institutionalist Analysis*, Basingstoke and London: Macmillan.

Vision Working Group (2000) *NorVision: A Spatial Perspective for the North Sea Region*.

Wates, N. and Knevitt, C. (1987) *Community Architecture*, London and New York: Penguin.

Watson, V. (2001) 'The usefulness of normative planning theories in the context of Africa', paper presented at the Oxford Planning Theory Conference, 20–1 June 2001.

Welbank, M., Davies, N. and Haywood, I. (2000) *Mediation in Planning*, London: DETR.

Westman, B. (1991) 'Devolution of power to local authorities', in Fredlund, A. (ed.) *Swedish Planning in Times of Transition*, Swedish Society for Town and Country Planning.

Wetterberg, G. (1991) 'Challenge to strategic policy making', in Fredlund, A. (ed.) *Swedish Planning in Times of Transition, Swedish Society for Town and Country Planning*.

Yiftachel, O. and Hague, E. (2002) 'Editorial: Excavating Nationalism: Theory, Space, and Crtique', *HAGAR, International Social Science Review*, 3(2), eds E. Hague and O. Yiftachel), 167–70.

WEBSITES

http://www.countryside.gov.uk/villagedesign
http://www.nifonline.org.uk
http://www.noordxxi.nl
http://www.placecheck.co.uk

INDEX